# Who Wants Candy?

### Jane Sharrock

HPBooks

HPBooks
Published by The Berkley Publishing Group
A division of Penguin Group (USA) Inc.
375 Hudson Street
New York, New York 10014

First HPBooks trade-paperback edition: August 2004

Visit our website at www.penguin.com

Library of Congress Cataloging-in-Publication Data

Sharrock, Jane.
    Who wants candy? / Jane Sharrock.—1st HPBooks pbk. ed.
        p. cm.
    ISBN 1-55788-432-3
    1. Candy. I. Title.

TX791.S46 2004
641.8'53—dc22
                                            2004047498

PRINTED IN THE UNITED STATES OF AMERICA

10  9  8  7  6  5  4  3  2

# Acknowledgments

I wish to thank the following:

Tom and Sherry Muchmore of the *Ponca City News* of Ponca City, Oklahoma, for allowing me to include recipes published in special editions of my hometown newspaper many years ago. I also wish to thank those who contributed, as well as my friends who contributed recipes to these special editions.

Kansas State University for allowing me to include recipes from the twenty-first edition of *Practical Cookery and the Etiquette and Service of the Table*, published in 1945. The book was first published in 1912 by the university's School of Home Economics. Those responsible for this book continue to educate long after their teaching careers have ended, as their words provided me with a basic understanding of candy-making principles.

My mother's former colleagues at the Department of Home Economics at Oklahoma A & M, now Oklahoma State University, for inspiring my mother, who in turn inspired me. The candy-making research conducted by Ms. Eula Morris in the early 1950s has given my family years of enjoyment.

Jim, Nancy, and Lynda, whose daily encouragement kept me going. I could not have done it without you.

My special friends at Epworth Villa retirement community who never once complained about getting free candy.

Oklahoma Lieutenant Governor Mary Fallon and Oklahoma's former First Lady Rhonda Walters for contributing their favorite recipes to this collection.

My family, friends, and neighbors, who supported this effort in every way imaginable, and especially Margaret who introduced me to some of my favorite recipes.

My publisher John Duff, my agent Coleen O'Shea, and my editor Jeanette Egan. Your vision, wisdom, experience, and patience were a blessing.

And most importantly, I wish to thank my mother and mentor for sharing the joy of candy making with a delighted young child. It is with great pleasure that I now share her joy and her lessons with you.

# Contents

# Preface

*Who Wants Candy?* is a fabulous collection of 375 recipes, many of which date back 50 years or more. It is an excellent addition to any kitchen library, offering both the novice and the experienced candy maker an incredible assortment of recipes to explore.

Compiled from my personal recipe collection and the collections of family and friends, *Who Wants Candy?* is also a tribute to generations past. Many of our mothers, grandmothers, and great-grandmothers were experts in the art of candy making, having learned their craft at the knees of the generation before them. Armed with a glob of butter the size of an egg or a pinch of soda the size of a bean, they could turn out a batch of homemade goodies that would rival even the most expensive of confections that we now purchase.

Few of us bother to make our own candies today, perhaps because we do not have time, or perhaps because we do not know how. Regardless of the reasons, the art of candy making is quickly vanishing from the American home. *Who Wants Candy?* is an effort to preserve the recipes of another generation, as well as the bit of Americana they represent, before they are lost to us forever.

J. S., 2004

# Basic Things to Know

Many of us are intimidated at the thought of making our own candies, but only because we have not mastered a few basic principles that every candy maker should know. By following just a few simple steps, even the novice candy maker can produce delicious homemade goodies that everyone will enjoy.

## Choosing the Right Candy Kettle

The ideal cooking pan is a saucepan or kettle made of heavy aluminum. Nonstick coatings are not required and make little difference in cooking or cleanup. The pan should have a sturdy handle to grip during stirring, beating, and pouring. Lids are required in some recipes but not all. Lightweight stainless steel pans are not recommended for most candies because ingredients such as milk, cream, and butter can easily scorch.

Saucepans with bowed sides are beautiful but not practical for candy making. The bowed sides often do not distribute the heat evenly throughout the pan, meaning that candy ingredients may not cook properly. Pans should have straight sides or rounded sides with an opening larger than the base. Place the saucepan or kettle on a burner that is as wide or wider than the sides of the pan so that the sides of the pan remain heated during cooking.

My official candy kettle is a deep 4.5-quart banged-up beauty that began life as an aluminum pressure cooker nearly 60 years ago. This coveted family heirloom has probably produced a thousand batches of candy, yet it still cooks as well today as it did when my mother first christened it "The Candy Pot" in the late 1940s. Similar pans are often available at garage sales or estate sales for only a few dollars. For smaller recipes, I use nonstick heavy aluminum saucepans from one of two sets of everyday cookware.

As I was putting the finishing touches on this book, one of my younger family members entertained me with tales about her first solo

1

batch of fudge. Her story reminded me that old candy makers sometimes forget to tell new candy makers a thing or two, like candy ingredients that barely cover the bottom of a huge kettle when cold may overwhelm the kitchen when hot. A boiling candy mixture has a tendency to take on a life of its own, with some increasing in volume by as much as 500 percent, especially if the recipe includes buttermilk and baking soda. To avoid a major cleanup effort, use a pan larger than you think you need.

## Cooking with Candy Thermometers

I strongly recommend investing in a good, sturdy candy thermometer. I rarely make candy without mine. Why toy with disaster when a little gadget will tell us all we need to know?

Candy thermometers should have very specific markings showing temperatures in 2-degree increments. Those encased in metal are often sturdier, easier to use, and less likely to break than those made only of glass. This type of thermometer is available at stores that sell kitchen supplies or candy-making equipment. Two brand names are Taylor and Comark, though other brands may work equally well. More expensive digital thermometers are also available in specialty stores. Glass thermometers are available in some grocery stores for only a few dollars, but the least expensive models can be difficult to read.

Clip the thermometer to the side of the pan so that the tip is covered by the candy mixture. Do not let the thermometer rest on the bottom of the pan where it can give a false reading. Most metal-encased thermometers have a bottom lip to prevent the glass portion from touching the pan. Depending on the size and shape of the pan, thermometers may also be placed in the middle of the pan, with the thermometer resting on the pan's outer edge. During cooking, it is important to move the thermometer occasionally and stir underneath it. Do not place the thermometer in the pan until after the sugar dissolves and the mixture comes to a boil.

To clean a thermometer, soak it in hot, soapy water until the sugar mixture dissolves, and then rinse it and pat it dry. Scrubbing a thermometer may erase the markings, making it difficult to read. Thermometers can be damaged if not carefully stored away from knives and other heavy cooking utensils.

If a candy thermometer is not available, refer to the Candy-Cooking Guide (page 7) for another method to tell when the candy is done.

## Final Cooking Temperatures

The purpose of cooking candy is to change the texture of ingredients by reducing or "cooking out" excess moisture. The temperature rises as the moisture evaporates, with sugar changing forms as it cooks. Cooked sugar gradually progresses through a series of stages known as the soft ball, medium ball, firm ball, hard ball, soft crack, and hard crack stages. Each of these stages defines a candy's moisture content and affects texture, which is why it is necessary to monitor cooking temperatures so closely.

Cooking temperatures can be adjusted for personal preferences as long as they fall within a range of temperatures appropriate for that type of candy. For example, one person may prefer a specific fudge recipe when cooked to 236°F, while another prefers that same recipe cooked to 234°F for a slightly softer fudge or to 238°F for a slightly firmer fudge. For this reason, many of the temperatures cited in this book are recommendations rather than edicts.

If a candy is too dry for your taste, cook it 1 to 2 degrees lower next time, thus letting it retain more moisture. If it is too soft, sticky, or tacky, cook it 1 to 2 degrees higher next time, thus decreasing the moisture. Record temperatures as you cook so that you can duplicate your best candies again.

## Cooking Candies in Humid Conditions

Most candy experts recommend cooking candies on a clear day if possible and increasing the temperature by 1 to 2 degrees on particularly damp or humid days. While bad weather is broadly thought to adversely affect candies, I have not found it to be a major factor in the success or failure of any particular recipe. I tend to pay more attention to seasons rather than cloud cover, cooking soft candies like fudge a little longer in the summer to fortify them against Oklahoma's notorious summer heat.

## Cooking Candies at High Altitudes

Those who live in high altitudes must adjust cooking temperatures for their specific altitude. To make these adjustments, insert a candy thermometer into a pan of cool water and place over medium heat. Bring the water to a boil, noting the precise temperature on the candy thermometer as the water reaches the boiling point. Subtract that temperature reading from 212°F (the boiling point of water at sea level), and then reduce the cooking temperature by the difference.

For example, if the water boils at 202°F, subtract 202°F from 212°F. The result is 10, meaning that candy cooked at that altitude will reach the desired consistency 10 degrees sooner than when cooked at sea level. There-fore, reduce the recommended cooking temperature of your candies by 10 degrees.

## Temperatures for Cooking Candies

Unless directed otherwise, candies should be cooked slowly over low or medium heat. Cooking too quickly can cause candies to scorch or become grainy.

## Stirring Candy

In candy making, the phrase "stir constantly" usually means slow, gentle stirring rather than fast, vigorous stirring. The purpose of stirring is simply to keep the mixture moving so that it does not scorch on the bottom or the sides of the pan. I often stir in a slow, rhythmic figure-eight pattern through the center of the pan, occasionally coming out of my trance long enough to lift the thermometer and stir underneath it. Too much stirring may cause candy to be grainy, so do not stir more than necessary.

Many old-time candy makers believe that candy should only be stirred or beaten with wooden spoons, often warning that anything but a wooden spoon will ruin the candy. While I usually use a wooden spoon, I have cooked with metal spoons without noticing any significant difference. In one recipe, Aunt Bill's Brown Candy (page 28), I often choose a metal spoon because it gives me a better feel for what is happening on the bottom of the kettle. If the metal spoon drags across the pan, I know that the caramelized sugar has not yet fully dissolved.

## Preventing Sugar Crystals

Some recipes call for removing sugar crystals that form on the sides of the pan as a result of sugar that has not fully dissolved. This can be a crucial step, as even one crystal can prompt a chain of crystals to form and make a candy grainy.

The two most common methods for removing crystals are (1) to place the lid on the pan for a few minutes so that crystals will dissolve in the trapped moisture or (2) to wash the crystals (or wipe them) from the sides of the pan with a damp pastry brush or cloth-wrapped fork while cooking. I prefer the lid method, but brushing the sides of the pan with a pastry brush that has been dipped in water can be equally effective. If in doubt about sugar crystals, cover the pan for 2 to 3 minutes just after it begins to boil. This requires very little effort and can only improve the candy, not harm it. Be aware that covered candy can boil over the sides of the pan very easily, so lift the lid occasionally to make sure you are not headed for disaster.

Some recipes may specify not to stir, move, or shake a mixture while it is cooking or to pour without scraping the sides or bottom of the pan. For example, Grace's Walnut Butter Fudge (page 98), calls for pouring the cooked mixture into a clean, dry container without scraping the pan. This is because moving, shaking, and scraping can prompt a chain of sugar crystals to form, making a candy grainy.

## Beating Candy

Unless directed otherwise, candies that require beating should be beaten by hand until they cool, lose their gloss, and begin to stiffen. These are signs that the chemical changes that affect texture are complete. Electric mixers are a poor substitute for hand beating and will not necessarily yield the same results. Additionally, many old-fashioned candies are too thick and heavy to beat with most electric mixers

without causing motor damage. Unless a recipe specifies to use an electric mixer, consider it a risk. The one exception may be fudges containing marshmallow creme. A few short minutes of beating with an electric mixer does not seem to hurt these candies and can often help them.

In most recipes, it is important to use a clean spoon for beating. For example, in Grace's Walnut Butter Fudge (page 98), the only time a spoon is used to stir the mixture is at the very beginning of the cooking process. If we later pick up that same spoon to beat the cooked candy, the undissolved sugar left on the spoon will be mixed into the candy and may cause a chain of sugar crystals to form.

## Cooling Candy

Many candies may be cooled in the refrigerator or freezer. Some candies, especially fudges, often cut more neatly if slightly chilled first. Occasionally, a candy cooled in the refrigerator or freezer develops a sticky coating. This is especially true of hard candies made from a mixture of sugar and corn syrup, such as Glass Candy (page 48), Horehound Candy (page 49), or Hardtack Candy (page 50). These types of candies should always be cooled at room temperature.

As a general rule, if a finished candy can be stored in the refrigerator or freezer, it can be cooled in the refrigerator or freezer. Cool others at room temperature.

## Storing Candy

Store candy in airtight containers to prevent drying. Refrigeration is often a matter of personal choice, though many candies will keep longer if properly covered and chilled.

Hard candies like toffees or brittles may absorb moisture and become sticky if stored with soft candies like fudge, so it is best to store them in separate containers.

Because most candies that come through my kitchen are ingested within a matter of hours, it is difficult to say exactly how long candies might keep in a home graced with willpower. Cooked candies such as fudge should retain their freshness at least 1 month if properly covered and stored in the refrigerator. Aunt Bill's Brown Candy (page 28) is rumored to keep indefinitely, though indefinitely has never visited my home. Some pralines seem to lose their eye appeal after only a few days yet are still tasty at least 2 weeks after cooking, especially when individually sealed in plastic wrap. Some truffles and ball-type candies may begin to show their age after a week or so, though the majority of these same candies can be frozen for later use. Certainly any candy containing raw, uncooked eggs should be stored in the refrigerator and eaten within 2 to 3 days, if not sooner. (See Cook's Note, page 145, concerning eating uncooked eggs.) This rule does not apply to divinity, as the hot syrup that is poured over the beaten egg whites should heat the whites sufficiently to consider them cooked.

## Packaging Candy for Gifts

Some craft stores and candy-making supply stores offer coated, direct-pour candy boxes in ½-pound or 1-pound sizes that are perfect for gift giving. Simply pour the warm candy into these boxes, allow the candy to cool, and then seal the box in plastic wrap. Place the lid on the box, tie it with a decorative bow, and the candy is ready to hand to a friend or ship across the country.

Any sturdy, decorative box can be made into a direct-pour candy box with a set of kitchen shears, a little parchment paper, and some butter. Cut a piece of parchment paper to exactly fit the bottom of the box, and then generously butter both the parchment paper and the sides of the box. Place the buttered parchment paper into the bottom of the box. Once the candy is finished as directed, simply pour the warm candy on top of the parchment paper. After the candy cools, seal the box in plastic wrap, and then add the lid and a decorative bow. Both types of boxes work very well for candies such as fudge, and the final presentation is worth the effort.

Cellophane bags are an impressive yet inexpensive way to present favorite toffees, brittles, barks, and hard candies to family, friends, and coworkers, especially when tied with a festive bow. These bags can also be used to package candies like fudges, pralines, or caramels, especially if each piece of candy is individually wrapped in plastic wrap first. Large craft store chains often sell packages of these bags near candy-making supplies. Shop early because cellophane bags seem to disappear from the shelves just as the holiday season approaches.

Most craft stores and some grocery stores carry small, fluted paper candy cups designed to hold bonbons, truffles, and other chocolate-dipped candies. When small candies are placed into these cups and then into a decorative box, they can be just as beautiful as professionally packaged candies. Coordinating the color of the candy cup with the candy's flavor, such as using red or pink candy cups for Luscious Raspberry-Fudge Truffles (page 177), is a nice way to let friends distinguish one chocolate-coated candy from another.

## The Candy Maker's Personality: Getting the Right Frame of Mind

I spent years wondering why my mother was more successful with some candy recipes than I was, finally uncovering the secret while writing this book. My mother has the ideal personality to be a candy maker. She never hurries her candy along, she never puts much effort into stirring, and she is more than happy to let some candies simmer quietly on the stove while tending to another task. Above all, she never worries, becomes frustrated, or takes shortcuts.

I, on the other hand, spent years turning the heat to the highest possible setting, often pushing it to the extreme. My spoon never stopped moving, as I was certain that the constant clatter in my kitchen would somehow make candy cook faster. I chained myself to the stove, watching every bubble, every degree, and every tick of the clock. Patience may be a virtue, but my mother got my share.

Eventually I discovered that the more patient I became, the better my candies tasted. My date and pecan rolls were smoother, my

## Safety First

Candy mixtures can be dangerously hot, especially for little ones standing underfoot. Use great caution when cooking, stirring, carrying, or pouring hot candy to prevent burns and spills on children, pets, and yourself. Nothing is more satisfying than introducing a child to candy making, but place safety above all else. Provide full-time adult supervision, and never leave a child alone with hot candies.

fudges creamier, and my Aunt Bill's Brown Candy (page 28) began to rival my mother's. That may be my finest achievement yet.

As a result of this "research," my single best piece of advice for anyone wanting to become a candy maker is to be slightly lazy about it. Pull up a chair, sit near the stove, turn down the heat, and daydream while you stir. Candy will cook at its own pace if you let it.

# Candy-Cooking Guide

## Cold Water Testing Procedure

Even though it is always recommended to use a candy thermometer, some cooks still depend on dropping the hot syrup into cold water to determine if the candy is ready. Some cooks like to check the temperature with a thermometer and do the cold water test.

First remove the saucepan from the heat so that the temperature does not rise during testing. Drop about ½ teaspoon of the boiling hot syrup into a glass of cold water. Test the firmness of the mixture by shaping it with your fingers. Use fresh cold water for each test.

### SOFT BALL STAGE * 234°F TO 240°F
*For fondants, fudges, and penuches*
Soft ball may be formed under cold water but flattens some when picked up.

### MEDIUM BALL STAGE * 241°F TO 244°F
(Not indicated on candy thermometers)
*For old-fashioned fudgelike candies*
Medium ball firmer than soft ball.

### FIRM BALL STAGE * 244°F TO 248°F
*For caramels*
Firm ball may be formed and holds its shape unless pressed.

### HARD BALL STAGE * 250°F TO 265°F
*For divinities, marshmallows, nougats, popcorn balls, and taffies*
Hard ball may be formed and retains its shape. The ball is hard enough to be rolled on a buttered surface.

### SOFT CRACK STAGE * 270°F TO 290°F
*For butterscotches*
Hard threads form as the hot syrup strikes the cold water. They will be chewy and stick to the teeth.

### HARD CRACK STAGE * 300°F TO 310°F
*For brittles and toffees*
Hard, brittle threads form as the hot syrup strikes the cold water.

# Skill Levels: What Do They Mean?

**M**any candy makers often want guidance in choosing recipes appropriate for their level of expertise. The recipes in this book can be classified into one of five categories, ranging from those candies that anyone can make to those best reserved for experienced candy makers. Keep in mind that most of these groupings are based upon the amount of skill required to make the recipe rather than the amount of time required.

## Novice, Super Simple

For the most part, Super Simple recipes require opening a few packages, measuring a few ingredients, and stirring a few things together. Even those who claim they cannot boil water should have no trouble with these recipes since no cooking is involved.

## Novice, Easy

Easy recipes do not require any exceptional culinary skill, though some may be time-consuming. For example, most chocolate-coated candies are stirred together, formed into balls, and dipped into melted chocolate. Recipes of this nature are not difficult, though shaping and dipping individual candies takes time. Most truffle recipes are also grouped into this category since they involve heating, mixing, and shaping ingredients. No-bake cookies also carry this rating.

## Average

Most candies in the Average category must be cooked to a specific temperature but do not require significant hand beating. Examples are marshmallow fudges, toffees, brittles, caramel popcorn, and most old-fashioned hard candies. Those who have a basic understanding of cooking procedures should make these candies successfully.

## Advanced

Candies in the Advanced category involve some level of precision cooking. Not only must the candies cook to a specific temperature, but most also require hand beating. Often, deciding when a candy is properly beaten is more of a judgment call than an exact science. Most traditional cooked candies and old-fashioned fudge recipes fall within this category, as do the divinity recipes.

## Expert

These candies involve extra time or multiple steps and should be attempted by those who are experienced candy makers or those who have excellent cooking skills. For example, Aunt Bill's Brown Candy (page 28) not only requires precision cooking, but it also requires cooking and stirring two mixtures simultaneously. Though it is a wonderful old recipe to be enjoyed by many, it is not the place for novices to begin.

# Jane's Top Forty

With so many delicious candies made from the four basic food groups of sugar, cream, butter, and chocolate, choosing my favorites can be impossible. These forty recipes are some of my top selections for candy makers of all ages and all skill levels for all occasions. Many of the candies on this list are recipes I have enjoyed for many years, with some being recent discoveries that are too good not to mention.

# The Science of Candy Making

Candy making is based upon sugar chemistry, with different ingredients and different methods producing different candies. Some fundamental knowledge of how the different ingredients interact with the sugar is very useful if we want to improve a candy's texture or compare one recipe to another.

Most traditional candies fall into one of two categories, crystalline or noncrystalline. Crystalline candies include old-fashioned fudges, penuches, divinities, nougats, pecan rolls, date rolls, and cooked fondants. All of these candies ideally contain very fine sugar crystals that form due to the combination of ingredients, the cooking temperature, and the beating process. If small crystals form slowly, the candy will be smooth and creamy. If large crystals form rapidly, the candy may become sugary or grainy. As candy makers, our job is to help the sugar crystals form slowly so that our candies will be extradelicious.

The purpose of cooking candies slowly and beating by hand is to encourage small crystals to form. Some crystalline candy recipes also recommend a cooling period between cooking and beating, often cooling the candy until it is lukewarm (110°F) or until you can comfortably hold your hand on the bottom of the pan. This cooling period is just one more step candy makers add to promote the formation of small crystals. Cooling is also a bonus for the cook because cooled candies usually require less beating than hot candies.

Ingredients also affect the crystallization process, with certain ingredients aiding crystallization and others hindering it. Some candy makers prefer recipes that include corn syrup, which is known for producing ultrasmooth candies. Butter and cream also reduce the size of sugar crystals and give our candies that silky texture that we love. Noncrystalline candies, such as brittles, toffees, butterscotches, caramels, and taffies, ideally do not contain any sugar crystals and, therefore, often call for large amounts of these ingredients. Acidic ingredi-

11

ents, such as vinegar, lemon juice, and cream of tartar, also work to prevent crystallization. Some of the creamiest candies in this collection often contain at least one, if not two, forms of acid, along with corn syrup, butter, and cream.

## Modifying Recipes

This example shows how to put this knowledge to practical use. I had the following recipe for pineapple fudge.

**3 cups granulated sugar**
**1 tablespoon light corn syrup**
**½ cup heavy cream**
**1 (8-ounce) can crushed pineapple, drained**
**2 tablespoons butter**
**½ teaspoon vanilla extract**
**1 cup coarsely chopped walnuts or black**
**    walnuts (optional)**

At first glance, I expected the candy to be creamy, but instead it was grainy and best used as a brick. The small amount of heavy cream did not give it the moisture it needed so the candy cooked too quickly, even when placed over low heat. I modified the recipe, adding slightly more corn syrup to prevent crystallization; plus I added ½ cup light cream to give it moisture. My second version was better, but it still was not what I wanted.

On the third try, I added lemon juice, cream of tartar, and a little more corn syrup. Because half-and-half has more moisture than heavy cream, I chose to use all half-and-half rather than a mixture of the two creams. Though I could have adjusted my cooking temperature down 1 or 2 degrees to correct the dryness, I added a little more butter after the candy was cooked. This is the modified list of ingredients.

**3 cups granulated sugar**
**3 tablespoons light corn syrup**
**1 cup half-and-half**
**1 (8-ounce) can crushed pineapple, drained**
**2 teaspoons lemon juice**
**¼ teaspoon cream of tartar**
**¼ cup butter**
**¼ teaspoon pure lemon extract**
**1 cup coarsely chopped walnuts (optional)**

In the end, I had an ultrasmooth, light-colored, pineapple-speckled fudge, which is exactly what I wanted when I started. My last-minute decision to use lemon extract versus vanilla extract was nothing more than an adventure, but it gave the flavor an extra boost and branded the recipe as my own.

## Comparison of Three Recipes for Pralines

As you can see, the science of making candy is not nearly as complicated as it first appears to be. Just a little knowledge helps us customize a recipe to our tastes. Understanding how ingredients interact with one another also helps us choose which recipes might have the texture we like.

For example, Perfect Pralines (page 56) tend to be somewhat creamier than most traditional pralines. This is due to the buttermilk used in the recipe, as buttermilk contains acid and acid helps prevent crystallization.

**INGREDIENTS FOR PERFECT PRALINES**
**1 cup buttermilk**
**2 cups granulated sugar**
**1 teaspoon baking soda**
**½ cup butter or margarine (butter preferred)**
**⅛ teaspoon salt**

**2½ cups pecans in large pieces**
**1 teaspoon vanilla extract**

Soft Pecan Pralines (page 59) do not contain any acid, but they do contain large quantities of corn syrup, cream, and butter or margarine, all of which are known to reduce the size of crystals. Therefore, we know that Soft Pecan Pralines may also be creamier than most traditional praline recipes.

INGREDIENTS FOR SOFT PECAN PRALINES
**2 cups granulated sugar**
**⅓ cup light corn syrup**
**⅔ cup heavy cream**
**Pinch of salt**
**2 cups pecans in large pieces**
**¼ cup butter or margarine**
**½ teaspoon vanilla extract**

Ruth's Angel Pralines (page 58) do not contain any acid; plus the recipe calls for relatively low amounts of cream and butter. If we think about sugar and what affects its crystallization, we know that this combination of ingredients is likely to produce sugary, traditional pralines.

INGREDIENTS FOR RUTH'S ANGEL PRALINES
**1 cup granulated sugar**
**1 cup packed light brown sugar**
**½ cup half-and-half**
**¼ teaspoon salt**
**2 tablespoons butter or margarine**
**1 cup pecans in large pieces**

Eventually, analyzing recipes becomes second nature as we learn which candies we like and which ingredients will produce them.

# Duplicating Lost Recipes

One of the purposes of including a wide variety of similar candies is to help cooks locate cherished recipes that may have been lost from one generation to the next. Often, the first step to finding a recipe similar to the one lost is to write down everything remembered about the candy.

For example, if you are trying to duplicate your mother's delicious date roll, what do you remember about the way she cooked? Did she like easy recipes that just involved mixing a few ingredients together in a bowl, or was she an old-fashioned candy maker who let candies simmer slowly on the stove?

Do you remember any special processes she may have used, such as hand beating or kneading? People often comment that their mothers kept date roll candy rolled in a damp towel, which is a sure sign that they are trying to duplicate an old-fashioned, slow-cooked date roll rather than a quick date roll. Any little tidbit of information, such as, Mom always cooked in an old iron skillet, can be a clue.

Did the candy have cherries, marshmallows, pineapple, or other unusual ingredients that could lead you to the recipe? Do you remember it having a brown sugar flavor, or was it just brown in color? For example, most date rolls are some shade of brown, but recipes that contain brown sugar often have a strong brown sugar taste. Candies containing melted, caramelized sugar also have a distinctive flavor, though it is a milder flavor than that of brown sugar.

Do you remember your mother using corn syrup in candies, cookies, or other kinds of recipes? If so, then it is likely that the recipe you want contains corn syrup because candy makers often follow patterns.

What kind of texture did the candy have? Was it sugary or smooth? By reading about The Science of Candy Making (page 11), it may be easier to determine the kinds of ingredients that can produce the texture you remember.

Once you have gathered every bit of information available about the candy you want to duplicate, select a few recipes to try. If you still do not have an exact match, consider modifying a near match by adjusting a few ingredients, using the information in The Science of Candy Making. For example, adding corn syrup often makes a candy smoother, and light cream or evaporated milk produces a richer candy than milk. A dry candy can often be made creamier by adding a little extra butter after cooking, and cocoa powder or unsweetened chocolate can usually be increased or decreased as desired. The amount of sugar in a recipe can often be modified slightly, though this may depend upon the particular recipe or type of candy being made. Ingredients such as salt and vanilla can be added or eliminated, and nuts are typically a matter of personal choice.

# Candy Glossary

The glossary includes old-fashioned phrases, such as "butter the size of an egg," to help you update any old family recipes that might be in your recipe collection or ones found in an old cookbook, as well as terms such as "candy coating," used in candy making today.

**BLOCK CHOCOLATE** High-quality, gourmet chocolate that is usually cut to order and sold by the pound from large blocks. It is available from a variety of chocolate manufacturers in many price ranges from high-end grocery stores and specialty stores in some major cities. Those who cannot purchase block chocolate can often substitute the highest quality chocolate available for block chocolate.

**BROWN SUGAR** Granulated sugar combined with molasses to make a soft brown sugar. The darker the color of the brown, the stronger the flavor a product made with it will have.

**BUTTER THE SIZE OF AN EGG** Usually in a much older recipe, 4 tablespoons butter.

**BUTTER THE SIZE OF A WALNUT** Often found in older recipes, 2 tablespoons butter.

**BUTTERMILK** In the days when families churned their own butter, they often used the milky substance drained from freshly churned butter for cooking purposes. This "buttermilk" was a staple in most rural kitchens and was commonly used in place of fresh milk. Today's cooks find buttermilk in the refrigerated section of most grocery stores. Used according to package directions, dried buttermilk works well in baked goods, but do not use dried buttermilk for candy recipes.

**CANDY-COATING SQUARES** A product used to coat the outside of candies such as truffles, bonbons, turtles, or other chocolate-dipped candies or fruits. The advantage to the candy-coating squares is that they are premixed with both chocolate and a firming agent so that the candy's outside coating dries very quickly. Coating squares are a more modern approach to making homemade chocolate-dipped candies than previous generations used, but all brands are not available in some parts of the country. Coating squares are available in milk chocolate, dark chocolate, white chocolate, and imitation chocolate flavoring. Not all manufacturers offer their product in the form of squares; some companies offer round discs or flat chips. Two brand names that may be found in some grocery stores are Ghirardelli and Baker's. Three brand names that may be available in specialty stores that feature candy-making supplies or via the Internet are Nestle, Bakel's, and Merckens.

**CHERRIES, CANDIED** The same syrup-coated cherries used in most fruitcake recipes. They are available in both red and green colors and are usually sold in clear plastic 4-ounce or 8-ounce containers. Two brand names are Seneca and Paradise. Grocers often display candied cherries in the produce department, in the baking aisle, with dried fruits and nuts, and/or with the seasonal fruitcake ingredients. Green candied cherries do not always have the same flavor as red candied cherries; use red candied cherries for the recipes in this book unless otherwise specified. Many grocers carry candied cherries as a seasonal holiday item, sometimes making them difficult to locate for about nine months of the year. Candied cherries may be tightly sealed and refrigerated or frozen for later use.

**CLABBER MILK** Unpasteurized milk that soured and thickened due to lack of refrigeration. It was used as a beverage and in cooking before refrigeration was common.

**CONFECTIONERS' SUGAR** Another name for powdered sugar (see page 19).

**CORN SYRUP** Light or dark corn syrup added to candies to prevent crystallization. The dark syrup is used when a caramel flavor is desired.

**CREAM OF TARTAR** An acid in powder form added to candies to make them creamier by retarding the formation of large crystals. Other acids sometimes added to candy include lemon juice or vinegar.

**CUBE OF MARGARINE OR BUTTER** Occasionally appearing in old recipes, the equivalent of 1 stick, ¼ pound, or ½ cup of butter or margarine.

**EVAPORATED MILK** Milk from which 60% of the water has been removed. It is typically sold in 5-ounce and 12-ounce cans. One 5-ounce can of evaporated milk contains slightly less than ⅔ cup. One 12-ounce can of evaporated milk contains 1½ cups. Evaporated milk and sweetened condensed milk are different products and cannot be used interchangeably.

**FLAVORED OILS** Flavored oils such as cinnamon oil, clove oil, or anise oil that are much more concentrated than extracts and appear most often in recipes for old-fashioned hard candies. Flavored oils usually come packaged in very small bottles, with cooks measuring them by drops rather than by teaspoons. Oils can often be found in stores that specialize in baking supplies, candy-making supplies, or craft items.

**GLYCERIN USP** A thick, slick liquid usually sold as a skincare product and a common ingredient in skin lotions. It can also be a home remedy for removing difficult stains, such as chocolate, from washable clothing. In candy making, glycerin may be added to fondant recipes to make very soft centers for bonbons. Occasionally, it can appear in other candy recipes such as those for taffy. Most pharmacies sell glycerin in small bottles of about 4 ounces each for just a few dollars. It is available in craft stores that sell cake and candy-making supplies. Leftover glycerin can be used as a skin protectant or softener.

**GRANULATED SUGAR** Common white sugar. If a recipe simply calls for sugar, this is the one to use.

**HEAVY CREAM** Whipping cream containing less moisture and a higher fat content than light cream or half-and-half.

**HOMOGENIZED MILK** Milk in which the size of the fat particles are distributed throughout the milk, staying in suspension. Today most of our milk is both pasteurized and homogenized. Pasteurization destroys any bacteria in the milk and makes it safe for consumption. The cream does not rise to the surface (see Top milk, on page 19) as it does in unhomogenized milk.

**LIGHT CREAM** A mixture of cream and milk. The definition of light cream often depends upon who answers the question. Older adults who grew up in rural America often think of light cream as a mixture of cream and milk that came from the family cow, or unhomogenized milk. The proportion of cream to milk often depended upon the type of milk cow the family owned and who was holding the dipper. In other words, the definition of light cream was a judgment call based upon experience, not on an exact science. Commercial light cream contains between 18% and 30% fat, but it is not available nationwide. Because we do not usually find a product called "light cream" on grocery store shelves, most of today's cooks interpret this term to mean half-and-half. For purposes of the recipes in this book, half-and-half, which contains between 10% and 12% fat, is used for any recipe that called originally for light cream.

**MAPLE SUGAR** A product derived from maple syrup harvested from sugar maple trees. It can be difficult to locate in grocery stores but can be ordered via the Internet. For a list of potential sources, visit the Vermont Maple Sugar Maker's Association web site at www.vermont maple.org.

**MAPLE SYRUP** Pure maple syrup boiled from the sap from maple trees. It is very expensive so often maple-blended syrups are used.

**MOLASSES** A sweetener made from the juice of the sugar cane. Use dark molasses for a strong molasses flavor.

**NUTS** Often called nutmeats in older recipes, an important ingredient in many candies. The type and quantity of nuts used in candies is often a personal choice, though most recipes that simply call for "nuts" assume the use of either pecans or walnuts. Be sure to buy fresh nuts and keep them in the refrigerator or freezer to prevent them from turning rancid. For most candies, I prefer to buy walnut or pecan halves and break them by hand into smaller pieces rather than chop them in a food processor, for hand breaking produces larger pieces. Fresh nuts are usually far more flavorful than the packaged nuts commonly found with baking ingredients and can make a significant contribution to the flavor of a candy. Avoid using finely chopped nuts available in the supermarket, if possible.

**OLEO OR OLEOMARGARINE** The original name of the vegetable oil spread that we now know as margarine. In most cases, if a recipe calls for oleo, either margarine or butter may be used.

**PARAFFIN WAX** Sometimes called paraffin, a product that was commonly used to seal jars of homemade jams, jellies, and preserves and added to chocolate to make shiny, hard coatings on dipped candies. However, paraffin wax is no longer approved by the U.S. Food and Drug Administration for use in food. For newer recipes for candy coatings, see page 151.

**PINEAPPLE, CANDIED** The same chopped, syrup-coated pineapple used in most fruitcake recipes. It is usually sold in clear plastic 4-ounce or 8-ounce containers. Two brand names are Seneca and Paradise. Grocers often display candied pineapple in the produce department, in the baking aisle, with dried fruits and nuts, and/or with the seasonal fruitcake ingredients. Many grocers carry candied pineapple as a seasonal holiday item, sometimes making it difficult to locate for about nine months of the year. Candied pineapple may be tightly sealed and refrigerated or frozen for later use.

**POWDERED SUGAR** Granulated sugar that has been ground into a powder. Cornstarch is added to prevent clumping. If clumps do form, measure the sugar and then sift it before using.

**RICH MILK** Much like top milk (see right), an ambiguous term once used to describe milk that was rich in fat, with exact proportions of

cream to milk left open for interpretation. Today's cook can use half-and-half or whole milk with 4% fat.

**SEA SALT** Sea salt is a coarse form of salt often used in gourmet cooking. It is usually found near table salt in large grocery stores.

**SORGHUM SYRUP OR PURE SORGHAM** A product made from the juice of certain types of sorghum cane. It is sometimes called sorghum molasses, but that term is now used for a combination of sorghum syrup and molasses.

**SUMMER CHOCOLATE COATING** Another term for candy coating.

**SUPERFINE SUGAR** Sugar that contains smaller granules than regular granulated sugar. It should not be substituted for the granulated sugar used in recipes in this book.

**SWEET MILK** An old term used to describe the fresh, unspoiled table milk that we now buy in grocery stores to pour over our cereal.

**SWEETENED CONDENSED MILK** A thick, highly concentrated form of milk with added sugar and about 60% of the water removed. It is typically sold in 14-ounce cans. Common brand names are Eagle Brand and Carnation. Sweetened condensed milk and evaporated milk cannot be used interchangeably. One 14-ounce can of sweetened condensed milk contains approximately 1¼ cups.

**TOP MILK** An ambiguous term once used to describe the creamy substance that rose to the top of the milk from the family cow or the grocery store before homogenization. As in light cream, the proportion of cream to milk often depended upon what type of milk cow the family owned and who was holding the dipper. Today's cook should use half-and-half for recipes requiring top milk.

**VANILLA EXTRACT** Choice of pure vanilla extract or imitation vanilla extract. While gourmet and imported vanilla extracts are now popular with many cooks, logic tells us that previous generations did not have these choices and thus used common brands of vanilla extracts in their candies. In some cases, gourmet or double-strength vanilla extracts may significantly alter the taste of a candy, sometimes overwhelming subtle flavors such as caramelized sugar or chocolate and completely changing the end product. For this reason, I use common brands of vanilla extract, such as Durkee's, McCormick's, or Adam's, reserving strongly flavored vanilla extracts for other foods.

**WHOLE MILK** Whole milk is milk containing 4% butterfat. Skim or nonfat milk (except for instant nonfat dry milk) is seldom used in candy making because some fat is needed to produce proper candy texture. Older recipes in particular assume that whole milk will be used, as lower-fat milk was most likely not available at the time the recipe was created. If desired, milk containing 2% butterfat may usually be substituted in recipes requiring whole milk, though the candy may be slightly less rich or less creamy than it would be if whole milk were used.

# Problems and Solutions

**N**o matter what problem you encounter in candy making, someone has probably had a similar or worse experience. If your first candy-making attempt is less than successful, do not stop trying. Candy making becomes easier with experience. Most problems can be diagnosed and corrected rather easily.

### CANDY IS TOO SOFT, TOO STICKY, OR LIKE SOUP

The candy is probably undercooked. Increase the temperature by 1 or 2 degrees next time (or by 3 or 4 degrees if the candy was really like thin soup). High humidity could also be a factor, as well as underbeating.

### CANDY IS TOO DRY, TOO BRITTLE, OR RESEMBLES A BRICK

The candy is probably overcooked. Decrease the temperature by 1 or 2 degrees next time (or by 3 or 4 degrees if you could use it to break a window). Also consider the cooking pot used. Even if you followed all instructions, cooking in a lightweight pot can ruin a batch of candy.

### CANDY IS TOO GRAINY

A number of factors contribute to graininess. If you followed all directions, then the most likely causes are (1) you stirred too vigorously, (2) the candy was cooked too rapidly at too high a temperature, or (3) the sugar crystals were not removed from the sides of the pan. See Basic Things to Know (page 1) and The Science of Candy Making (page 11).

### CANDY IS TOO DARK, WOULD NOT COOK PROPERLY, AND TEXTURE IS INCORRECT

The saucepan or kettle used for cooking can make the difference between a good batch of candy and a "strange" one. Most candies should be cooked in a heavyweight pan made of a material such as aluminum, not in pans made of lightweight stainless steel. Candies cooked in stainless steel pots often cook too quickly, causing them to scorch. If the heat is reduced to accommodate the stainless steel pan, then the candy may cook so slowly that the sugar caramelizes.

Also check to see that the stove's heating element is working properly. The removable metal elements in electric burners can become old and worn, causing them to conduct heat unevenly or improperly.

## What to Do with Candy Failures

These are some interesting ideas other candy makers have shared about what they did with less-than-perfect candy.

If the candy is too soft and undercooked, stir in some powdered sugar before turning it into the pan. Another thought is to roll the candy into balls, and then roll the balls into coconut or chopped nuts.

When one woman had chocolate soup instead of fudge, she sprinkled a layer of coconut in the bottom of several small disposable dishes, poured her soup on top, and served it with a spoon. Her son thought it was so good that he asked her to make more.

A friend crumbled scorched toffee into small bits and added them to chocolate chip cookie dough. She said the cookies were delicious.

# Dipping Candies in Chocolate

A few years before writing this book, I read an article criticizing some of the older and more common products and techniques used for dipping candies in chocolate. I thought of all the "inferior" homemade candies I have enjoyed the past few decades. Many of these candies relied on melting chocolate with paraffin wax to give the candy a firm outer shell. Though millions of candy makers have used this combination successfully, we must now find other solutions, as the U. S. Food and Drug Administration does not considers paraffin wax safe for human consumption. Fortunately, we can now purchase specially designed chocolate candy coating products that offer the same firming qualities that paraffin wax once provided. For further information on these products, see Chocolate Coatings (page 151). If these products are not available locally, they can be ordered via the Internet.

Most candy makers eventually develop their own blends of chocolate and their own dipping techniques using tools and products that are commonly available. For example, I may combine dark chocolate candy coating with semisweet chocolate or milk chocolate to give my coatings a personal touch; sometimes adjusting the combination to accommodate different types of recipes. Occasionally I dip one type of candy using a specially designed dipping tool, and then dip another type of candy using a toothpick. How we go about coating our candies is often a matter of personal preference rather than a steadfast rule.

The focus of this chapter is to describe some of the methods others have used so that new candy makers have a starting point for developing their own techniques. Certainly, those who want to experiment with very high-quality chocolates and professional methods are encouraged to do so. Candy-making supply stores usually offer products, tools, and books to help you get started.

## Heating Chocolate

Professional chocolatiers heat high-quality chocolates through a process known as tempering, which involves the repeated heating and cooling of the chocolate to very specific temperatures. Tempering is what gives gourmet chocolate candies the beautiful gloss that we associate with luxury. The majority of home candy makers need not worry about tempering as long as they understand one basic fact: Chocolate can burn.

The purpose of melting chocolate in the top of a double boiler over hot water, not boiling water, is to prevent the chocolate from scorching. Chocolate that has been heated too long or at too high a temperature "seizes" and becomes an unsalvageable, grainy mess. Melted chocolate will also seize if a drop of water gets into it. The only way to recover from a seized batch of melted chocolate is to throw it away and start again.

Most candy makers take great care to keep chocolate from overheating because chocolate that has overheated can also lose its gloss. The exceptionally careful candy maker heats water in a pan, removes the pan from the heat, and then places the top double boiler pan containing the chocolate over the hot water, stirring until the chocolate has melted. This works best when working with very small amounts of chocolate.

I am not that careful or that patient, usually preferring to place the entire double boiler pan over very low heat, stirring the chocolate until melted. I remove the pan from the heat while dipping my candies, sometimes warming the pan again slightly as the chocolate cools and becomes too thick for coating.

Many people are not as careful or patient as I am, choosing to melt chocolate in the microwave rather than in a double boiler. This must be done with great care, especially if dealing with white chocolate and milk chocolate. The lighter the chocolate, the more easily it burns.

## Dipping Methods

One of the easiest and most common methods for dipping candies is to insert a toothpick into the center of the candy, dip the candy into the melted chocolate, and then drop it onto waxed paper to dry. Generations of Americans have successfully used this method, though it does have its drawbacks. The warm chocolate often pools underneath the candy as it dries, meaning that candies such as bonbons or truffles may have a flat bottom rather than being attractive, round balls. The toothpick also leaves a hole in the top of the candy. Dabbing a tiny amount of melted chocolate over the hole is one solution, but it can be time-consuming.

Another method is to drop the candy into the melted chocolate, remove it from the chocolate using either one or two forks, and then drop it onto waxed paper to dry. Unfortunately, the forks usually leave imprints on the outer chocolate coating. Though rolling the candy into chopped nuts will cover the imprints, not all of us want nut-coated candies.

When I first began making Chocolate-Dipped Strawberries (page 158), I developed my own method for dipping that eliminates the chocolate pools. Place a plastic colander on waxed paper, turning the colander upside down so that the rounded bottom is upright. Insert a toothpick into the strawberry or candy center, dip it into the melted chocolate, and then insert the toothpick into a hole on the colander. The excess chocolate drips off the candy onto the waxed paper rather than pooling underneath the coated ball or berry. Let the candies stand until firm or refrigerate the colander filled with the candies or berries until the chocolate cools. A large piece of hard foam or similar material could be used in place of the colander.

This homespun method offers a few improvements but is certainly not foolproof. Soft-centered candies such as truffles may fall off the toothpicks, ruining the candies and creating quite a mess. Once the coating is dry and the toothpicks removed, the candies still have holes in them, though at least the holes are at the bottom of the candies instead of on the top. For most candies this may not matter, but in the case of some soft-centered candies, such as Luscious Raspberry-Fudge Truffles (page 177), these holes must be covered with chocolate or the filling will ooze out of the hole.

By far, the best method for dipping fruits or candies is to use specially designed candy dipping tools. These tools are often available at large craft stores or candy-making supply stores for a very reasonable price. While very inexpensive plastic models are available, I prefer a moderately priced, two-piece wood and metal set made by Wilton. One tool is a long two-pronged fork; the other is a long hollow spoon that resembles a flat basket. Drop the ball or the candy into the melted chocolate, slide the hollow spoon or fork underneath it, lift, and gently tap the handle on the side of the double boiler to remove the excess chocolate. With a flip of the wrist, turn the candy over and drop it onto waxed paper. The hollow spoon often leaves an attractive swirl pattern on the top of the candy, making it appear professionally dipped. With just a little practice, you will wonder why you did not invest in a set of dipping tools long ago.

# Heirloom Candies

Like that bit of handmade lace found tucked in an old family cedar chest, the recipes in this collection are the legacies of another generation, each telling a story of the families who once held them dear. They remind us of

a different era in our country, a time when traditions passed from father to son, from mother to daughter, rooting each generation in the family history. Homemade candy was often at the center of these traditions, bringing excitement and adventure to everyday lives and marking special occasions with delectable treats.

Families once gathered in the heart of their homes, building fires to warm cold fingers and toes while Granddad told tall tales of bear hunting or sang silly ditties to amuse the children. They would shell fresh nuts scavenged in the woods, skim fresh cream from the pail of cow's milk left cooling in the water well, then marvel as a penny turned over upon Granddad's command. Homemade candy was as common as homespun entertainment, with fiddles, harmonicas, and taffy pulls bringing families and communities together for a night of

old-fashioned fun.

Some of the most delicious candies we have today are those once cherished by our grandmothers. They gave us extraordinary recipes such as Aunt Bill's Brown Candy, Patience Candy, or Penuche Nut Roll plus unusual recipes such as Holiday Pineapple Candy and Peanut Butter Cracker Candy, which is far more interesting than it sounds. They reminded us to use damp tea towels to shape date rolls, to remove any sugar crystals from the sides of the pan, and to beat divinity until the candy becomes very stiff. They taught us to make brittles and chocolate-topped toffees, to cook Black Walnut Caramels slowly, and to be inventive in the combinations we use. They wrapped pecans in rich white cream and coconut in sumptuous orange, mixed peanut butter with cinnamon or apricots and mashed potatoes with powdered sugar, delighting us with their novel ideas. They loved hard candies flavored with oils of peppermint, lemon, or anise and festive, colorful candies such as Fruit Fancies and the rich, nutty flavor of Perfect Pralines. They dazzled us with Caramel Pecan Rolls and brightened our day with Lollypops, showering us with sweet memories we can never forget.

Reminiscent of days gone by, these recipes are the legacies of our grandmothers, now gathered into one rare collection for you to enjoy. Even the most experienced candy makers will find new flavors and new adventures to explore. Many of these candies have brought joy to generation after generation for one simple reason: they truly are superb.

# Old-Fashioned Cooked Candies

## Aunt Bill's Brown Candy

### Skill Level: Expert

*Aunt Bill's Brown Candy is Oklahoma's pride and joy. This wonderful old recipe has circulated throughout my home state for at least 70 years and is rumored to have originated with an Oklahoma pioneer. No one seems to know exactly who Aunt Bill was, but we do know that she made one of the richest, smoothest, and most distinctivly flavored homemade candies that we have ever tasted.*

*One of my favorite stories about Aunt Bill's candy comes from a special hometown friend. For many years, LaVelle made this candy during the holidays much to her son-in-law's delight. Eventually when she grew older and retired from candy making, she framed her old handwritten recipe and gave it to him as a remembrance of the tradition they had shared.*

*Once my mother's signature candy, this recipe is challenging though not impossible. It takes two hours to make this caramel-colored, pecan-packed confection, but those of us who adore Aunt Bill's candy believe that no holiday is complete without it. If you have never made a candy such as this, consider recruiting a friend to help. I made my first batch with a dear friend over 20 years ago, and she and I still remember it as one of the best times we ever had together.*

*My family prefers the texture that comes from using evaporated milk, but some candy makers use whole milk or half-and-half, with a few choosing heavy cream or buttermilk. No matter how you make it, Oklahoma's beloved tradition is always a tasty adventure.*

✳ MAKES ABOUT 3 POUNDS

**6 cups granulated sugar, divided**
**2 cups evaporated milk**
**¼ teaspoon baking soda**
**½ cup margarine**
**1 teaspoon vanilla extract**
**2 cups pecans in large pieces**

Butter a 9 × 13-inch pan.

Place 2 cups of the sugar into a heavy aluminum or cast-iron skillet. Place the remaining 4 cups sugar and the milk into a heavy 5-quart kettle.

Melt the sugar in the skillet slowly over low heat, stirring constantly to prevent scorching. When fully melted, the caramelized sugar should be a golden brown liquid; it will take about 30 minutes.

While the sugar is melting, cook the sugar and milk slowly over low heat, stirring constantly but gently to prevent scorching. (Both the sugar in the skillet and the sugar and milk in the kettle must be stirred simultaneously.) The sugar and milk mixture should reach a slow boil 2 to 3 minutes before the sugar in the skillet is completely melted. If the sugar and milk begins to boil before the sugar in the skillet is almost completely melted, reduce the heat slightly, maintaining a slow, steady boil.

Slowly pour the melted sugar into the boiling sugar and milk mixture in a thin stream no larger than a knitting needle, stirring across the bottom of the kettle at all times to prevent the melted sugar from clumping. Any clumps of sugar that form may be dissolved later through cooking and stirring, but the candy is best when no large clumps are allowed to form. If the sugar and milk mixture begins to boil over the sides of the pan while adding the melted sugar, reduce the heat but maintain a slow, steady boil.

Cook the combined mixture, stirring slowly but constantly, over low heat to the firm ball stage (246°F), 35 to 40 minutes.

Remove from the heat. Add the baking soda; stir vigorously until the mixture foams and nearly doubles in volume, about 1 minute. Stir in the margarine just until melted. Set the candy away from the heat. Cool 20 minutes.

Add the vanilla. Using a sturdy wooden spoon, beat the candy by hand until it is thick and heavy and has a dull appearance, 20 to 25 minutes. Stir in the pecans. Turn into the buttered pan. Cool and cut into squares.

Store the candy in an airtight container. If covered and refrigerated, it will stay moist and delicious almost indefinitely.

COOK'S NOTES: Many believe that this recipe requires two cooks, and though it is nice to have an extra set of hands, one experienced candy maker can make this candy alone.

My mother was successful cooking Aunt Bill's to 244° F; I have better luck cooking it to 246°F. Do not vary the cooking temperature beyond this 2 degree range.

Proper beating is critical to this candy's texture. If in doubt about how to judge when this candy is properly beaten, set a kitchen timer for 20 minutes just as you begin beating. When the timer rings, the candy is usually ready for the pecans.

Strongly flavored or double-strength vanilla extracts can overwhelm the subtle caramelized sugar flavor of this candy and are not recommended. Brands of vanilla extract that are commonly found in most grocery stores, such as McCormick's, Adam's, or Durkee's, are recommended. Pure vanilla extract is best, but imitation vanilla extract may also be used. For the ultimate flavor, use fresh Oklahoma pecans. These can be purchased from Oklahoma pecan farmers via the Internet.

# Brown Sugar Candy

## Skill Level: Advanced

*With a strong brown sugar flavor, some may think of this as caramel fudge.*

✳ MAKES ABOUT 6 POUNDS

3 cups granulated sugar
3 cups packed light brown sugar
1 cup heavy cream
½ cup light corn syrup
½ cup water
2 teaspoons vanilla extract
2 cups chopped pecans or walnuts (optional)

Butter a 9 × 13-inch pan.

In a heavy 5-quart kettle over medium heat, bring the sugars, cream, corn syrup, and water to a boil, stirring until the sugars dissolve and the mixture begins to boil. Reduce the heat to medium low. Cover and cook 2 to 3 minutes to dissolve the sugar crystals on the sides of the pan. Remove the lid. Cook slowly, without stirring, over low to medium-low heat to the medium ball stage (242°F).

Remove from the heat. Cool about 1 hour to lukewarm (110°F).

Stir in the vanilla. Beat by hand until the candy loses its gloss and becomes creamy. Stir in the nuts, if desired. Pour into the buttered pan. Cool and cut into squares. Store in an airtight container.

COOK'S NOTES: The recipe may be reduced by half, cooked in a heavy 3-quart saucepan, and poured into a buttered 8- or 9-inch square pan.

For a similar candy, see Wildcat Maple Sugar Fudge (page 127).

- - - - - - - - - - - - - - - - - - - - - -

## Candy for the Troops

Candy has long been considered the ultimate comfort food, with homemade candy receiving top billing. Some military families have a long-standing tradition of sending homemade candy to family members serving our nation, sending the same candies to their loved ones today that their mothers and grandmothers sent to loved ones sixty years ago.

During World War II, our country rationed sugar so that soldiers on the battlefield could have a sweet reminder of home. The candy packaged in their C rations (now called MREs or meals ready to eat) was often the highlight of an exhausted GI's day. Sugar rationing in the U.S. lasted a little over five years, ending in June 1947.

# Golden Butter Nut Candy

## Skill Level: Advanced

*This golden, pecan-packed candy from the* Ponca City News *is far more interesting than the ingredients suggest, reminding some of Aunt Bill's Brown Candy (page 28).*

✳ MAKES ABOUT 6 POUNDS

**7 cups granulated sugar**
**2 cups dark corn syrup**
**1 cup butter**
**1 (12-ounce) can evaporated milk**
**2 cups pecans in large pieces**

Butter a 9 × 13-inch pan.

In a heavy 5-quart kettle over medium heat, bring the sugar, corn syrup, butter, and milk to a boil, stirring until the sugar dissolves and the mixture begins to boil. Cook, stirring frequently to prevent scorching, at a rolling boil to the high end of the soft ball stage or the medium ball stage (240°F to 242°F), about 17 minutes.

Remove from the heat. Stir in the pecans. Beat by hand until the candy becomes creamy and begins to hold its shape, 30 to 40 minutes. Pour into the buttered pan. Cool and cut into squares. Store in an airtight container.

### VARIATION

*Nut Candy Loaf:* Use 6 cups granulated sugar. Add 1 teaspoon vanilla extract to the candy while beating. Use 3 cups walnuts and 1 cup pecans in large pieces (or add the nuts to taste). Do not add the nuts until after the candy has been beaten and begins to hold its shape.

- - - - - - - - - - - - - - - - - - - - - -

# Fresh Buttermilk Candy

## Skill Level: Advanced

*If you have never had a candy such as this, you are missing one of the richest, most delectable treats invented. This caramel-colored, nut-packed confection has a soft texture and a deep, robust flavor.*

✳ MAKES ABOUT 1½ POUNDS

2 cups granulated sugar
⅔ cup buttermilk
1 teaspoon baking soda
¼ cup butter or margarine
1 teaspoon vanilla extract
1 cup pecans in large pieces

Butter a 9 × 5-inch loaf pan.

In a heavy 5-quart kettle over low heat, bring the sugar, buttermilk, and baking soda to a boil, stirring constantly to prevent scorching. The mixture will foam rapidly and rise in the kettle when it begins to boil. Cook, stirring constantly to prevent scorching, to the soft ball stage (234°F to 240°F, with 236°F recommended).

Remove from the heat. Add the butter and vanilla. Beat by hand until the candy thickens and loses its gloss. Stir in the pecans. Pour into the buttered pan. Cool and cut into squares. Store in an airtight container.

COOK'S NOTES: The buttermilk mixture can scorch very easily, making low heat and stirring a must.

If preferred, the finished candy may be dropped by spoonfuls onto waxed paper rather than poured into a pan.

For candies with a similar flavor, see Sinfully Rich Buttermilk Fudge (page 125), Perfect Pralines (page 56), Texas Pralines (page 56), and Ultra-Creamy Buttermilk Pralines (page 57).

# Sweet Buttermilk Candy

## Skill Level: Advanced

*This unusual and somewhat crispy candy looks and tastes like sweetened buttermilk.*

✳ MAKES ABOUT 1 POUND

2 cups granulated sugar
1 cup buttermilk
1 tablespoon butter
1 cup chopped pecans

Butter a 9 × 5-inch loaf pan or a plate.

In a heavy 3-quart saucepan over low heat, bring the sugar and buttermilk to a boil, stirring until the sugar dissolves and the mixture begins to boil. Cook, without stirring, to the soft ball stage (234°F to 240°F, with 234°F recommended).

Remove from the heat. Add the butter. Beat by hand until the candy thickens slightly. Add the pecans a few at a time, beating until the candy begins to lose its gloss. Quickly pour into the buttered pan. Cool and cut into squares. Store in an airtight container.

COOK'S NOTE: For a softer candy with a similar flavor, see Extra-Buttery Buttermilk Fudge (page 124).

# Butterscotch Nut Marshmallows

## Skill Level: Average

*The kid inside you will love these fluffy, white marshmallows coated in rich, gooey butterscotch and crispy chopped nuts.*

✳ MAKES 25 TO 35 MARSHMALLOWS

1½ cups pecans, finely chopped
1½ cups packed light brown sugar
¾ cup half-and-half or evaporated milk
¼ teaspoon salt
½ teaspoon vanilla extract (optional)
25 to 35 large marshmallows

Cover a large countertop area or a large baking sheet with waxed paper. Place the chopped pecans into a small dish.

In a heavy 1- or 2-quart saucepan over low to medium-low heat, bring the sugar, half-and-half, and salt to a boil, stirring until the sugar dissolves and the mixture begins to boil. Cook, stirring occasionally to prevent scorching, to the soft ball stage (234°F to 240°F, with 238°F recommended).

Remove from the heat. Stir in the vanilla, if using. Set the saucepan into a pan or sink filled with hot water to keep the butterscotch warm. (Do not allow the hot water to seep into the butterscotch mixture.) Using a fork, toothpick, or specially designed dipping tool, dip the marshmallows, one at a time, into the hot butterscotch mixture. Roll the coated marshmallows in the chopped pecans. Place on the waxed paper to cool. Store in an airtight container.

COOK'S NOTES: If the butterscotch becomes too stiff to coat the marshmallows, warm it over low heat until the candy reaches the desired consistency.

For smaller-sized servings, cut the marshmallows in half before dipping.

. . . . . . . . . . . . . . . . . . . . .

# Orange Creams

## Skill Level: Advanced

*One word comes to mind when I think of this rich, creamy, fudgelike candy: "Yum!" Try adding a little extra orange peel or substituting chopped pecans for the coconut.*

✳ MAKES ABOUT 1¾ POUNDS

3 cups granulated sugar
1¼ cups half-and-half or evaporated milk
½ teaspoon salt
3 tablespoons light corn syrup
2 tablespoons freshly grated orange zest
2 tablespoons butter
1½ cups sweetened flaked coconut

Butter an 8-inch square pan.

In a heavy 3-quart saucepan over low heat, bring the sugar, half-and-half, salt, and corn syrup to a boil, stirring until the sugar dissolves and the mixture begins to boil. Cover and cook 2 to 3 minutes to dissolve the sugar crystals on the sides of the pan. Remove the lid. Cook slowly, stirring occasionally to prevent scorching, over low heat to the soft ball stage (234°F to 240°F, with 240°F recommended).

Remove from the heat. Add the orange zest and butter; do not stir. Cool to lukewarm (110°F), 45 minutes to 1 hour.

Beat by hand until the candy begins to thicken and lose its gloss. Stir in the coconut.

Beat by hand until the candy thickens and is creamy. Pour into the buttered pan. Cool and cut into squares. Store in an airtight container in the refrigerator.

### VARIATION

If preferred, the candy may be shaped into small balls and rolled in additional coconut.

COOK'S NOTE: The coconut adds moisture to this candy, making it fairly soft. For a firmer candy, cook to a medium ball stage (242°F).

# Peanut Butter Cracker Candy

### Skill Level: Advanced

*No one but you will ever guess that this surprisingly delicious, old-time favorite is made with soda crackers.*

✳ MAKES ABOUT 1 POUND

1 cup granulated sugar
1 cup packed light brown sugar
1/3 cup evaporated milk
2 tablespoons butter or margarine
2 tablespoons smooth peanut butter
1 teaspoon vanilla extract
24 soda crackers (saltines), finely crushed

Butter a 9 × 5-inch loaf pan.

In a heavy 2-quart saucepan over medium heat, bring the sugars, milk, and butter to a boil, stirring until the sugars dissolve and the mixture begins to boil. Cook, stirring frequently to prevent scorching, to the soft ball stage (234°F to 240°F, with 236°F recommended).

Remove from the heat. Stir in the peanut butter, vanilla, and cracker crumbs. Beat by hand until the candy begins to thicken and cool, about 5 minutes. Pour into the buttered pan. Cool and cut into squares. Store in an airtight container.

# Fruit Fancies

### Skill Level: Advanced

*What could be more festive than cherries, pineapple, and three kinds of nuts wrapped in a light, creamy candy? This 1950s-style recipe is sure to tickle your fancy and delight your family and friends.*

✳ MAKES ABOUT 4 POUNDS

3 cups granulated sugar
1 cup light corn syrup
1½ cups half-and-half
½ teaspoon salt
1 teaspoon vanilla extract
1 cup Brazil nuts, cut lengthwise in halves
1 cup walnuts in large pieces
1 cup pecan halves
1 cup candied cherries, chopped
1 cup candied pineapple, chopped

Line a 9 × 5-inch loaf pan with waxed paper, leaving a 1-inch overhang over the sides of the pan.

In a heavy 5-quart kettle over medium-low heat, bring the sugar, corn syrup, half-and-half, and salt to a boil, stirring until the sugar dissolves and the mixture begins to boil. Cook, stirring occasionally to prevent scorching, to the soft ball stage (234°F to 240°F, with 238°F recommended).

Remove from the heat. Cool 20 minutes.

Add the vanilla. Beat by hand until the candy begins to thicken. Stir in the nuts and fruits. Beat by hand until the candy loses its gloss. The mixture will be thick and sticky. Using a wet spoon, pack the candy into the lined loaf pan. Tightly cover with plastic wrap or aluminum foil. Refrigerate 24 hours. The sticky syrup will become firm, creamy, and lighter in color after a few hours of refrigeration.

Lift the candy from the loaf pan. Cut into ½-inch-thick slices. Cut each slice into finger-length pieces or cubes. Store in an airtight container.

# Nut Cream Loaf

## Skill Level: Advanced

*The flavor of this vanilla fudgelike candy improves with age as the candy absorbs the nut flavors.*

✳ MAKES ABOUT 1½ POUNDS

> 2 cups granulated sugar
> ½ cup light corn syrup
> 1 cup half-and-half
> 1 tablespoon butter or margarine
> 1 tablespoon vanilla extract
> 1 cup chopped pecans or walnuts

Butter a 9 × 5-inch loaf pan.

In a heavy 3-quart saucepan over medium-low to medium heat, bring the sugar, corn syrup, and half-and-half to a boil, stirring until the sugar dissolves and the mixture begins to

boil. Cook, stirring occasionally to prevent scorching, to the soft ball stage (234°F to 240°F, with 240°F recommended).

Remove from the heat. Add the butter and vanilla. Beat by hand until the candy thickens and loses its gloss. Stir in the nuts. Pour into the buttered pan. Cool and cut into squares. Store in an airtight container.

COOK'S NOTE: For similar candies, see Creamy Blonde Fudge (page 131) and Creamy White Fudge (page 132).

# Three-Nut Candy

## Skill Level: Advanced

*Only mildly sweet, this is a candy for those who love nuts. Try substituting your favorite combination of nuts for those listed, keeping the proportions the same.*

✳ MAKES ABOUT 4½ POUNDS

> 3 cups granulated sugar
> 2 cups half-and-half
> 1 cup light corn syrup
> 2 cups walnuts, in large pieces or halves
> 2 cups pecans, in large pieces or halves
> 2 cups Brazil nuts, in large pieces or halves
> 1 teaspoon vanilla extract

Line a 9 × 13-inch pan or 2 (9 × 5-inch) loaf pans with waxed paper or foil, leaving a 1-inch overhang over the sides of the pan. Butter the lining generously or spray with nonstick spray.

In a heavy 5-quart kettle over medium-low heat, bring the sugar, half-and-half, corn syrup, and nuts to a boil, stirring until the sugar dissolves and the mixture begins to boil. Cover and cook 2 to 3 minutes to dissolve the sugar crystals on the sides of the pan. Remove the lid. Cook, stirring gently only a few times to prevent scorching, over low to medium-low heat to the soft ball stage (234°F to 240°F, with 236°F recommended), 30 to 40 minutes.

Remove from the heat. Cool about 5 minutes.

Add the vanilla. Beat by hand until the candy begins to stiffen. The candy will be sticky. Using a wet spoon, pack the candy into the prepared pan(s). Cover tightly with plastic wrap or aluminum foil. Let ripen at room temperature 24 hours.

Lift the candy from the pan. Peel off the lining. Wrap the entire block of candy in aluminum foil and store, covered. Cut into paper-thin slices as needed. The beaten candy may also be cut into squares, but each piece must be individually wrapped in plastic wrap. To cut into individual pieces, place the block of candy on a cutting board. Using a sharp knife and a sawing motion, cut the block into 1-inch strips, and then cut each strip into squares. Wrap each piece in plastic wrap and store in an airtight container.

COOK'S NOTES: The basic recipe used for this candy is very similar to the recipe for Fruit Fancies (page 33), but this version produces very different results. This candy has twice as many nuts as Fruit Fancies, plus a darker color and a much deeper nut flavor because the nuts are cooked with the candy.

The recipe may be reduced by half and cooked in a 3-quart pan.

# Pralines-in-a-Pan

## Skill Level: Advanced

*Originally known as Pecan Candy, this recipe tastes so much like pralines that it earned a new name. One easy way to serve this golden brown pecan candy is to break it into pieces somewhat like a bark.*
✳ MAKES ABOUT 1½ POUNDS

> 2 cups granulated sugar
> 1 cup milk
> 2 tablespoons butter or margarine
> 2 tablespoons light corn syrup
> ¼ teaspoon salt
> ¼ teaspoon baking soda
> 1 cup chopped pecans
> 1 teaspoon vanilla extract

Butter an 8-inch square pan.

In a heavy 5-quart kettle over low heat, bring the sugar, milk, butter, corn syrup, salt, and baking soda to a boil, stirring until the sugar dissolves and the mixture begins to boil. The mixture will foam rapidly and rise in the kettle when it begins to boil. Stir in the pecans. Cook, stirring occasionally to prevent scorching, over low heat to the soft ball stage (234°F to 240°F, with 236°F recommended).

Remove from the heat. Add the vanilla. Beat by hand until the candy thickens and begins to hold its shape. Pour into the buttered pan. Cool and cut into squares or break into serving-size pieces similar to a bark. Store in an airtight container.

COOK'S NOTE: If preferred, this candy may be dropped by spoonfuls onto waxed paper, creating individual praline-type candies.

# Patience Candy

## Skill Level: Expert

*This charming old recipe immediately conjures up images of a very sweet lady, perhaps even a grandmother, carefully writing her favorite recipe for a young, inexperienced bride.*

*Though it is impossible to verify the recipe's age or origin, it is easy to imagine that it is quite old and perhaps one used by Oklahoma pioneers. The candy is somewhat similar to Aunt Bill's Brown Candy (page 28), which is thought to be a pioneer recipe, and the language certainly suggests another era in our nation's history. For example, "sweet milk" is a term that was commonly used to describe fresh, unspoiled milk in the days before electricity and refrigeration, and "butter the size of an egg" reminds us of a time when women churned their own butter, poured it into a bowl, and scooped it out as needed.*

*Regardless of age, Patience Candy is a very tasty and unusual candy. My thanks go to the* **Ponca City News** *for allowing me to share this delightful recipe. It brings a smile to my face every time I read it.*

*These are the original instructions: Take a large pan so candy will not boil over. Put 1 cup granulated sugar in pan and place over fire; stir constantly until melted and brown like syrup. After all is melted, slowly stir in 1 cup (scant) sweet milk, in which has been dissolved a pinch of soda the size of a bean. Do not get scared, but stir and boil until smooth. Then add a second cup of sweet milk (scant), 2 cups of sugar, and butter the size of an egg. Boil until the candy forms a soft ball. Remove from fire and beat until the candy starts to grain. Add nuts if you wish. May be rolled in powdered sugar or poured. This candy is very delicious and worth your patience.*

✳ **MAKES 1½ TO 2 POUNDS**

> **3 cups granulated sugar, divided**
> **¼ teaspoon baking soda**
> **Scant 2 cups milk, divided**
> **¼ cup butter**
> **¾ to 1 cup chopped pecans (optional)**
> **Powdered sugar (optional)**

Butter an 8-inch square pan.

In a large heavy aluminum skillet over low to medium-low heat, slowly melt 1 cup sugar, stirring constantly to prevent scorching. While the sugar is melting, dissolve the baking soda into 1 scant cup milk.

When the sugar is fully melted to a brown liquid, slowly stir the milk-soda mixture into the melted sugar. The mixture will foam rapidly and rise in the skillet as it begins to boil. Cook, stirring constantly, until the mixture is smooth.

Slowly add the remaining 1 scant cup milk, remaining 2 cups sugar, and butter. Cook, stirring constantly, to the soft ball stage (234°F to 240°F, with 234°F recommended).

Remove from the heat. Beat by hand until the candy is thick and loses its gloss. Add the pecans if desired. The candy may be formed into a log and rolled in powdered sugar or poured into a buttered pan. Cool and slice as needed or cut into squares. Store in an airtight container.

# Holiday Pineapple Candy

## Skill Level: Average

*This delicately flavored, ultrasweet confection has been at the center of one hometown family's holiday tradition since the 1930s, with the recipe being passed from one generation to the next.*

✳ MAKES ABOUT 1½ POUNDS

3 cups granulated sugar
2 tablespoons light corn syrup
1 cup crushed pineapple with juice
24 large marshmallows
2 tablespoons butter
1 teaspoon vanilla extract
1½ cups pecans in large pieces

Butter an 8-inch square pan.

In a heavy 2-quart saucepan over medium-low heat, bring the sugar, corn syrup, and pineapple to a boil, stirring until the sugar dissolves and the mixture begins to boil. Cook, stirring frequently to prevent scorching, to the soft ball stage (234°F to 240°F, with 238°F recommended).

Remove from the heat. Add the marshmallows, butter, and vanilla. Let stand until the marshmallows are partially melted, about 3 minutes. Stir the candy until the marshmallows are completely melted and the mixture is well blended. Stir in the pecans. Pour into the buttered pan. Cool and cut into squares. Store in an airtight container in the refrigerator.

### VARIATIONS

*Hawaiian Pineapple Candy:* Substitute 2 cups granulated sugar and 1 cup packed light brown sugar for the 3 cups granulated sugar.

**COOK's NOTE:** The original recipe contained 3 cups pecans. The quantity may be adjusted to personal tastes.

# Pineapple Cremes

## Skill Level: Advanced

*Brown sugar and half-and-half give this candy a darker color and heavier texture than Holiday Pineapple Candy (at left), making this recipe somewhat similar to light brown fudge.*

✳ MAKES ABOUT 1 POUND

1 cup granulated sugar
½ cup packed light brown sugar
¼ cup half-and-half
⅛ teaspoon salt
½ cup crushed pineapple, well drained
2 tablespoons butter or margarine
12 large marshmallows
½ teaspoon vanilla extract or lemon juice
½ cup chopped pecans (optional)

Butter a platter or 9 × 5-inch loaf pan.

In a heavy 1- to 2-quart saucepan over medium-low heat, bring the sugars, half-and-half, salt, and pineapple to a boil, stirring until the sugar dissolves and the mixture begins to boil. Cook, stirring occasionally to prevent scorching, to the firm ball stage (244°F to 248°F, with 244°F recommended).

Remove from the heat. Add the butter and the marshmallows, stirring only until blended. Cool to lukewarm (110°F), 30 to 45 minutes.

Add the vanilla. Beat by hand until creamy. Stir in the pecans, if using. Pour into the prepared pan. Cool and cut into squares. Store in an airtight container.

# St. Patty's Pineapple Candy

## Skill Level: Advanced

*What better way to celebrate St. Patty's Day than with a batch of this pineapple-packed green candy?*
＊ MAKES ABOUT 1½ POUNDS

> 3 cups granulated sugar
> ½ cup half-and-half
> 2 tablespoons light corn syrup
> 1 (8-ounce) can crushed pineapple, undrained
> 3 tablespoons butter or margarine
> Few drops green food coloring

Butter a 9 × 5-inch loaf pan.

In a heavy 3-quart saucepan over medium-low heat, bring the sugar, half-and-half, corn syrup, pineapple with juice, and butter to a boil, stirring until the sugar dissolves and the mixture begins to boil. Cook, stirring occasionally to prevent scorching, to the soft ball stage (234°F to 240°F, with 236°F recommended).

Remove from the heat. Stir in green food coloring. Beat by hand until the candy thickens and begins to lose its gloss. Pour into the buttered pan. Cool and cut into squares. Store in an airtight container.

COOK'S NOTE: For a similar candy, see The Preacher's Pineapple Fudge (page 130).

# Sour Cream Candy

## Skill Level: Advanced

*Ultrarich and creamy, this fudgelike brown-sugar candy retains a hint of sour cream.*
＊ MAKES ABOUT 1 POUND

> ½ cup sour cream
> 2 cups packed light brown sugar
> 2 tablespoons butter or margarine
> 1 teaspoon vanilla extract
> Few grains of salt
> 1 cup chopped pecans (optional)

Butter a 9 × 5-inch loaf pan.

In a heavy 2-quart saucepan over medium-low heat, bring the sour cream and sugar to a boil, stirring until the sugar dissolves and the mixture begins to boil. Cook, stirring occasionally to prevent scorching, to the soft ball stage (234°F to 240°F, with 236°F recommended).

Remove from the heat. Add the butter without stirring. Cool to lukewarm (110°F), 30 to 45 minutes.

Add the vanilla and salt. Beat by hand until the candy loses its gloss and begins to hold its shape. Stir in the nuts if using. Pour into the prepared pan. Cool and cut into squares if needed. Store in an airtight container.

COOK'S NOTE: If preferred, the beaten candy may be dropped by spoonfuls onto waxed paper.

# Brittles

## Almond Brittle

### Skill Level: Average

*With this brittle being only mildly sweet and smooth as glass, nut lovers will be "nuts" for this candy because most of the flavor comes from the almonds, which roast during cooking. Try substituting pecans for the almonds.*

✳ MAKES ABOUT 1½ POUNDS

2 cups granulated sugar
½ cup light corn syrup
⅓ cup water
¼ teaspoon salt
3 tablespoons butter or margarine
1¼ cups halved or coarsely chopped blanched almonds
1 teaspoon vanilla extract

Butter 2 large baking sheets.

In a heavy 3-quart saucepan, combine the sugar, corn syrup, water, salt, and butter. Bring to a boil over medium to medium-high heat, stirring until the sugar dissolves and the mixture begins to boil. Stir in the almonds and bring to a second boil. Cook, stirring frequently, to the hard crack stage (300°F).

Remove from the heat. Quickly stir in the vanilla. Pour onto the baking sheets. Cool and break into pieces. Store in an airtight container.

## Aunt Lucy's Extra-Buttery Brittle

### Skill Level: Average

*My aunt sent me this recipe several years ago with a note saying, "Extra buttery," but she forgot to say, "Extra good." Do not be surprised if friends tell you this is the best brittle they have ever tasted.*

✳ MAKES ABOUT 2½ POUNDS

3 cups raw, unsalted peanuts, almonds, cashews, pecans, walnuts, macadamia nuts, or pine nuts
2 cups granulated sugar
1 cup light corn syrup
½ cup water
1 cup butter
1 teaspoon baking soda

Butter 2 large baking sheets. If using large nuts, cut or break the nuts into smaller pieces.

In a heavy 5-quart kettle over medium heat, bring the sugar, corn syrup, and water to a boil, stirring until the sugar dissolves and the mixture begins to boil. When the mixture reaches a full, rolling boil, stir in the butter until melted. Reduce the heat slightly to medium low, maintaining a medium boil. Cook, stirring frequently, to the soft crack stage (280°F).

Stir in the nuts. Cook, stirring frequently, to the hard crack stage (300°F).

Remove from the heat. Stir in the baking

soda until well blended. Quickly pour the mixture onto the buttered baking sheets, spreading evenly across both pans. If desired, use two forks or the back the spoon to spread the candy into an extrathin layer. Cool and break into pieces. Store in an airtight container.

COOK'S NOTES: This candy may be cooked in a heavy 3-quart saucepan but must be watched carefully to prevent the mixture from boiling over the sides of the pan.

Because raw, unsalted cashews can be difficult to locate, roasted, salted cashews may be substituted. If roasted cashews are used, cook the candy mixture slightly longer to 285°F or 290°F before adding the cashews so that the nuts are not roasted again during cooking.

# Munchabuncha Peanut Brittle

## Skill Level: Average

*In the words of Robert Palmer, "Simply Irresistible." This extra-crunchy version is one of my favorite peanut brittles of all time.*

❋ MAKES ABOUT 1½ POUNDS

    **1 cup granulated sugar**
    **1 cup light corn syrup**
    **1 tablespoon water**
    **2 cups raw, unsalted peanuts or pecans**
    **1 teaspoon baking soda**

Butter a large baking sheet.

In a heavy 3-quart saucepan over medium to medium-high heat, bring the sugar, corn syrup,

and water to a boil, stirring until the sugar dissolves and the mixture begins to boil. Cook, without stirring, to the soft crack stage (280°F).

Stir in the peanuts. Cook, stirring occasionally to prevent the peanuts from settling on the bottom of the pan, to the hard crack stage (300°F).

Remove from the heat. Gently stir in the baking soda until well blended. Pour onto the baking sheet. Cool and break into pieces. Store in an airtight container.

# Pistol Pete Peanut Brittle

## Skill Level: Average

*Named for the Oklahoma State University mascot, this classic version of an old Southern favorite was one of the candies tested in the OSU test kitchen during the early 1950s. Add your own touch with coconut or pecans.*

❋ MAKES ABOUT 2 POUNDS

    **2 cups granulated sugar**
    **1 cup light corn syrup**
    **½ cup water**
    **1 teaspoon salt**
    **2 cups raw, unsalted peanuts**
    **2 tablespoons butter or margarine**
    **2 teaspoons baking soda**
    **1 teaspoon vanilla extract**

Butter 2 large baking sheets.

In a heavy 5-quart kettle over medium heat, bring the sugar, corn syrup, water, and salt to a boil, stirring until the sugar dissolves and the mixture begins to boil. Cover and cook 3 minutes to dissolve the sugar crystals on the sides of the pan. Remove the lid. Cook, without stirring, to 260°F.

Stir in the peanuts and butter. Cook, stirring occasionally to prevent the peanuts from settling on the bottom of the pan, to the hard crack stage (300°F).

Remove from the heat. Add the vanilla and baking soda without stirring, allowing the mixture to foam rapidly. Gently stir just until blended; too much stirring will cause this candy to become dense rather than porous. Quickly pour onto the baking sheets. Cool and break into pieces. Store in an airtight container.

### VARIATIONS

*Pistol Pete Coconut Peanut Brittle:* Add ½ cup sweetened flaked coconut when adding the vanilla and baking soda.

*Pistol Pete Pecan Brittle:* Substitute 2 cups pecans in large pieces for the peanuts.

½ **teaspoon salt**
1½ **tablespoons butter or margarine**
1 **teaspoon baking soda**

Butter a large baking sheet.

In a heavy 2-quart saucepan over medium-high heat, bring the sugar, corn syrup, and water to a boil, stirring until the sugar dissolves and the mixture begins to boil. Cook, without stirring, to the soft crack stage (280°F).

Stir in the peanuts. Cook, stirring occasionally to prevent the peanuts from settling on the bottom of the pan, to the hard crack stage (300°F).

Remove from the heat. Add the salt, butter, and baking soda, stirring until well mixed. Pour onto the baking sheet. Using the back of a wooden spoon, a flat metal spatula, or two forks, spread or pull the mixture into a very thin layer until the brittle is so thin that you can almost see through it. Cool and break into pieces. Store in an airtight container.

# Farmers' Market Peanut Brittle

## Skill Level: Average

*The friendly folks at the local farmers' market are always glad to share a few of their favorite recipes, such as this one for extrathin peanut brittle.*

✳ MAKES ABOUT 1½ POUNDS

1½ **cups granulated sugar**
½ **cup light corn syrup**
2 **tablespoons water**
1½ **cups raw, unsalted peanuts**

# Reece's Microwave Peanut Brittle

## Skill Level: Novice, Easy

*Nothing beats my neighbor's microwave candy for speed, ease, and taste, all features appreciated by today's grandmothers.*

✳ MAKES ABOUT 1 POUND

1 cup granulated sugar
1 teaspoon salt
½ cup light corn syrup
1 cup raw, unsalted peanuts
1 tablespoon butter or margarine
1 teaspoon vanilla extract
1 teaspoon baking soda

Butter a large baking sheet.

In a 2-quart microwave-proof bowl, stir together the sugar, salt, corn syrup, and peanuts. Microwave, uncovered, on High for 4 minutes. Stir the candy and turn the dish.

Microwave on High 4 minutes. Stir in the butter and vanilla.

Microwave on High 1 to 1½ minutes. Gently stir in the baking soda; the mixture will become light and foamy. Pour onto the baking sheet. Cool and break into pieces. Store in an airtight container.

# Toffees

## Marry Me Toffee

### Skill Level: Average

*I first tasted my signature candy in the late 1980s when my neighbor Julie gave me a bag for Christmas. After the first bite, I had to have the recipe. Since then, I have made several hundred batches of this mouthwatering toffee for people all over the country, and almost everyone agrees that it is one of the most delicious and addictive candies they have ever tasted. This buttery, chocolate-topped candy is particularly popular with men, hence the name.*

✳ MAKES ABOUT 2¼ POUNDS

2 to 2½ cups chopped, toasted almonds, divided

6 (1.55-ounce) Hershey's milk chocolate bars

1 pound good-quality butter (do not use margarine)

2 cups granulated sugar

3 tablespoons water

1 teaspoon vanilla extract

Scatter about half of the almonds over 2 baking sheets (one large baking sheet and one small to medium baking sheet), reserving the remaining almonds for the topping. Break the chocolate bars into pieces.

In a heavy 3-quart saucepan over medium heat, bring the butter, sugar, and water to a boil, stirring until the sugar dissolves and the mixture begins to boil. Cook, stirring constantly, to the hard crack stage (300°F).

Remove from the heat. Quickly stir in the vanilla. Immediately pour a thin layer of hot toffee over the almonds on the baking sheets. (The toffee will not completely cover the baking sheets.) Immediately place the chocolate pieces on top of the hot toffee; the chocolate will melt within a few minutes.

Using a flat metal spatula or a knife, spread the melted chocolate in an even layer over the toffee.

Sprinkle with the reserved almonds, lightly pressing the almonds into the chocolate with the palms of your hands. Let stand until the chocolate is firm. The toffee may be cooled in the refrigerator or freezer if preferred. Break into pieces. Store in an airtight container at room temperature, in the refrigerator, or in the freezer as desired. Do not store in a container with other candies.

COOK'S NOTES: This candy is extradelicious when made with toasted almond topping sold in ice cream specialty stores such as Braum's, Häagen-Dazs, or Ben & Jerry's. Remember to use high-quality ingredients, because the better the butter, the better the toffee.

It takes about 45 minutes to make this candy. The recipe may be doubled and cooked in a heavy 5-quart kettle.

# English Toffee

## Skill Level: Average

*Just a tablespoon of corn syrup makes this traditional English toffee extra smooth.*

✳ **MAKES ABOUT 1¼ POUNDS**

> **1 cup butter (do not use margarine)**
> **1 cup granulated sugar**
> **2 tablespoons water**
> **1 tablespoon light corn syrup**
> **¾ cup finely chopped walnuts or toasted almonds**
> **4 to 8 ounces German's sweet chocolate, semisweet chocolate, or milk chocolate bars, melted**

Line a large baking sheet with foil; butter the foil or spray with nonstick spray.

In a heavy 2-quart saucepan over low to medium-low heat, slowly melt the butter, being careful not to allow it to burn. Stir in the sugar and cook, stirring constantly, until the mixture begins to bubble. Remove from the heat temporarily. Stir in the water and corn syrup, mixing well. Return to the heat and cook, stirring as needed to prevent scorching, to the hard crack stage (300°F).

Remove from the heat. Stir in the nuts. Immediately pour the hot mixture onto the prepared baking sheet, spreading into a thin layer with the back of a spoon. Cool at room temperature.

Spread 4 ounces melted chocolate over the toffee. Let stand until the chocolate is firm. If desired, turn the coated toffee over and spread 4 ounces melted chocolate on other side. Let stand until the chocolate is firm. Break into pieces. Store in an airtight container in the refrigerator.

**VARIATION**

*Nut-Topped English Toffee:* If desired, additional chopped or ground nuts may be sprinkled on top of the warm chocolate. Without these nuts, the candy must remain refrigerated or the chocolate coating may become soft and somewhat sticky.

# The Candy Dance

Nothing can tell of America's continued love of homemade candy quite like the story of the Candy Dance. In 1919, the ladies of the tiny community of Genoa, Nevada, held a dance and passed out homemade candy to raise funds for community streetlights. The Candy Dance was such an overwhelming success that they made it an annual event. In the 1970s, the Candy Dance became a two-day affair when organizers added an arts and crafts show. Held in late September, attendance at the annual Candy Dance has steadily risen over the years, with thousands of visitors pouring into this small community to sample the candy and join in the fun. Volunteers make up to 4,000 pounds of candy in the weeks preceding the event, most of which is sold during the first day.

# Butternut Toffee

## Skill Level: Average

*With a mild walnut taste and a rich, dark chocolate topping, this candy often becomes the toffee of choice. The recipe also contains half the butter of some toffee recipes.*

✳ MAKES ABOUT 1 POUND

½ cup butter (do not use margarine)
1 cup granulated sugar
½ teaspoon salt
¼ cup water
¾ cup finely chopped walnuts, divided
1 cup semisweet chocolate chips, melted

Butter a large baking sheet.

In a heavy 2-quart saucepan over medium heat, bring the butter, sugar, salt, and water to a boil, stirring until the sugar dissolves and the mixture begins to boil. Cook, stirring constantly, to the hard crack stage (300°F).

Remove from the heat. Stir in ½ cup of the walnuts. Immediately pour the hot mixture onto the buttered baking sheet, spreading into a thin layer with the back of a spoon. Cool.

Spread the melted chocolate over the toffee. Sprinkle with the remaining walnuts. Let stand until the chocolate is firm. Break into pieces. Store in an airtight container.

# Almond Butter Toffee

## Skill Level: Average

*This unusual toffee recipe contains baking soda, giving it an extracrunchy texture.*

✳ MAKES ABOUT 1¼ POUNDS

½ cup butter
1 cup granulated sugar
1 tablespoon water
½ cup chopped, toasted almonds
½ teaspoon vanilla extract
¾ teaspoon baking soda
¼ cup ground or finely chopped, toasted almonds
1 to 1½ cups semisweet chocolate chips, divided

Line a large baking sheet with foil. Butter the foil or spray with nonstick spray.

In a heavy 2-quart saucepan over medium heat, bring the butter, sugar, and water to a boil, stirring until the sugar dissolves and the mixture begins to boil. Cook, stirring constantly, to the hard crack stage (300°F).

Remove from the heat. Stir in the chopped almonds and vanilla. Add the baking soda. When the candy foams, immediately pour it onto the prepared baking sheet in a thin layer about ¼ inch thick. Cool.

In the top pan of a double boiler over hot, but not boiling water, melt half of the chocolate chips, stirring until smooth. Spread the chocolate on one side of the cooled toffee; sprinkle with half of the finely chopped almonds. Let stand until the chocolate is firm. Melt the remaining chocolate chips using the same method. Turn the toffee and spread the uncoated side with chocolate. Sprinkle with the remaining nuts. Let stand until the chocolate is firm. Break into pieces. Store in an airtight container.

## Butter Pecan Toffee

### Skill Level: Average

*Everyone will want samples of this delicious toffee, shared by my cousin Susan's friend Donna, of Huntsville, Arkansas.*

✳ **MAKES ABOUT 2¼ POUNDS**

> 1 pound butter (do not use margarine)
> 2 cups granulated sugar
> 2 teaspoons light corn syrup
> ½ cup water
> 2 cups chopped pecans
> 12 ounces milk chocolate chips

Line 2 baking sheets with foil.

In a heavy 3-quart saucepan over medium heat, bring the butter, sugar, corn syrup, and water to a boil, stirring until the sugar dissolves and the mixture begins to boil. Cook, stirring constantly, to just below the hard crack stage (295°F).

Remove from the heat. Stir in the pecans. Pour in a thin layer onto the baking sheets. Sprinkle the chocolate chips over the hot mixture; let stand a few minutes to melt. Using a knife or spatula, spread the melted chocolate across the toffee in an even layer. Let stand until the chocolate is firm. Break into pieces. Store in an airtight container in the refrigerator.

## One-in-a-Million Toffee

### Skill Level: Average

*Professional toffee tasters have named this pecan toffee as a worthy opponent to my signature candy, Marry Me Toffee (page 43), with a few, including my own brother, hinting that this candy might even be better.*

✳ **MAKES ABOUT 2¼ POUNDS**

> ½ to ¾ cup chopped pecans
> 6 (1.55-ounce) Hershey's milk chocolate bars
> 1 pound butter
> 2 cups sugar
> 1 to 1½ cups very finely chopped pecans

Scatter the chopped pecans across a 10 × 15-inch jelly roll pan. Break the chocolate bars into pieces.

In a heavy 3-quart saucepan over medium heat, bring the butter and sugar to a boil, stirring until the sugar dissolves and the mixture begins to boil. Cook, stirring constantly, to the hard crack stage (300°F).

Remove from the heat. Quickly pour a thin layer of hot toffee over the pecans in the jelly roll pan. Immediately place the chocolate pieces on top of the hot toffee; the chocolate will melt within a few minutes.

Using a flat metal spatula or knife, spread the melted chocolate in an even layer over the toffee. Sprinkle with the very finely chopped pecans. Let stand until the chocolate is firm. Place a sheet of waxed paper over the cooled toffee and break into pieces using a small hammer. Store in an airtight container.

# Buttercrunch Candy

## Skill Level: Average

*Finally, a candy that we can burn! The slightly scorched flavor of this special toffee may remind you of a Heath candy bar.*

✳ **MAKES ABOUT 2 POUNDS**

> 6 (1.55-ounce) Hershey's milk chocolate bars, melted
> 1 pound butter, softened (do not use margarine)
> 2 cups granulated sugar
> 1 cup finely chopped pecans, divided

Have a large unbuttered baking sheet ready. Break the milk chocolate bars into pieces.

In a heavy 3-quart saucepan, cream the butter and sugar together until well blended. Cook, stirring constantly, over medium-high to high heat to the hard crack stage (300°F). Allow the candy to cook slightly past the hard crack stage, to about 303°F, or until it appears slightly scorched.

Remove from the heat. Stir in ½ cup of the pecans. Immediately pour in a thin layer onto the baking sheet. Immediately place the chocolate pieces on top of the hot toffee; the chocolate will melt within a few minutes.

Using a flat metal spatula or knife, spread the melted chocolate in an even layer over the toffee. Sprinkle with the remaining pecans, lightly pressing the nuts into the chocolate with the palms of your hands. Let stand until the chocolate is firm. (The candy may be cooled in the refrigerator or freezer if preferred.) Break into pieces. Store in an airtight container at room temperature, in the refrigerator, or in the freezer as desired. Do not store in a container with other candies.

# Microwave Toffee

## Skill Level: Novice, Super Simple

*Though the microwave version may not be as smooth as most traditional toffees, it can certainly satisfy a craving.*

✳ **MAKES ABOUT ¾ POUND**

> 1 cup chopped pecans, walnuts, or toasted almonds, divided
> 1 cup granulated sugar
> ¼ cup water
> ½ teaspoon salt
> ½ cup butter, thinly sliced (do not use margarine)
> 2 (1.55-ounce) Hershey's milk chocolate bars, coarsely chopped into pieces

Line an 8-inch square pan with aluminum foil. Sprinkle half of the nuts evenly across the bottom of the pan.

In a medium microwave-proof bowl, combine the sugar, water, and salt until well mixed. Add the butter. Microwave on High 3 minutes. Stir. Microwave on High 3 minutes. Stir again. Microwave on High 1 to 5 minutes, or until the mixture reaches a light golden brown; watch carefully and stir every 1 to 2 minutes. Pour the browned sugar mixture over the nuts in the pan. Cool.

In a small microwave-proof dish, microwave the chocolate on High 30 seconds to 1 minute, or until mostly melted; watch carefully so that the chocolate does not burn. Stir until the chocolate is completely melted. Spread over the cooled toffee. Sprinkle with the remaining nuts. Cool and break into pieces. Store in an airtight container.

# Old-Fashioned Hard Candies

## Glass Candy

### Skill Level: Average

*A friend once gave me a lovely glass water pitcher. It was tied with a bow and filled with bright red, cinnamon-flavored Glass Candy. Not only was the candy delicious, it turned the pitcher into a beautiful and ingenious presentation.*

※ MAKES ABOUT 1½ POUNDS

> 2 cups granulated sugar
> 2 cups light corn syrup
> 1 teaspoon cinnamon oil
> 1 teaspoon red food coloring

Have 2 large baking sheets ready to receive the candy.

In a 3-quart saucepan over medium heat, bring the sugar and corn syrup to a boil, stirring until the sugar dissolves and the mixture begins to boil. Cook, without stirring, to the hard crack stage (300°F).

Remove from the heat. Quickly stir in the cinnamon oil and food coloring. Pour the hot syrup onto the baking sheets in thin, even layers. Cool at room temperature in a dry location. Break into small pieces. Store in an airtight container.

COOK'S NOTE: Cinnamon oil may damage plastic measuring spoons; it's better to use metal spoons if possible. Be cautious using flavored oils. The fumes are very strong when added to the hot candy. Turn on the exhaust fan and do not lean over the pan.

· · · · · · · · · · · · · · · · · · · · · · · · ·

## Licorice

### Skill Level: Average

*Unlike the soft, stretchy licorice we ate as kids, this recipe makes the old-fashioned kind of licorice, which is a hard, black candy with licorice flavoring.*

※ MAKES ABOUT 1½ POUNDS

> 3 cups granulated sugar
> 1 cup water
> 1 cup light corn syrup
> 1 teaspoon anise oil
> ¼ teaspoon black vegetable coloring (see Cook's Note opposite)

Line 2 baking sheets or pans with foil; butter the foil.

In a 3-quart saucepan over medium heat, bring the sugar, water, and corn syrup to a boil, stirring until the sugar dissolves and the mixture begins to boil. Cook, without stirring, to 290°F.

Remove from the heat. Quickly stir in the anise oil (see Cook's Note at left regarding using flavored oils) and the vegetable coloring. Pour the hot syrup onto the baking sheets in thin, even layers. When lukewarm, deeply

# Old-Fashioned Hard Candies

The candies in this collection are similar to the first candies enjoyed by our ancestors. According to the National Confectioners Association, hard candies made of boiled sugar were gaining popularity with American colonists as early as the 17th century. By the early 1800s, improvements in technology brought this type of candy making into the home, where cooks flavored their candies with lemon, peppermint, and other common flavorings. Our tastes have not changed over the years, for who can resist savoring one of these candies for as long as they will last?

score the slabs of candy into ½ × 1½-inch bars. When cold, carefully break into pieces along the score lines. Wrap each piece individually in waxed paper.

COOK'S NOTES: Black vegetable coloring can often be purchased at stores specializing in baking and candy-making supplies.

Other flavorings and colorings may be substituted for the anise oil and the black vegetable coloring.

# Horehound Candy

## Skill Level: Average

*In the 1920s, my great-grandfather was known for carrying a few pieces of horehound candy in his pocket but keeping his main stash hidden from his thirty-five grandchildren. When his stash disappeared, he knew that his grandkids were better at playing hide-and-seek than he was.*

*Horehound, sometimes spelled hoarhound, is a flowering plant that grows wild along the roadsides in Europe. Early settlers brought horehound to North America, planting it near homesteads. Today we find dried, crushed horehound in health food stores that specialize in herbs or herbal teas. Sometimes called "soldier's tea," horehound has been used in cough remedies for centuries. Thanks to Kansas State University, I can share this interesting old recipe.*

✴ MAKES ABOUT ½ POUND

¾ cup boiling water
2 teaspoons crushed dried horehound
¼ cup light corn syrup
1 cup granulated sugar

Pour the boiling water over the horehound and let stand 10 to 20 minutes. Strain the horehound through a cheesecloth, discarding the horehound and reserving the water. Butter a large baking sheet.

Combine the horehound water, sugar, and syrup in a 2-quart saucepan. Cook slowly, without stirring, to the hard crack stage (300°F). Pour onto the buttered baking sheet. Cut into squares before it hardens. Store in an airtight container.

COOK'S NOTES: The easiest way to make this recipe is to use two single-serving packets of horehound tea, which usually contain about 1 teaspoon horehound per bag. Because the horehound is sealed in a tea bag, no straining is needed. Steep the tea bags in ¾ cup boiling water for the number of minutes directed on the tea package (about 3 minutes). If the tea bags are steeped for 10 to 20 minutes as directed above, the candy may develop a bitter taste.

Horehound has a fairly mild and not particularly sweet menthol-type flavor. Most commercial horehound candies contain additional flavoring, such as oil of root beer, to make the candy more interesting. If desired, ¼ to ½ teaspoon of flavoring oil may be stirred into this recipe just before pouring the candy onto the baking sheet.

. . . . . . . . . . . . . . . . . . .

# Hardtack Candy

## Skill Level: Average

*Like many hard candies, this recipe can be flavored and colored any way the cook chooses. See the Cook's Notes for suggestions.*

❋ MAKES ABOUT 1 POUND

  2 cups granulated sugar
  1 cup water
  ¾ cup light corn syrup
  ½ teaspoon oil flavoring of choice
  ½ to 1 teaspoon food coloring of choice

Line a 9 × 13-inch baking pan or a large baking sheet with aluminum foil.

In a 2-quart saucepan over medium heat, bring the sugar, water and corn syrup to a boil, stirring until the sugar dissolves and the mix-

ture begins to boil. Cook, without stirring, to the hard crack stage (300°F).

Remove from the heat. Quickly stir in the flavoring and food coloring of choice. Pour the hot syrup into the lined pan in a thin, even layer. When lukewarm, deeply score the slab of candy into squares or triangles as desired. When cold, carefully break into pieces along the score lines. Wrap each piece individually in waxed paper. Store at room temperature.

COOK'S NOTES: Some suggested flavorings are wintergreen oil, peppermint oil, cinnamon oil, clove oil, and anise oil. The candy may be tinted to a color that complements the flavoring. For example, use green food coloring for candy flavored with oil of lime and yellow food coloring for candy flavored with oil of lemon.

If preferred, this recipe can be made using ⅔ cup light corn syrup and cooked to 295°F. These changes will make very little difference in the finished candy.

. . . . . . . . . . . . . . . . . . .

# Lollypops

## Skill Level: Advanced

*To liven up your lollypops, try decorating them with a few multicolored sprinkles while the candy is still warm.*

❋ MAKES ABOUT 12

  2 cups granulated sugar
  ⅔ cup light corn syrup
  1 cup water
  ½ teaspoon food coloring of choice
    (see Cook's Note, above)

**½ teaspoon oil flavoring of choice (see Cook's Note, page 50)**

Butter 2 large baking sheets.

In a 2-quart saucepan over medium heat, bring the sugar, corn syrup, and water to a boil, stirring until the sugar dissolves and the mixture begins to boil. Cover and cook 2 to 3 minutes to dissolve the sugar crystals on the sides of the pan. Remove the lid. Cook, without stirring, to the hard crack stage (300°F).

Remove from the heat. Quickly add the coloring and flavoring, stirring only until mixed. Quickly drop from the tip of a large spoon onto the buttered baking sheet, making certain the drops are round. Press a wooden skewer or lollypop stick into the edge of each lollypop before it hardens. Press any decorations into the lollypop at the same time. Loosen the lollypops from the pan before they get too cold or they will crack. To store, wrap the cooled lollypops in cellophane or waxed paper.

# Caramels

## Dorothy's Never-Fail Caramels

### Skill Level: Average

*Hometown friend Dorothy often used this recipe to teach home economics students about candy making. If teenagers can make these caramels, you can, too.*

✳ MAKES ABOUT 2 POUNDS

2 cups granulated sugar
1 cup packed light brown sugar
1 cup light corn syrup
1 cup half-and-half
1 cup milk
1 cup butter
4 teaspoons vanilla extract

Generously butter a 9 × 13-inch pan.

In a heavy 5-quart kettle over medium heat, bring the sugars, corn syrup, half-and-half, milk, and butter to a boil, stirring until the sugars dissolve and the mixture begins to boil. Reduce the heat to medium low. Cook, stirring constantly, to the firm ball stage (244°F to 248°F, with 248°F recommended).

Remove from the heat. Stir in the vanilla. Pour into the buttered pan. Cool and cut into squares. Individually wrap each piece in plastic wrap or waxed paper. Store in an airtight container.

### VARIATION

*Dorothy's Never-Fail Caramels with Pecans:* 2 cups pecans in large pieces may be added with the vanilla.

. . . . . . . . . . . . . . . . . . . . . . . .

## Oklahoma Pecan Squares

### Skill Level: Average

*Chewy, gooey, and richer than an Oklahoma oil baron, these homespun pecan squares are more than just OK. Even polite people will lick their chins to get every drop of this caramel-like candy.*

✳ MAKES ABOUT 3 POUNDS

2 cups granulated sugar
1 cup packed light brown sugar
1 (12-ounce) can evaporated milk
1 cup heavy cream
1½ cups light corn syrup
1 cup butter (do not use margarine)
¼ teaspoon salt
2½ cups pecans in large pieces
½ teaspoon vanilla extract

Butter a 10 × 15-inch jelly roll pan.

In a heavy 5-quart kettle over medium-low heat, bring the sugars, milk, cream, syrup, butter, and salt to a boil, stirring until the sugars dissolve and the mixture begins to boil. Cover and cook 2 to 3 minutes to dissolve the sugar crystals on the sides of the pan. Remove the lid. Cook slowly, stirring occasionally to prevent scorching, over medium-low heat to the soft ball stage (234°F to 240°F, with 238°F recommended), about 40 minutes.

Remove from the heat. Add the pecans and vanilla extract, stirring only to blend. Pour into the buttered pan. Cool and cut into squares. Wrap each square individually in plastic wrap. Store in an airtight container.

. . . . . . . . . . . . . . . . . . . . . . .

# Black Walnut Caramels

## Skill Level: Advanced

*Attention, black walnut lovers: Get ready for the best caramel of your life.*

*Black walnuts are a native American nut with a pronounced flavor. They are available in some supermarkets, farmers' markets, and by mail order.*

✳ MAKES ABOUT 2½ POUNDS

¾ **cup finely chopped black walnuts**
2 **cups pecans in large pieces**
2½ **cups granulated sugar**
¾ **cup light corn syrup**
½ **cup butter (do not use margarine)**
¼ **teaspoon cream of tartar**
2½ **cups whole milk, divided**
1 **teaspoon vanilla extract**

Butter a 9 × 13-inch pan. Sprinkle the black walnuts across the bottom of the pan. Sprinkle the pecans over the walnuts.

In a heavy 5-quart kettle over medium-low heat, combine the sugar, corn syrup, butter, cream of tartar, and 1 cup of the milk, stirring until the sugar dissolves. Cook, stirring constantly, 15 minutes. (The mixture should reach the boiling point 7 or 8 minutes into cooking.) Add ½ cup milk.

Cook, stirring constantly, 15 minutes. Add ½ cup of the milk.

Cook, stirring constantly, 10 minutes. Add the remaining ½ cup milk. Cook, stirring constantly, to the high end of the soft ball stage (240°F).

Remove from the heat. Gently add the vanilla, stirring as little as possible. Pour the hot caramel mixture over the nuts in the pan. Cool and cut into squares. Individually wrap each piece in plastic wrap. Store in an airtight container.

COOK'S NOTES: These are firm caramels and hold their shape well.

The black walnuts give this candy a strong and distinctive flavor. If preferred, the black walnuts may be decreased or omitted and replaced with walnuts or additional pecans. You can use up to a total of 3 cups nuts.

This recipe takes about 1½ hours to complete, but caramel lovers will say it is worth it.

. . . . . . . . . . . . . . . . . . . . . . . . .

# Chocolate Caramels

## Skill Level: Average

*The only thing better than a smooth, creamy caramel is a smooth, creamy chocolate caramel.*

✳ **MAKES ABOUT 2¼ POUNDS**

1 cup butter or margarine
1 pound light brown sugar
1 cup light corn syrup
1 (14-ounce) can sweetened condensed milk
2 ounces unsweetened baking chocolate, very finely chopped
1½ teaspoons vanilla extract

Butter a 9-inch square pan.

In a heavy 3-quart saucepan over medium heat, melt the butter. Stir in the brown sugar and corn syrup, blending well. Gradually stir in the milk, mixing well. Stir in the chocolate. Cook, stirring frequently to prevent scorching, to the firm ball stage (244°F to 248°F, with 246°F recommended).

Remove from the heat. Stir in the vanilla. Pour into the buttered pan. Cool and cut into squares. Individually wrap each piece in plastic wrap. Store in an airtight container.

# Honey Walnut Caramels

## Skill Level: Average

*The use of honey in place of sugar makes these caramels less sweet than most candies. Use good-quality honey, because the honey is what adds the flavor.*

✳ **MAKES ABOUT 1 POUND**

1 cup half-and-half or evaporated milk
1 cup honey
2 teaspoons flour
½ teaspoon salt
¼ cup butter or margarine
1 teaspoon vanilla extract
1 cup chopped walnuts

Butter an 8 × 4-inch or a 9 × 5-inch loaf pan.

In a heavy 1- to 2-quart saucepan over medium heat, combine the half-and-half, honey, flour, and salt, stirring to dissolve the sugar and any lumps that form from the flour. Add the butter. Bring to a boil over medium heat, stirring constantly until the mixture begins to boil. Cook, stirring frequently, to the firm ball stage (244°F to 248°F, with 248°F recommended).

Remove from the heat. Stir in the vanilla and walnuts. Pour into the buttered pan. Cool and cut into squares. Individually wrap each piece in plastic wrap. Store in an airtight container.

# Clusters, Patties, and Pralines

## Creamy Peanut Patties

### Skill Level: Advanced

*With peanuts as Oklahoma's second largest crop, it is no surprise that red peanut patties are staples in many local stores. This super creamy version is the best I have ever tasted.*

✳ MAKES ABOUT 45

2½ cups granulated sugar
1 cup half-and-half
⅔ cup light corn syrup
Dash salt
2½ cups raw peanuts
2 tablespoons butter or margarine
1 teaspoon vanilla extract
4 to 6 drops red food coloring

Cover a large countertop area or 2 large baking sheets with waxed paper.

In a heavy 4- to 5-quart kettle over medium-low to medium heat, bring the sugar, half-and-half, corn syrup, and salt to a boil, stirring until the sugar dissolves and the mixture begins to boil. Stir in the peanuts. Cook, stirring frequently to prevent scorching, to the medium ball stage (242°F).

Remove from the heat. Add the butter, vanilla, and food coloring. Beat by hand until the candy thickens, looks opaque, and holds its shape. Quickly drop by spoonfuls onto the waxed paper. Cool. Store in an airtight container.

COOK'S NOTE: If preferred, these peanut patties may be dropped into small buttered muffin tins.

. . . . . . . . . . . . . . . . . . . . . . .

## Microwave Peanut Patties

### Skill Level: Average

*This microwave version of peanut patties is slightly easier to cook than the traditional version but still requires some hand beating.*

✳ MAKES ABOUT 36

2 cups granulated sugar
½ cup light corn syrup
½ cup half-and-half
1½ cups raw peanuts
2 tablespoons butter
1 teaspoon vanilla extract
Few drops red food coloring

Cover a large countertop area or 2 large baking sheets with waxed paper.

In a medium microwave-proof bowl, combine the sugar, corn syrup, and half-and-half. Microwave on High 3 minutes. Stir in the peanuts. Microwave on High 4½ minutes. Stir the mixture. Microwave on High 4½ minutes.

Remove the bowl from the microwave. Stir in the butter and vanilla. Stir in a few drops of red food coloring as desired. Beat by hand until the candy is creamy and holds its shape. Quickly drop by spoonfuls onto the waxed paper. Cool. Store in an airtight container.

**COOK'S NOTE:** Milk may be substituted for the half-and-half, but the half-and-half makes a creamier candy.

. . . . . . . . . . . . . . . . . . . . . . . .

# Perfect Pralines

### Skill Level: Advanced

*These semismooth, melt–in–your–mouth nut clusters are a personal favorite. The buttermilk makes them extrarich, and the pecans are slightly soft because they are cooked along with the candy. These pralines are a little darker than most, so don't be surprised if your friends think they are eating chocolate.*

✳ MAKES ABOUT 30 PRALINES

1 cup buttermilk
2 cups granulated sugar
1 teaspoon baking soda
$\frac{1}{2}$ cup butter or margarine (butter preferred)
$\frac{1}{8}$ teaspoon salt
2$\frac{1}{2}$ cups pecans in large pieces
1 teaspoon vanilla extract

Cover a large countertop area or large baking sheet with waxed paper.

In a heavy 8-quart kettle over medium-low heat, bring the buttermilk, sugar, and baking soda to a boil, stirring constantly. The mixture will foam rapidly and rise in the kettle as it begins to boil. Boil, stirring constantly, for 7 minutes.

Stir in the butter, salt, and pecans. Cook,

stirring constantly, to the soft ball stage (234°F to 240°F, with 236°F recommended).

Remove from the heat. Stir in the vanilla. Beat by hand until the candy is thick and creamy. Quickly drop by spoonfuls onto the waxed paper. Cool. Store in an airtight container.

**COOK'S NOTES:** The candy may be cooked in a 6-quart kettle but is likely to boil over the sides of the pan if not very carefully watched.

If the candy becomes too stiff to drop, stir in a few drops of half-and-half, evaporated milk, or milk until the candy is smooth.

. . . . . . . . . . . . . . . . . . . . . . . .

# Texas Pralines

### Skill Level: Advanced

*These pralines come with a triple endorsement. The recipe began with a lady in Louisiana named Carol and passed through at least two other kitchens before making it to mine. Adding the nuts after the candy is cooked keeps them extracrispy.*

✳ MAKES ABOUT 30

1 cup buttermilk
2 cups granulated sugar
1 teaspoon baking soda
1 tablespoon butter or margarine
1 teaspoon vanilla extract
2 cups pecan pieces or halves

Cover a large countertop area or a large baking sheet with waxed paper.

In a heavy 8-quart kettle over medium heat, bring the buttermilk, sugar, and baking soda to a boil, stirring until the sugar dissolves and the mixture begins to boil. The mixture will foam rapidly and rise in the kettle as it begins to boil. Cook, stirring constantly, to the soft ball stage (234°F to 240°F, with 236°F recommended).

Remove from the heat. Add the butter, vanilla, and pecans. Beat by hand until the candy is thick and creamy. Quickly drop by spoonfuls onto the waxed paper. Cool. Store in an airtight container.

**COOK'S NOTE:** If the candy becomes too stiff to drop, place the kettle back on the burner for a few seconds and stir, continuing to drop the candies when the mixture softens again.

# Ultra-Creamy Buttermilk Pralines

## Skill Level: Advanced

*With a flavor similar to Perfect Pralines (page 56) and Texas Pralines (page 56), this recipe is a good choice for those who prefer candies containing corn syrup.*

✳ MAKES ABOUT 38

    1 cup buttermilk
    3 cups granulated sugar
    1 teaspoon baking soda
    ¾ cup light corn syrup
    ⅛ teaspoon salt
    2 cups pecan pieces or halves
    1 teaspoon vanilla extract
    1 tablespoon margarine

Cover a large countertop area or 2 large baking sheets with waxed paper.

In a heavy 8-quart kettle over medium heat,

bring the buttermilk, sugar, baking soda, corn syrup, and salt to a boil, stirring until the sugar dissolves and the mixture begins to boil. The mixture will foam rapidly and rise in the kettle as it begins to boil. Cook, stirring constantly, to the soft ball stage (234°F to 240°F, with 236°F recommended).

Remove from the heat. Stir in the pecans, vanilla, and margarine. Beat by hand until the candy is thick and creamy. Quickly drop by spoonfuls onto the waxed paper. Cool. Store in an airtight container.

**COOK'S NOTE:** If the candy becomes too stiff to drop, stir in a few drops of half-and-half, evaporated milk, or milk until the candy is smooth.

# New Orleans Roasted Pecan Pralines

## Skill Level: Advanced

*Anyone who has eaten New Orleans's famous "prah-leens" will be happy to have my cousin Margaret's authentic recipe for these traditional sugary candies from a New Orleans cooking school. Be bold; try one of the unusual flavors.*

✳ MAKES 25 TO 30

    1½ cups pecans in large pieces
    1½ cups granulated sugar
    ¾ cup packed light brown sugar
    ⅔ cup milk
    6 tablespoons butter
    1 teaspoon vanilla extract

To roast the pecans, preheat the oven to 275°F. Spread the pecans in a shallow pan. Bake for 20 to 25 minutes, or until the pecans are slightly browned and the smell of roasted pecans permeates the room.

Cover a large countertop area or a large baking sheet with buttered waxed paper, buttered foil, or parchment paper.

In a heavy 3-quart saucepan, combine the sugars and milk, stirring to dissolve the sugar. Add the butter and pecans. Bring to a boil over medium heat, stirring constantly. Cook, stirring constantly, to the soft ball stage (234°F to 240°F, with 238°F recommended).

Remove from the heat. Beat by hand until the candy thickens and becomes creamy and cloudy, and the pecans stay suspended in the mixture. Quickly drop by spoonfuls onto the buttered paper or foil. Cool. Store in an airtight container.

### VARIATIONS

*Flavored and Spiced Pralines:* Add 1 teaspoon of your favorite flavoring, such as coffee or brandy, or ½ to 1 teaspoon of your favorite spice, such as ground ginger or nutmeg, to the mixture before cooking.

*Praline Sauce:* Add ½ cup light corn syrup to the mixture before cooking. Follow the directions above but do not drop onto waxed paper. Serve the sauce warm over ice cream or other desserts.

*Chocolate-Covered Pralines:* Dip the cooled pralines into melted chocolate to coat, placing on waxed paper until the chocolate hardens. See Dipping Candies in Chocolate (page 23) and Chocolate Coatings (page 150) for further instructions and ideas.

**COOK'S NOTE:** If using waxed paper, protect the countertop by placing newspaper or parchment paper underneath the waxed paper so that hot wax from the paper does not transfer onto the countertop.

. . . . . . . . . . . . . . . . . . . . . . . .

# Ruth's Angel Pralines

## Skill Level: Advanced

*Ruth Hoeflin, former dean of home economics at Kansas State University, was known for sending annual greetings to hundreds of friends during her summer break. She always included a few new recipes she discovered that year, such as this one for traditional sugary pralines.*

✳ **MAKES ABOUT 24**

> 1 cup granulated sugar
> 1 cup packed light brown sugar
> ½ cup half-and-half
> ¼ teaspoon salt
> 2 tablespoons butter or margarine
> 1 cup pecans in large pieces

Cover a large countertop area or a large baking sheet with waxed paper or foil.

In a heavy 2-quart saucepan over medium-low heat, bring the sugars, half-and-half, and salt to a boil, stirring until the sugars dissolve and the mixture begins to boil. Cook to 228°F, stirring gently to prevent scorching. Stir in the butter and pecans. Cook, stirring frequently to prevent scorching, to the soft ball stage (234°F to 240°F, with 236°F recommended).

Remove from the heat. Cool 5 minutes.

Beat by hand until the candy is slightly thickened. (The candy coats the nuts but does not lose its gloss.) Quickly drop by spoonfuls onto the waxed paper. Cool. Store in an airtight container.

COOK'S NOTE: If the candy becomes too stiff to drop, stir in a few drops of half-and-half, evaporated milk, or milk until the candy is smooth.

# Prizewinning Pralines

## Skill Level: Advanced

*Made with a combination of brown and white sugar, these creamy, golden brown nut clusters took second prize in the 1972 recipe contest sponsored by the* Ponca City News.

❋ MAKES ABOUT 40

2 cups light brown sugar
1 cup granulated sugar
3 tablespoons light corn syrup
1⅓ cups milk
⅓ cup butter or margarine
2 teaspoons vanilla extract
2 to 2½ cups pecans in large pieces

Cover a large countertop area or 2 large baking sheets with waxed paper.

In a heavy 4- to 5-quart kettle over medium heat, bring the sugars, corn syrup, and milk to a boil, stirring until the sugars dissolve and the mixture begins to boil. Reduce the heat to medium low. Cook, stirring occasionally to pre-

vent scorching, to the soft ball stage (234°F to 240°F, with 236°F recommended).

Remove from the heat. Add the butter without stirring. Cool slightly, about 10 minutes.

Add the vanilla. Beat by hand until the candy thickens and loses its gloss. Stir in the nuts. Quickly drop by spoonfuls onto the waxed paper. Cool. Store in an airtight container.

COOK'S NOTE: If the candy becomes too stiff to drop, stir in a few drops of half-and-half, evaporated milk, or milk until the candy is smooth.

# Soft Pecan Pralines

## Skill Level: Advanced

*Heavy cream makes these pralines unusually soft and light in color.*
❋ MAKES ABOUT 35

2 cups granulated sugar
⅓ cup light corn syrup
⅔ cup heavy cream
Pinch salt
2 cups pecans in large pieces
¼ cup butter or margarine
½ teaspoon vanilla extract

Cover a large countertop area or 2 large baking sheets with waxed paper.

In a heavy 3-quart saucepan over medium-low heat, bring the sugar, corn syrup, cream, and salt to a boil, stirring until the sugar dissolves and the mixture begins to boil. Cover and cook 2 to 3 minutes to dissolve the sugar crystals on the sides of the pan. Remove the lid. Cook, stirring only as needed to prevent scorching, to the soft ball stage (234°F to 240°F, with 238°F recommended).

Remove from the heat. Add the pecans, butter, and vanilla. Beat by hand until the candy thickens and becomes creamy. Quickly drop by spoonfuls onto the waxed paper. Cool. Store in an airtight container.

**COOK'S NOTE:** If the candy becomes too stiff to drop, stir in a few drops of half-and-half, evaporated milk, or milk until the candy is smooth.

occasionally to prevent scorching, to the soft ball stage (234°F to 240°F, with 238°F recommended).

Remove from the heat. Add the butter and pecan halves. Beat by hand until the candy is thick and creamy. Quickly drop by spoonfuls onto the waxed paper. Cool. Store in an airtight container.

**COOK'S NOTE:** If the candy becomes too stiff to drop, stir in a few drops of half-and-half, evaporated milk, or milk until the candy is smooth.

# Creamy Pecan Pralines

## Skill Level: Advanced

*It is extremely rare to find baking soda in a candy recipe that does not also contain buttermilk.*
❋ MAKES ABOUT 30

2 cups granulated sugar
¾ teaspoon baking soda
1 cup half-and-half or evaporated milk
1½ tablespoons butter
2 cups pecan halves

Cover a large countertop area or a large baking sheet with waxed paper.

In a heavy 5-quart kettle, combine the sugar and baking soda, mixing well. Stir in the half-and-half. Bring to a boil over medium heat, stirring until the sugar dissolves and the mixture begins to boil. The mixture will foam rapidly and rise in the kettle as it begins to boil. Reduce the heat to medium low. Cook, stirring

# Caramel-Pecan Pralines

## Skill Level: Expert

*These rich, sugary brown pralines have a distinctive flavor that only caramelized sugar can give.*
❋ MAKES ABOUT 40

2½ cups granulated sugar, divided
1 cup evaporated milk
2 tablespoons butter or margarine
Dash salt
1 teaspoon vanilla extract
2 cups pecans in large pieces

Cover a large countertop area or 2 large baking sheets with waxed paper.

In a small, heavy saucepan or skillet over low heat, slowly melt ½ cup of the sugar, stirring constantly to prevent scorching. In a heavy 5-quart kettle over medium-low heat, combine the remaining 2 cups sugar and the milk. While the sugar slowly melts in the saucepan or skillet, slowly bring the sugar-milk mixture to a gentle boil, gently stirring to prevent scorching.

When sugar is fully melted and caramelized, slowly pour it into the kettle containing the boiling sugar-milk mixture, stirring constantly to prevent the caramelized sugar from clumping on the bottom of the kettle.

Cook, stirring constantly to prevent scorching, to the soft ball stage (234°F to 240°F, with 236°F recommended).

Remove from the heat. Add the butter, salt, and vanilla. Beat by hand until the candy begins to thicken. Stir in the pecans. Quickly drop by spoonfuls onto the waxed paper. Cool. Store in an airtight container.

COOK'S NOTES: These pralines can "sugar" within a few days. To help avoid this, let the candy cool about 20 minutes before beating.

If the candy becomes too stiff to drop, stir in a few drops of half-and-half, evaporated milk, or milk until the candy is smooth.

Evaporated milk gives the candy a richer texture, but milk may be substituted.

. . . . . . . . . . . . . . . . . . . . . . . . . . .

# Love Me Pralines

### Skill Level: Advanced

*When I was testing recipes for this book, it was not unusual to see me toting candy samples wherever I went. On the day that I took a few of these marshmallow-smooth pralines to a group of dentists, I had a rather unforgettable message from a dentist I had never met.*

*"Tell her I love her," he said.*

*It is amazing how easily candy makers make friends.*

✳ MAKES ABOUT 32

1½ cups granulated sugar
½ cup packed light brown sugar
3 tablespoons light corn syrup
½ cup half-and-half
6 large marshmallows
2 tablespoons butter or margarine
1 teaspoon vanilla extract
1½ cups pecans in large pieces

Cover a large countertop area or 2 large baking sheets with waxed paper or buttered foil.

In a heavy 2-quart saucepan over medium heat, bring the sugars, corn syrup, and half-and-half to a boil, gently stirring until the sugars dissolve and the mixture begins to boil. Cover and cook 2 to 3 minutes to dissolve the sugar crystals on the sides of the pan. Remove the lid. Cook, stirring occasionally to prevent scorching, to the soft ball stage (234°F to 240°F; with 236°F recommended).

Remove from the heat. Add the marshmallows and butter, stirring until melted. Add the vanilla and pecans. Beat by hand until the candy begins to stiffen. Quickly drop by spoonfuls onto the waxed paper. Store in an airtight container.

COOK'S NOTE: If the candy becomes too stiff to drop, stir in a few drops of half-and-half, evaporated milk, or milk until the candy is smooth.

. . . . . . . . . . . . . . . . . . . . . . . . . . .

# Butterscotch Pecan Pralines

## Skill Level: Advanced

*When my cousin Patti told me that butterscotch-flavored pralines were all the rage in Austin, I enjoyed telling her that this scrumptious candy has been around since we were kids and took first prize in the 1964 recipe contest sponsored by our hometown newspaper, the* Ponca City News.

✳ MAKES ABOUT 18 TO 24

> 1 (3.5-ounce) package butterscotch pudding
>    mix (not instant)
> 1 cup granulated sugar
> ½ cup packed light brown sugar
> ½ cup evaporated milk
> 1 tablespoon butter
> ½ teaspoon vanilla extract (optional)
> 1½ cups pecans in large pieces

Cover a large countertop area or a large baking sheet with waxed paper.

In a heavy 2-quart saucepan over medium-low heat, bring the pudding mix, sugars, milk, and butter to a boil, gently stirring until the sugar dissolves and the mixture begins to boil. Cook, stirring occasionally to prevent scorching, to the soft ball stage (234°F to 240°F, with 234°F recommended).

Remove from the heat. Add the vanilla, if using, and pecans. Beat by hand until the candy is creamy and begins to thicken. Quickly drop by spoonfuls onto the waxed paper. Cool. Store in an airtight container.

COOK'S NOTES: For a firmer praline, cook to 236°F.

If the candy becomes too stiff to drop, stir in a few drops of half-and-half, evaporated milk, or milk until the candy is smooth.

# Evelyn's Maple Pralines

## Skill Level: Advanced

*A longtime favorite with Evelyn who lives in the retirement community with my mother, these ultra-smooth, light-colored pralines have a wonderful maple taste. For exceptional flavor, use good-quality maple syrup.*

✳ MAKES ABOUT 30

> 2 cups granulated sugar
> ⅔ cup half-and-half
> 1 cup maple syrup
> 2 cups pecans in large pieces

Cover a large area of the countertop or a large baking sheet with waxed paper.

In a heavy 3-quart saucepan over medium heat, bring the sugar, half-and-half, and maple syrup to a boil, stirring until the sugar dissolves and the mixture begins to boil. Cook, stirring occasionally to prevent scorching, to the soft ball stage (234°F to 240°F, with 238°F recommended).

Remove from the heat. Beat by hand until the candy thickens and becomes creamy. Stir in the pecans. Quickly drop by spoonfuls onto the waxed paper. Cool. Store in an airtight container.

COOK'S NOTES: For softer pralines, cook to 236°F.

The cooked candy may be removed from the heat and cooled slightly before beating, about 5 minutes, to reduce the beating time.

This candy sets in the pan very quickly. If the candy becomes too stiff to drop, stir in a few drops of half-and-half, evaporated milk, or milk until the candy is smooth.

# Maple Pecan Pralines

## Skill Level: Advanced

*A hint of maple flavoring makes these smooth, pow-dered sugar pralines hard to beat.*

✳ MAKES ABOUT 30

2 cups powdered sugar
½ cup evaporated milk
1 cup maple syrup, preferably good quality
Dash salt
1 tablespoon butter or margarine
1 teaspoon vanilla extract
1 to 1½ cups pecans in large pieces

Cover a countertop area or large baking sheet with waxed paper or buttered foil.

In a heavy 3-quart saucepan over medium heat, bring the sugar, milk, syrup, and salt to a boil, stirring until the sugar dissolves and the mixture begins to boil. Cook, stirring occasion-ally to prevent scorching, to the soft ball stage (234°F to 240°F, with 236°F recommended).

Remove from the heat. Add the butter, vanilla, and pecans. Beat by hand until the candy is opaque and creamy. Quickly drop by spoonfuls onto the waxed paper or foil. Cool. Store in an airtight container.

COOK'S NOTES: For softer pralines, cook to 234°F.

To reduce the beating time, add the butter, vanilla, and pecans without stirring. Let the candy cool slightly, about 5 minutes, before beating.

# Molasses Pralines

## Skill Level: Advanced

*These dark, nontraditional, almost bittersweet pra-lines are included for those trying to duplicate a lost praline recipe containing molasses.*

✳ MAKES ABOUT 30

2 cups packed light brown sugar
½ cup hot water
2 tablespoons molasses
1 tablespoon butter or margarine
1 to 1½ cups pecans in large pieces

Cover a large countertop area or a large baking sheet with waxed paper.

In a heavy 3-quart saucepan over medium heat, bring the sugar, water, and molasses to a boil, stirring until the sugar dissolves and the mixture begins to boil. Cook, stirring only as needed to prevent the candy from boiling over the sides of the pan, to the soft ball stage (234°F to 240°F, with 236°F recommended).

Remove from the heat. Add the butter. Beat by hand until the candy begins to thicken. Stir in the pecans. Quickly drop by spoonfuls onto the waxed paper. Cool. Store in an airtight con-tainer.

COOK'S NOTE: Either mild flavor or full flavor molasses may be used.

# Coconut Pralines

## Skill Level: Advanced

*Light brown and ultrasugary, these pralinelike candies contain coconut, instead of nuts.*

＊ **MAKES ABOUT 50**

 **2 cups packed light brown sugar**
 **1 cup granulated sugar**
 **1 cup water**
 **1 teaspoon cider vinegar**
 **1 tablespoon butter or margarine**
 **2 cups sweetened flaked coconut**

Cover a large countertop area or 2 large baking sheets with waxed paper.

In a heavy 2-quart saucepan over medium heat, bring the sugars, water, and vinegar to a boil, stirring until the sugar dissolves and the mixture begins to boil. Cook, stirring only a few times to prevent scorching, to the soft ball stage (234°F to 240°F, with 236°F recommended).

Remove from the heat. Add the butter. Cool about 5 minutes to reduce the beating time. Add the coconut. Beat by hand until the candy begins to thicken and hold its shape. Quickly drop by spoonfuls onto the waxed paper. Cool. Store in an airtight container.

**COOK'S NOTES:** Half-and-half or evaporated milk may be substituted for the water in this recipe, but the brown sugar will still give the pralines a very sugary texture.

For firmer pralines, cook to 238°F.

# Mexican Orange Drops

## Skill Level: Expert

*Surprise your guests by serving these chewy, orange-flavored pralines at your next Mexican dinner party.*

＊ **MAKES ABOUT 36**

 **3 cups granulated sugar, divided**
 **1 cup evaporated milk**
 **¼ cup orange juice**
 **¼ teaspoon salt**
 **Grated zest of 2 oranges**
 **1 cup pecans in large pieces**

Cover a large countertop area or 2 large baking sheets with waxed paper. Spray with nonstick spray.

In a heavy 3-quart saucepan over medium-low heat, slowly melt 1 cup of the sugar, stirring constantly to prevent scorching. While the sugar is melting, in a very heavy saucepan or in the top pan of a double boiler pan over hot, but not boiling water, heat the milk until it is very hot. Do not allow the milk to boil. Heat the orange juice in the microwave until boiling.

When the sugar has fully melted into a rich, brown liquid, slowly stir the boiling orange juice into the sugar, being careful that the hot mixture does not splatter. Slowly stir the hot milk into the sugar-orange juice mixture, stirring until the mixture is blended.

Gradually add the remaining 2 cups sugar and the salt, stirring until the sugar dissolves. Bring to a boil over medium-low heat. Cover and cook 2 to 3 minutes to dissolve the sugar crystals on the sides of the pan. Remove the lid. Cook slowly over low or medium-low heat, without stirring, to the soft ball stage (234°F to 240°F, with 236°F recommended). Just before the candy reaches the desired temperature, gently stir in the orange zest.

Remove from the heat. Cool to lukewarm (110°F), 45 minutes to 1 hour.

Beat by hand until the candy thickens and loses its gloss. Stir in the pecans. Quickly drop by spoonfuls onto the waxed paper. Cool. Store in an airtight container.

COOK'S NOTES: Boiling water may be substituted for the orange juice, but the orange juice gives a better flavor.

If preferred, the candy may be beaten without cooling to lukewarm, but the cooling period reduces the beating time.

The beaten candy may be pressed into a well-buttered 8- or 9-inch square pan, cooled, and then cut into squares.

If the candy becomes too stiff to drop, stir in a few drops of half-and-half, evaporated milk, or milk until the candy is smooth.

. . . . . . . . . . . . . . . . . . . . . . . . . . . . . .

# Mexican Candy

## Skill Level: Expert

*This very interesting recipe for orange-flavored candy is almost a cross between Mexican Orange Drops (page 64) and Aunt Bill's Brown Candy (page 28).*

✳ MAKES ABOUT 36 PIECES OR 1½ POUNDS

> 3 cups granulated sugar, divided
> 1½ cups evaporated milk
> Grated zest of 2 oranges
> Pinch salt
> ½ cup butter
> 1 cup pecans in large pieces

Cover a large countertop area or 2 large baking sheets with waxed paper. Spray with nonstick spray.

In a heavy 4- to 5-quart kettle over low heat, slowly melt 1 cup of the sugar, stirring constantly to prevent scorching. While the sugar is melting, in a very heavy saucepan or in the top pan of a double boiler pan over hot, but not boiling water, heat the milk until it is very hot. Do not allow the milk to boil.

When the sugar has fully melted into a rich, brown liquid, slowly stir the hot milk into the melted sugar, being careful that the hot mixture does not splatter. Stir until the mixture is blended.

Gradually add the remaining 2 cups sugar, stirring until the sugar dissolves. Bring to a boil over medium-low heat. Cook, stirring frequently to prevent scorching, to the firm ball stage (244°F to 248°F, with 246°F recommended).

Remove from the heat. Stir in the zest, salt, and butter. Cool 20 minutes.

Beat by hand until the candy is creamy and loses its gloss. Stir in the nuts. Quickly drop by spoonfuls onto the waxed paper. Cool. Store in an airtight container.

COOK'S NOTES: If preferred, the candy may be poured onto a buttered platter or into an 8- or 9-inch square buttered pan and cut into squares when cool.

If the candy becomes too stiff to drop, stir in a few drops of half-and-half, evaporated milk, or milk until the candy is smooth.

. . . . . . . . . . . . . . . . . . . . . . . . . . . . . .

# Mexican Pecan Candy

### Skill Level: Advanced

*These traditional Mexican candies are a very sugary form of American pralines.*
✳ MAKES ABOUT 18

> 2 cups granulated sugar
> 1 cup water
> 1½ cups pecan halves

Cover a large countertop area or a large baking sheet with waxed paper.

In a heavy 2-quart saucepan over medium heat, bring the sugar, water, and pecans to a boil, stirring until the sugar dissolves and the mixture begins to boil. Cook, stirring occasionally to prevent the nuts from settling on the bottom of the pan, to the soft ball stage (234°F to 240°F, with 236°F recommended).

Remove from the heat. Cool slightly, about 10 minutes. Beat by hand until the mixture thickens and becomes difficult to beat. Quickly drop by spoonfuls onto the waxed paper. Cool. Store in an airtight container.

COOK'S NOTE: If the candy becomes difficult to drop, add a drop or two of hot water, stirring until well blended.

# Coconut Haystacks

### Skill Level: Average

*These light brown coconut haystacks may be nothing like the coconut haystacks that you might buy in a candy store, but they may be a favorite of coconut lovers. Nut lovers might like to toss a few chopped pecans into the candy before dropping it onto waxed paper.*
✳ MAKES ABOUT 36

> ¾ cup packed light brown sugar
> ¾ cup evaporated milk
> 6 tablespoons light corn syrup
> 2 tablespoons butter
> 3 cups sweetened flaked coconut

Cover a large countertop area or 2 large baking sheets with waxed paper.

In a heavy 1- to 2-quart saucepan over medium heat, bring the sugar, milk, corn syrup, and butter to a boil, stirring until the sugar dissolves and the mixture begins to boil. Cook, stirring occasionally to prevent scorching, to the soft ball stage (234°F to 240°F, with 238°F recommended).

Remove from the heat. Stir in the coconut until well blended. Quickly drop by spoonfuls onto the waxed paper. To create the haystacks, dip your fingers into cold water and shape the candy into cones 1½ inches high while the candy is still warm. Cool. Store in an airtight container.

COOK'S NOTES: For a similar candy that is chocolate coated, see Chocolate-Covered Haystacks (page 156).

If preferred, the butter may be added after the candy is cooked to make the candy slightly softer and creamier.

# Nut Cream Drops

## Skill Level: Advanced

*Those needing a quick sugar fix will be glad to know that they can make these rich little drops in about 15 minutes.*

✳ MAKES ABOUT 24

1½ cups granulated sugar
¼ cup milk
2 tablespoons light corn syrup
Dash salt
1 teaspoon vanilla extract
½ cup chopped walnuts, pecans, or sweetened
   flaked coconut

Cover a large countertop area or a large baking sheet with waxed paper.

In a heavy 1- to 2-quart saucepan over medium-low to medium heat, bring the sugar, milk, corn syrup, and salt to a boil, stirring until the sugar dissolves and the mixture begins to boil. Cook, stirring frequently to prevent scorching, to the soft ball stage (234°F to 240°F, with 236°F recommended).

Remove from the heat. Stir in the vanilla and nuts. Beat by hand until the candy is thick and creamy and begins to lose its gloss. Quickly drop by spoonfuls onto the waxed paper. Cool. Store in an airtight container.

COOK'S NOTE: For a richer candy, substitute half-and-half for the milk.

# Divinities, Nougats, and Similar Candies

## Mom's Divinity

### Skill Level: Advanced

*My mother's divinity recipe is one of the few versions of this traditional Southern favorite that calls for cooking the syrup in one stage rather than two. When I asked my mother why she chose this recipe, she jokingly said, "I never wanted to make things more difficult than they had to be!"*

*Like mother, like daughter, because this is my favorite divinity recipe, too. It is one of the easiest classic divinity recipes you will find.*

✳ **MAKES ABOUT 30 TO 36 PIECES**

2 extra-large or large egg whites
2⅔ cups granulated sugar
⅔ cup light corn syrup
½ cup water
1 teaspoon vanilla extract
⅔ cup pecans in large pieces

See Tips for Making Divinity (page 69).

Cover a large countertop area or a large baking sheet with waxed paper. Butter 2 small spoons.

In a large mixing bowl, beat the egg whites with an electric mixer on high speed until the whites form very stiff peaks, but not so long that they lose their gloss and become dry.

In a 1- to 2-quart saucepan over medium-high heat, bring the sugar, corn syrup, and water to a boil, stirring just until the sugar dissolves and the mixture begins to boil. Cook, without stirring, to the hard ball stage (260°F).

Remove the syrup from the heat. Turn the electric mixer to medium-high speed and beat the egg whites again while gradually pouring the hot syrup in a thin stream over the top of the egg whites. Continue beating while adding the vanilla. Beat with the electric mixer until the candy becomes slightly dull and holds its shape when dropped from a spoon. If the candy becomes too stiff to beat with an electric mixer, finish beating by hand.

Stir in the pecans by hand. Quickly drop the candy onto the waxed paper using the tip of a buttered spoon. Cool. Store in an airtight container at room temperature.

**COOK'S NOTES:** Experienced candy makers may prefer to beat the egg whites while the syrup is cooking.

Use 1 less tablespoon water on humid days.

# Tips for Making Divinity

Divinity is not a difficult candy to make but does have three failure points. If any one of these steps is not completed accurately, the divinity will not hold its shape.

* The egg whites must be properly beaten.
* The syrup must be properly cooked.
* The combined mixture must be properly beaten.

The egg whites should be beaten until they form very stiff peaks. This means that when the beaters are lifted from the egg whites, the tips should stand up straight. If the tops curl to one side, beat the egg whites 1 to 2 minutes longer, and then stop the mixer and lift the beaters again. Knowing exactly when the egg whites are ready usually requires stopping the mixer and checking their progress several times during beating. As soon as the egg whites stand in very stiff peaks, stop beating.

Though old-time candy makers know how to test divinity syrup by dropping it into cold water, the best way to know when the syrup is properly cooked is to use a candy thermometer.

The combined egg white–syrup mixture must be beaten until the candy holds its shape when dropped from a spoon. As one cousin put it, "Beat that stuff until the mixer begins to smoke." While it is not necessary to damage the mixer's motor, divinity does need to be beaten until it cools and stiffens, which is quite a bit longer than most people think. If a test candy spreads even slightly on the waxed paper after being dropped from a spoon, the candy has not been beaten long enough. Properly beaten divinity is usually so stiff that it is difficult to stir by hand.

# Down-Home Divinity

## Skill Level: Advanced

*My mother often refers to visiting her family in Arkansas as going "down home," so it seemed quite natural for me to name my aunt Mary and aunt Erma's divinity recipe, "Down-Home Divinity."*

*While both aunts could agree that this classic two-step recipe was a favorite, they could not agree on what to do with it once it was cooked. Aunt Mary, who began making divinity in the early 1930s using a rotary beater, preferred to pour or "pack" it into a buttered pan and cut it into squares, but Aunt Erma insisted that proper Southern divinity must be dropped from the tip of a buttered spoon. Now that they are both gone, I can privately admit that I tend to agree with Aunt Erma.*

✳ MAKES ABOUT 48 PIECES

### Part 1
3 extra-large or large egg whites
3 cups granulated sugar
1 cup light corn syrup
¾ cup water

### Part 2
1 cup granulated sugar
½ cup water
1 teaspoon vanilla extract
2 cups pecans in large pieces

See Tips for Making Divinity (page 69).

TO MAKE PART 1: Cover a large countertop area or 2 large baking sheets with waxed paper. Butter 2 small spoons.

In a large mixing bowl, beat the egg whites with a heavy-duty electric mixer on high speed until the egg whites form very stiff peaks, but not so long that they lose their gloss and become dry.

In a 2-quart saucepan over medium-low heat, bring the sugar, corn syrup, and water to a boil, stirring just until the sugar dissolves and the mixture begins to boil. Cook, without stirring, to the hard ball stage (265°F).

Remove the syrup from the heat. Turn the

## A Southern Favorite

In the early days, making divinity was quite a project. Not only did candy makers have to judge the syrup by look and by feel, but they also had to beat both the egg whites and the candy by hand until stiff. Those who owned modern handheld rotary beaters were considered the lucky ones. Given all the effort this candy once required, it is no wonder that serving a perfect batch of divinity became a sign of Southern hospitality; only really nice people would work that hard and then share their candy with guests.

With candy thermometers and electric mixers, divinity is now relatively simple to make. It remains a perennial favorite, with some loving the taste and some loving the tradition. Each of the recipes in this collection offers something a little different from the others. Whether you make divinity in one step or two, or prefer nuts or candied cherries, this collection will have y'all coming back for more.

electric mixer to medium-high speed and beat the egg whites again while gradually pouring the hot syrup in a thin stream over the top of the egg whites. Leave the mixer on while placing Part 2 over the heat, turning the mixer off when the mixture is well blended.

TO MAKE PART 2: In a very small saucepan over medium-low heat, bring the sugar and water to a boil, stirring just until the sugar dissolves and the mixture begins to boil. Cook, without stirring, to the hard ball stage (265°F).

Remove the syrup from the heat. Turn the electric mixer to medium-high speed and gradually pour the hot syrup over the top of the candy mixture, beating constantly. Continue beating while adding the vanilla. Beat with the electric mixer until the candy becomes slightly dull and holds its shape when dropped from a spoon.

Stir in the pecans by hand. Quickly drop the candy onto the waxed paper using the tip of a buttered spoon. Cool. Store in an airtight container at room temperature.

COOK'S NOTES: Experienced candy makers may prefer to beat the egg whites while Part I of the syrup is cooking.

The heat settings in this recipe were those my aunts used. Both syrups may be cooked over medium-high heat rather than medium-low heat if preferred.

If preferred, the divinity may be turned into a buttered 9 × 13-inch pan and cut into squares when firm.

# Louisiana Double Divinity Delight

## Skill Level: Advanced

*Occasionally, one of my cousins goes astray and finds a recipe that she thinks is better than her mother's. Such is the case with my cousin Margaret, whose mother helped make Down-Home Divinity (page 70), a family institution. Margaret's supersized, one-step divinity recipe is a sure winner, especially when entertaining large crowds down on the bayou.*
✳ MAKES 70 TO 90 SMALL PIECES

> 4 extra-large or large egg whites
> ⅛ teaspoon salt
> 6 cups granulated sugar
> 1 cup light corn syrup
> 4 cups water
> 1 tablespoon vanilla extract
> 2 cups chopped pecans

See Tips for Making Divinity (page 69).

Cover a large countertop area with newspapers or heavy brown wrapping paper to protect it from the heat and wax. Place waxed paper on top of the newspapers and spray with nonstick spray. Butter 2 small spoons.

In a large mixing bowl, beat the egg whites and salt with a heavy-duty electric mixer on high speed until the egg whites form very stiff peaks, but not so long that they lose their gloss and become dry.

In a 4- to 5-quart kettle over high heat, bring the sugar, corn syrup, and water to a boil, stirring just until the sugar dissolves and the mixture begins to boil. Cook, without stirring, to the hard ball stage (250°F). Watch the thermometer closely; the temperature increases rapidly during the last 5 degrees of cooking.

Remove the syrup from the heat. Turn the electric mixer to medium-high speed and beat the egg whites again while gradually pouring the hot syrup in a thin stream into the center of the egg whites. Beat with the electric mixer until the candy becomes slightly dull, stiffens, and holds its shape when dropped from a spoon. When properly beaten, the mixture will look as if it has wrinkles in it, and the wrinkles will lay flat and hold their shape.

Stir in the vanilla and nuts by hand. Quickly drop the candy onto the waxed paper using the tip of a buttered spoon. Cool. Store in an airtight container at room temperature.

COOK'S NOTES: Because of the volume of this recipe, it is essential to use a heavy-duty electric mixer such as a KitchenAid to beat the candy. Lighter models of electric mixers may not be able to manage this recipe without causing damage to the motors.

This divinity has a slightly softer center than recipes that cook the syrup to a higher temperature.

. . . . . . . . . . . . . . . . . . . . . . . . . . . . .

# Cowboy Divinity

## Skill Level: Advanced

*Cowboy Divinity is one of several recipes in this book that comes from a 1950s Oklahoma State University test kitchen managed by Eula Morris. It has the least amount of sugar of any of the divinity recipes in this collection. Try one of Eula's fun and delicious variations using her divinity recipe or your own favorite divinity recipe.*

✳ MAKES 30 TO 36 PIECES

**2 extra-large or large egg whites**
**2 cups granulated sugar**
**½ cup light corn syrup**
**½ cup water**
**⅛ teaspoon salt**
**1 teaspoon vanilla extract**
**½ cup pecans in large pieces**

See Tips for Making Divinity (page 69).

Cover a large countertop area or a large baking sheet with waxed paper. Butter 2 small spoons.

In a large mixing bowl, beat the egg whites with a heavy-duty electric mixer on high speed until the egg whites form very stiff peaks, but not so long that they lose their gloss and become dry.

In a 2-quart saucepan over medium heat, bring the sugar, corn syrup, water, and salt to a boil, stirring just until the sugar dissolves and the mixture begins to boil. Cover and cook 2 to 3 minutes to dissolve the sugar crystals on the sides of the pan. Remove the lid. Cook, without stirring, to the soft ball stage (234°F).

Remove the syrup from the heat. Turn the mixer to medium-high speed and beat the egg whites again while gradually pouring one-third of the hot syrup over the top of the egg whites. Leave the mixer on while returning the remaining syrup to the heat, turning the mixer off when the mixture is well blended.

Cook the remaining syrup, without stirring, to the soft crack stage (272°F).

Remove the syrup from the heat. Turn the electric mixer to medium-high speed and gradually pour the remaining hot syrup over the top of the candy mixture, beating constantly. Continue beating while adding the vanilla. Beat with the electric mixer until the candy becomes slightly dull and holds its shape when dropped from a spoon.

Stir in the pecans by hand. Drop quickly onto the waxed paper using the tip of a buttered spoon. Cool. Store in an airtight container at room temperature.

### VARIATIONS

*Chocolate Marbled Divinity:* Substitute ¾ cup semisweet chocolate chips for the nuts. The chocolate will melt as it is added to the candy mixture, creating a marbled effect.

*Cherry Divinity:* Reduce the amount of chopped pecans to ⅓ cup. Stir in ⅓ cup well-drained, finely chopped maraschino cherries with the nuts. If preferred, use ⅓ cup sweetened flaked coconut or coarsely chopped walnuts in place of the pecans.

*Orange Divinity:* Stir in ¾ cup chopped orange jelly candy slices or candied orange peel before dropping the pieces.

COOK'S NOTE: If preferred, the divinity may also be turned into a buttered pan and cut into squares when firm.

· · · · · · · · · · · · · · · · · · · · · · · ·

# Sweetheart Divinity

## Skill Level: Advanced

*If you are sweet on sweets, this is the divinity recipe for you. It contains more sugar than any other divinity recipe in this collection.*

✳ MAKES ABOUT 60 PIECES

**5 cups granulated sugar**
**1½ cups light corn syrup**
**1½ cups water**

**2 extra-large or large egg whites**
**1 teaspoon vanilla extract**
**2 cups coarsely chopped walnuts**

See Tips for Making Divinity (page 69).

In a large mixing bowl, combine the sugar, corn syrup and water, stirring until well blended. Let the mixture stand at room temperature several hours or overnight if possible, stirring often. (See Cook's Note below.)

Cover a large countertop area or 2 large baking sheets with waxed paper. Butter 2 small spoons.

In a large mixing bowl, beat the egg whites with a heavy-duty electric mixer on high speed until the egg whites form very stiff peaks, but not so long that they lose their gloss and become dry.

Transfer the sugar mixture to a 3- to 4-quart saucepan. Bring the sugar mixture to a boil over medium-high heat, stirring just until the sugar dissolves and the mixture begins to boil. Cover and cook 2 minutes to dissolve the sugar crystals on the sides of the pan. Remove the lid. Cook, without stirring, to the firm ball stage (244°F).

Remove the syrup from the heat. Turn the electric mixer to medium-high speed and beat the egg whites again while gradually pouring half of the hot syrup over the top of the egg whites. Leave the mixer on while returning the remaining syrup to the heat, turning the mixer off when the mixture is well blended.

Cook the remaining syrup, without stirring, to the hard ball stage (260°F).

Remove the syrup from the heat. Turn the electric mixer to medium-high speed and gradually pour the remaining hot syrup over the top of the candy mixture, beating constantly. Continue beating while adding the vanilla. Beat with the electric mixer until the candy becomes slightly dull and holds its shape when dropped from a spoon.

Stir in the walnuts by hand. Quickly drop the candy onto the waxed paper using the tip of a buttered spoon. Cool. Store in an airtight container at room temperature.

COOK'S NOTE: It is not essential that the sugar, corn syrup, and water mixture be blended in a separate bowl and left to stand several hours before making this recipe, but it is interesting to see the different ways that divinity can be made.

# Holiday Divinity

## Skill Level: Advanced

*This prize-winning recipe from the 1970* Ponca City News *recipe contest puts a new twist on an old favorite by adding colorful candied fruits.*

✳ MAKES 30 TO 36 PIECES

2 extra-large or large egg whites
2½ cups granulated sugar
½ cup light corn syrup
½ cup water
¼ teaspoon salt
1 teaspoon vanilla extract
1 cup coarsely chopped walnuts or pecans
¼ cup chopped candied cherries
¼ cup chopped candied pineapple

See Tips for Making Divinity (page 69).

Cover a large countertop area or a large baking sheet with waxed paper. Butter 2 small spoons.

In a large mixing bowl, beat the egg whites with a heavy-duty electric mixer on high speed until the egg whites form very stiff peaks, but not so long that they lose their gloss and become dry.

In a 1- to 2-quart saucepan over medium-high heat, bring the sugar, corn syrup, water, and salt to a boil, stirring just until the sugar dissolves and the mixture begins to boil. Cook, without stirring, to the firm ball stage (248°F).

Remove the syrup from the heat. Turn the electric mixer to medium-high speed and beat the egg whites again while gradually pouring half of the hot syrup over the top of the egg whites. Leave the mixer on while returning the remaining syrup to the heat, turning the mixer off when the mixture is well blended.

Cook the remaining syrup, without stirring, to the soft crack stage (272°F).

Remove the syrup from the heat. Turn the electric mixer to medium-high speed and gradually pour the remaining hot syrup over the top of the candy mixture, beating constantly. Continue beating while adding the vanilla. Beat with the electric mixer until the candy becomes slightly dull and holds its shape when dropped from a spoon.

Stir in the nuts and candied fruits by hand. Quickly drop the candy onto the waxed paper using the tip of a buttered spoon. Cool. Store in an airtight container at room temperature.

# Rainbow Divinity

## Skill Level: Advanced

*Every time I think of this recipe, I have visions of white-gloved ladies in pillbox hats carrying fluffy pastel candies into the local church social. This fruit-flavored never-fail divinity recipe was popular in my hometown during the 1960s and early 1970s, with slightly different variations appearing year after year in the* Ponca City News Annual Recipe Edition.

✳ MAKES ABOUT 45 PIECES

> 2 extra-large or large egg whites
> 3 tablespoons strawberry-, cherry-, or lime-flavored gelatin, about ½ of 1 (3-ounce) package
> 3 cups granulated sugar
> ¾ cup light corn syrup
> ¾ cup water
> Pinch salt
> 1 teaspoon vanilla extract
> 1 cup chopped pecans
> ¾ cup sweetened flaked coconut, tinted if desired (see Cook's Notes below), or ½ cup chopped candied cherries (optional)

See Tips for Making Divinity (page 69).

Cover the countertop or 2 large baking sheets with waxed paper. Butter 2 spoons.

In a large mixing bowl, beat the egg whites with a heavy-duty electric mixer on high speed until the egg whites form very stiff peaks, but not so long that they lose their gloss and become dry. Gradually add the gelatin, beating constantly while adding. Beat until well blended; the mixture will be thin.

In a 2-quart saucepan over medium-high heat, bring the sugar, corn syrup, water, and salt to a boil, stirring just until the sugar dis-solves and the mixture begins to boil. Cook, without stirring, to the hard ball stage (250°F).

Remove the syrup from the heat. Turn the electric mixer to medium-high speed and beat the egg whites again while gradually pouring the hot syrup in a thin stream over the top of the egg white–gelatin mixture. Continue beating while adding the vanilla. Beat with the electric mixer until the candy holds its shape when dropped from a spoon.

Stir in the pecans and coconut or cherries, if using, by hand. Quickly drop from a buttered spoon onto waxed paper. Cool. Store in an air-tight container at room temperature.

COOK'S NOTES: To tint the coconut, place the coconut in a small plastic bag and sprinkle lightly with water. Add a few drops of food coloring to the bag. Seal the bag and shake well.

Because this recipe contains gelatin, this candy cools and sets very quickly, especially once the nuts and coconut are added. As a result, the best-looking candies are usually the first to be dropped. If preferred, do not stir the nuts and coconut into the candy. Instead, sprinkle these ingredients on the tops of the candies to decorate, lightly pressing them into the candies before they cool.

# Easy-Do Divinity

## Skill Level: Average

*This mock divinity recipe is a delicious treat for those who do not want to take the time to beat the egg whites required for classic divinity.*

✳ MAKES 18 TO 20 PIECES

1 (7-ounce) jar marshmallow creme
2 cups granulated sugar
½ cup water
Pinch salt
1 teaspoon vanilla extract
½ cup chopped pecans

Cover a countertop area or a large baking sheet with waxed paper. Spray with nonstick spray if desired. Butter 2 small spoons.

Spoon the marshmallow creme into a heat-proof bowl.

In a 1-quart saucepan over medium-high heat, bring the sugar, water, and salt to a boil, stirring just until the sugar dissolves and the mixture begins to boil. Cook, without stirring, to the hard ball stage (250°F).

Remove the syrup from the heat. Gradually pour the hot syrup over the marshmallow creme in the bowl, stirring the marshmallow creme while adding the syrup. Stir by hand until the mixture begins to cool and stiffen. Stir in the vanilla and pecans. Quickly drop the candy onto the waxed paper using the tip of a buttered spoon. Cool. Store in an airtight container at room temperature.

COOK'S NOTE: Once the cooked syrup and marshmallow creme are well blended, place the bowl in the freezer for 1 to 2 minutes to help the mixture cool and thicken. This step reduces the stirring time.

# Sea Foam Candy

## Skill Level: Advanced

*Sea Foam Candy is a form of divinity made with brown sugar rather than granulated sugar. With a darker color and heavier texture than classic white divinity, this candy also carries a distinctive brown sugar flavor. Though few Southerners seem to be familiar with this candy, a New Jersey native told me that it was a part of her mother's holiday tradition.*

✳ MAKES ABOUT 36 PIECES

1 extra-large or large egg white
2 cups packed light brown sugar
½ cup water
½ teaspoon vanilla extract
½ cup pecans in large pieces

See Tips for Making Divinity (page 69).

Cover a large countertop area or a large baking sheet with waxed paper. Butter 2 spoons.

In a small mixing bowl, beat the egg white with a heavy-duty electric mixer on high speed until the egg white forms very stiff peaks, but not so long that it loses its gloss and becomes dry.

In a 1-quart saucepan over medium-high heat, bring the sugar and water to a boil, stirring just until the sugar dissolves and the mixture begins to boil. Cook, without stirring, to the hard ball stage (250°F).

Remove the syrup from the heat. Turn the electric mixer to medium-high speed and beat the egg white again while gradually pouring the hot syrup in a thin stream over the top of the egg white. Continue beating while adding the vanilla. Beat with the electric mixer until the candy becomes slightly dull and holds its shape when dropped from a spoon. Do not overbeat this candy or it may become dry.

Stir in the pecans by hand. Quickly drop the candy onto the waxed paper using the tip of a buttered spoon. Cool. Store in an airtight container at room temperature.

. . . . . . . . . . . . . . . . . . . . . .

# Dainty Mint Puffs

## Skill Level: Advanced

*Perfect for a bridal or baby shower, these delightful pastel candies look like small bites of divinity but have a smooth and creamy mint center.*
✳ MAKES ABOUT 40 PIECES

  **1 extra-large or large egg white**
  **1½ cups granulated sugar**
  **2 tablespoons light corn syrup**
  **¼ cup water**
  **¼ teaspoon peppermint or mint extract**
  **5 drops food coloring of choice**

See Tips on Making Divinity (page 69).

Cover a large countertop area or large baking sheet with waxed paper. Butter 2 small spoons.

In a small mixing bowl, beat the egg white with an electric mixer on high speed until the egg white forms very stiff peaks, but not so long that it loses its gloss and becomes dry.

In a 1-quart saucepan over medium-high heat, bring the sugar, corn syrup, and water to a boil, stirring just until the sugar dissolves and the mixture begins to boil. Cook, without stirring, to the soft ball stage (240°F).

Remove the syrup from the heat. Turn the electric mixer to medium-high speed and beat the egg white again while gradually pouring the hot syrup in a thin stream over the top of the egg white. Continue beating while adding the flavoring and food coloring, dropping the food coloring into the mixture a little at a time. Beat with the electric mixer until the candy becomes slightly dull and holds its shape when dropped from a spoon.

Quickly drop the candy onto waxed paper from the tip of a spoon, making pieces no larger than 1 inch in diameter. Cool. Store in an airtight container at room temperature.

. . . . . . . . . . . . . . . . . . . . . .

# Marshmallows

## Skill Level: Advanced

*Use your imagination and creativity to turn this treasured old recipe into any size, shape, and color of marshmallows that you desire. Just add a little food coloring and pull out the cookie cutters, because the possibilities are endless.*
✳ MAKES ABOUT 1 POUND OR 50 PIECES DEPENDING
  ON SIZE

  **About ¼ cup powdered sugar**
  **2 tablespoons unflavored gelatin powder**
  **¾ cup cold water**
  **2 cups granulated sugar**
  **½ cup hot water**
  **¾ cup light corn syrup**
  **Few grains salt**
  **1 teaspoon vanilla extract**
  **About 2 cups powdered sugar, finely chopped
    pecans or walnuts, or sweetened flaked
    coconut, for rolling**

Generously dust a 13 × 9-inch pan with ¼ cup powdered sugar. Using the back of a spoon, spread the powdered sugar across the bottom and sides of the pan until the bottom surface is completely covered, using slightly more powdered sugar if necessary.

In a small bowl, combine the gelatin and cold water, stirring to blend. Set aside.

In a 1-quart saucepan over medium heat, bring the sugar, hot water, corn syrup, and salt to a boil, stirring until the sugar dissolves and the mixture begins to boil. Cook, without stirring, to the soft ball stage (234°F to 240°F, with 236°F recommended).

Remove from the heat. Stir in the gelatin mixture. Pour the combined mixture into a large mixing bowl. Using a heavy-duty electric mixer, beat the mixture on medium-high speed until it holds its shape, blending in the vanilla while beating. Pour the marshmallow mixture into the prepared pan. Let stand until firm, about 20 minutes.

Using a sharp knife or cookie cutters dipped in hot water, cut into squares, triangles, or other shapes. Roll each marshmallow in powdered sugar, nuts, or coconut as desired. If using powdered sugar, tap the marshmallows lightly to remove the excess sugar. Store in an airtight container.

COOK'S NOTES: A 13 × 9-inch pan produces marshmallows about ¾-inch tall. For extra-tall marshmallows, use a 9-inch square pan. If preferred, the marshmallow mixture may be dropped by spoonfuls into a large pan generously coated with powdered sugar or into small molds generously dusted with powdered sugar. If using this method, work very quickly so that the marshmallow mixture does not set in the bowl.

For tinted marshmallows, add a few drops of food coloring during beating. For flavored marshmallows, substitute ¾ cup fruit juice for the cold water used to dissolve the gelatin.

If preferred, the marshmallows can be dipped into melted chocolate.

. . . . . . . . . . . . . . . . . . . . . . . .

# Cherry-Nut Nougat

## Skill Level: Advanced

*Extremely popular in Europe, nougat is a chewy, white candy that is somewhat similar to divinity, especially in the way it is prepared, but the syrup is cooked to a higher temperature. This recipe from a 1942 cookbook published by Kansas State University's School of Home Economics can be adjusted for different tastes by using a variety of nuts or fruits. This candy is particularly delicious when almond extract is added.*

✳ **MAKES ABOUT 2½ POUNDS**

> 3 extra-large or large egg whites
> 5 cups granulated sugar
> 1 cup light corn syrup
> 1 cup water
> 1 cup chopped walnuts, pecans, hazelnuts, or pistachio nuts, or sliced toasted almonds
> 1 cup candied cherries, chopped

See Tips for Making Divinity (page 69).

Line a 9 × 5-inch loaf pan or a mold with waxed paper, leaving a 1- to 2-inch overhang over the sides.

In a large mixing bowl, beat the egg whites with a heavy-duty electric mixer on high speed until the egg whites form very stiff peaks, but not so long that they lose their gloss and become dry.

In a 3-quart saucepan over medium-high heat, bring the sugar, corn syrup, and water to a boil, stirring just until the sugar dissolves and the mixture begins to boil. Cook, without stirring, to the soft ball stage (234°F).

Remove the syrup from the heat. Turn the electric mixer to medium-high speed and beat the egg whites again while gradually pouring about 1 cup of the hot syrup over the top of the egg whites. Leave the mixer on while returning the remaining syrup to the heat, turning the mixer off when the mixture is well blended.

Cook the remaining syrup, without stirring, to the hard crack stage (300°F).

Remove the syrup from the heat. Turn the electric mixer to medium-high speed and gradually pour the remaining hot syrup over the top of the candy mixture, beating constantly. Beat just until the mixture begins to hold its shape. Do not overbeat, or the candy may be dry.

Quickly stir in the nuts and cherries by hand. Immediately pack the candy into the lined pan or mold. Tightly cover the pan with plastic wrap or foil. Let the candy stand at room temperature 12 to 24 hours before cutting. The flavor improves if the candy ripens without being exposed to air.

To serve, invert the loaf pan or mold onto a cutting board. Remove the waxed paper and slice into pieces about ¾- to 1-inch thick. Cut each slice into cubes or squares. Each piece may be individually wrapped in plastic wrap or waxed paper if desired. Store in an airtight container at room temperature.

### VARIATIONS

Candied pineapple, candied orange peel, raisins, or similar ingredients may be substituted for the cherries.

*Cherry-Almond Nougat:* For a robust flavor, add 1 teaspoon pure almond extract to the candy mixture after adding the last of the syrup. Use 1 cup toasted sliced almonds for the nuts.

# Old-Fashioned Candy Rolls

## Cowboy Date Roll

### Skill Level: Advanced

*If you have never tasted date roll candy, this is a good place to start. This semismooth version from an early 1950s test kitchen at Oklahoma State University is my favorite of the two date roll recipes my mother used. My father preferred Dad's Date Loaf (page 81) for its more sugary texture.*

✳ MAKES ABOUT 30 SLICES

    3 cups granulated sugar
    2 tablespoons light corn syrup
    ¼ teaspoon salt
    1¼ cups half-and-half or evaporated milk
    1 cup pitted dates, chopped or quartered
    1 cup chopped pecans
    10 maraschino cherries, chopped and drained
       (optional)
    ½ cup powdered sugar (optional)

In a heavy 3-quart saucepan over low heat, bring the sugar, corn syrup, salt, and half-and-half to a boil, stirring just until the sugar dissolves and the mixture begins to boil. Cover and cook 3 minutes to dissolve the sugar crystals on the sides of the pan. Remove the lid. Cook very slowly over low heat, without stirring, to the soft ball stage (234°F to 240°F, with 238°F recommended). Add the dates and cook 1 minute longer, gently stirring to prevent the fruit from sticking together.

Remove from the heat. Cool to lukewarm (110°F), about 1 hour.

Dampen a clean dish towel (not terry cloth). Beat the candy by hand until it begins to stiffen. Add the pecans and cherries (if using). Finish beating by hand until creamy.

Turn the candy out onto the damp towel. Shape the candy into a roll about 1¼ inches in diameter. Wrap the candy in the damp towel and store in the refrigerator, slicing as needed. If desired, roll the candy in powdered sugar just before slicing.

COOK'S NOTES: The recipe may be reduced by half and cooked in a heavy 2-quart saucepan.

If the cooked candy is too soft to shape into a roll, work a little powdered sugar into the candy while kneading.

## Delicate Apricot Roll

### Skill Level: Advanced

*With the delicate flavor of apricots wrapped in rich, white cream, it is no wonder that family members say this candy is a favorite.*

✳ MAKES ABOUT 30 SLICES

    3 cups granulated sugar
    2 tablespoons light corn syrup
    ¼ teaspoon salt
    1 cup evaporated milk

**1 cup finely chopped or ground dried apricots**
**1 teaspoon vanilla extract**
**½ cup chopped pecans**
**½ cup powdered sugar (optional)**

In a heavy 3-quart saucepan over low heat, bring the sugar, corn syrup, salt, and milk to a boil, stirring just until the sugar dissolves and the mixture begins to boil. Cover and cook 3 minutes to dissolve the sugar crystals on the sides of the pan. Remove the lid. Cook very slowly over low heat, without stirring, to the soft ball stage (234°F to 240°F, with 238°F recommended).

Remove from the heat. Stir in the apricots and vanilla. Cool to lukewarm (110°F), about 1 hour.

Dampen a clean dish towel (not terry cloth). Beat the candy by hand until it begins to stiffen. Add the pecans. Finish beating by hand until creamy.

Turn the candy out onto the damp towel. Shape the candy into a roll about 1¼ inches in diameter. Wrap the candy in the damp towel and store in the refrigerator, slicing as needed. If desired, roll the candy in powdered sugar just before slicing.

COOK'S NOTES: The recipe may be reduced by half and cooked in a heavy 2-quart saucepan.

If the cooked candy is too soft to shape into a roll, work a little powdered sugar into the candy while kneading.

# Dad's Date Loaf

## Skill Level: Advanced

*Oh, how my father loved this sugary date loaf! Without a doubt, his favorite Christmas present always came wrapped in an old, damp tea towel.*

*This recipe from a 1942 cookbook published by Kansas State University is one of two date loaf candies my mother often made.*

✳ **MAKES 25 TO 30 SLICES**

**2½ cups granulated sugar**
**1 cup milk**
**8 ounces pitted dates, chopped**
**¾ cup chopped pecans, or to taste**

In a heavy 2-quart saucepan over low to medium-low heat, bring the sugar, milk, and dates to a boil, stirring until the sugar dissolves and the mixture begins to boil. Cover and cook 2 to 3 minutes to dissolve the sugar crystals on the sides of the pan, lifting the lid a few times to prevent the mixture from boiling over the sides of the pan. Cook, stirring only as needed to prevent scorching, to the soft ball stage (234°F to 240°F, with 236°F to 238°F recommended).

Remove from the heat. Cool to lukewarm (110°F), 45 minutes to 1 hour.

Dampen a clean dish towel (not terry cloth). Beat the candy by hand until it begins to thicken and hold its shape. Add the pecans and turn onto the damp towel. Shape the candy into a roll 2 inches in diameter. Wrap the candy in the damp towel and store in the refrigerator, slicing as needed. This candy will keep several weeks if tightly covered.

## VARIATIONS

*Aunt Erma's Date Loaf:* Add ¼ cup light corn syrup when combining the sugar, milk, and dates. Complete the recipe as described above.

*Old-Fashioned Apricot Roll:* Substitute 1 cup finely chopped dried apricots for the dates. Before beginning the recipe, cover the apricots with water and soak for about 30 minutes or until soft. Drain thoroughly. Do not cook the apricots with the sugar and milk. Add the apricots to the beaten candy along with the pecans.

# Pioneer Date Loaf

## Skill Level: Advanced

*This two-sugar version from the* **Ponca City News** *came with the following note: "Stores well if there is any left."*

✳ **MAKES 35 TO 40 SLICES**

> 2 cups granulated sugar
> 2 cups packed light brown sugar
> 1⅓ cups milk
> 2 tablespoons butter or margarine
> 1½ teaspoons vanilla extract
> 1 cup chopped, pitted dates
> 1 cup chopped pecans or ½ cup chopped
>     pecans and ½ cup chopped walnuts

In a heavy 3-quart saucepan over low to medium-low heat, bring the sugars and milk to a boil, stirring until the sugars dissolve and the mixture begins to boil. Cover and cook 2 to 3 minutes to dissolve the sugar crystals on the sides of the pan, lifting the lid a few times to prevent the mixture from boiling over the sides of the pan. Cook slowly to 234°F, stirring only as needed to prevent scorching. Add the butter. Cook, stirring just enough to blend in the butter, to the soft ball stage (234°F to 240°F, with 236°F to 238°F recommended).

Remove from the heat. Dampen a clean dish towel (not terry cloth). Beat the candy by hand until it begins to thicken and hold its shape. Stir in the vanilla, dates, and nuts. Turn onto the damp towel. Shape the candy into a roll 2 inches in diameter. Wrap the candy in the damp towel and store in the refrigerator. Let the candy ripen 24 hours in the refrigerator, if desired, before serving, slicing as needed.

### VARIATIONS

*Five-Cup Date Roll:* Omit the butter and vanilla extract. Use 1 cup each of granulated sugar, packed light brown sugar, and milk. Cook to 238°F. Stir the dates and pecans into the beaten candy before shaping it into rolls.

*Buttercup Date Roll:* Omit the 2 tablespoons butter and the vanilla extract. Use 1½ cups each of granulated sugar and packed light brown sugar and 1 cup milk. Cook to 238°F. Stir 1 teaspoon butter into the candy while beating. Stir the dates and pecans into the beaten candy before shaping it into rolls.

# Delta Date Loaf

## Skill Level: Advanced

*Extra butter makes this date loaf extraspecial.*

✳ **MAKES ABOUT 30 SLICES**

> 3 cups granulated sugar
> 1 cup evaporated milk
> 8 ounces pitted dates, chopped

¼ cup butter
1 cup chopped pecans
1 teaspoon vanilla extract (optional)
¼ teaspoon salt (optional)

In a heavy 3-quart saucepan over low to medium-low heat, bring the sugar, milk, and dates to a boil, stirring until the sugar dissolves and the mixture begins to boil. Cook, stirring only as needed to prevent scorching, to the soft ball stage (234°F to 240°F, with 240°F recommended).

Remove from the heat. Dampen a clean dish towel (not terry cloth). Add the butter, pecans and the vanilla and salt, if using. Beat by hand until the candy begins to thicken and hold its shape. Shape the candy into a roll 2 inches in diameter. Wrap the candy in the damp cloth and store in the refrigerator, slicing as needed.

# Granny's Extra-Sweet Date Roll

## Skill Level: Advanced

*This old-fashioned, sugary date roll can be made with a kitchen timer rather than a candy thermometer, though checking the temperature with either a candy thermometer or the softball test often helps ensure success.*

✳ MAKES 35 TO 40 SLICES

4 cups granulated sugar
1 cup milk
1 pound pitted dates, chopped
1 tablespoon butter

1 teaspoon vanilla extract
1 cup chopped pecans

In a heavy 5-quart kettle over low to medium-low heat, bring the sugar, milk, dates, butter, and vanilla to a rolling boil, stirring until the sugar dissolves and the mixture begins to boil. Continue to boil, stirring as needed to prevent scorching, 8 minutes, or to the soft ball stage (234°F to 240°F, with 238°F recommended).

Remove from the heat. Cool slightly, about 10 minutes. Beat by hand until the candy is thick. Divide the candy into two parts; shape into 2 (about 1½-inch-diameter) rolls. Roll the

# Old-Fashioned Candy Rolls

The mere mention of homemade candy seems to spark fond memories, yet no one type of candy prompts more discussion among my friends than recipes for old-fashioned date rolls. Time and time again, people smile and tell of the special treat that Granny kept hidden in the refrigerator underneath an old, damp towel.

Those longing for Granny's candy can now savor it once again. Whether you are looking for an old favorite or a new one, this collection of date, apricot, pecan, and peanut butter rolls is certain to hold something for everyone. Just remember to cook these candies slowly so that they will not become too sugary.

candy in the pecans. Wrap the candy rolls in waxed paper and chill in the refrigerator 24 hours before serving. Store covered, slicing as needed.

COOK'S NOTE: If desired, an additional 1 cup chopped pecans may be cooked with the candy.

. . . . . . . . . . . . . . . . . . . . . . . . . . . .

# Caramel-Coated Date Roll

## Skill Level: Advanced

*The caramel coating may be used with this date roll recipe or with your own favorite version.*
✳ MAKES 25 TO 30 SLICES

*Date Roll*
2 cups granulated sugar
1 cup evaporated milk
1 tablespoon light corn syrup
8 ounces pitted dates, chopped
1 cup chopped pecans

*Caramel Coating*
1 pound caramels
2 tablespoons evaporated milk

1½ to 2 cups chopped pecans

TO MAKE THE DATE ROLL: In a heavy 2-quart saucepan over low to medium-low heat, bring the sugar, milk, and corn syrup to a boil, stirring until the sugar dissolves and the mixture begins to boil. Cook, stirring only as needed to prevent scorching, to the soft ball stage (234°F to 240°F, with 236°F to 238°F recommended).

Remove from the heat. Cool to lukewarm (110°F), 45 minutes to 1 hour.

Beat the candy by hand until it begins to thicken and hold its shape. Stir in the dates and nuts. Shape the candy into 4 (1½- to 2-inch-diameter) rolls. Wrap the rolls in waxed paper and refrigerate until firm.

TO MAKE THE CARAMEL COATING: In a large, heavy skillet over low heat, melt the caramels and milk, stirring until smooth.

Spread the pecans onto a sheet of waxed paper.

TO COAT: Holding both ends of the chilled rolls with forks, dip the rolls into the hot caramel, rolling to coat. Quickly roll the dipped candy in the pecans. Let the rolls stand on waxed paper until the coating is firm. To store, tightly wrap the rolls in plastic wrap, aluminum foil, or waxed paper, slicing as needed. The rolls may be stored in the refrigerator if desired. Bring the candy to room temperature before slicing and serving.

. . . . . . . . . . . . . . . . . . . . . . . . . . . .

# Dreamy Date Roll

## Skill Level: Average

*With a texture similar to fudge, this ultracreamy candy is a date lover's dream.*
✳ MAKES ABOUT 5 POUNDS

4 cups granulated sugar
1 (12-ounce) can evaporated milk
¼ cup butter or margarine
1 pound pitted dates, chopped
1 (7-ounce) jar marshmallow creme
1 teaspoon vanilla extract
4 cups chopped pecans

Butter a 10 × 15-inch jelly roll pan.

In a heavy 5-quart kettle over medium heat, bring the sugar, milk, and butter to a boil, stirring until the sugar dissolves and the mixture begins to boil. Cook, stirring constantly to prevent scorching, to the soft ball stage (234°F to 240°F, with 234°F recommended). Add the dates and cook 1 to 2 minutes more, stirring to separate the dates.

Remove from the heat. Add the marshmallow creme, stirring until well blended. Stir in the vanilla and pecans. Pour into the buttered pan to cool. Tear 3 large sheets of waxed paper.

When the candy is cool enough to handle, divide it into 3 portions, placing each portion on a large sheet of waxed paper. Shape the candy into 3 (2-inch-diameter) rolls. Cover and refrigerate until firm. To serve, bring the rolls to room temperature and slice into ½-inch slices. Store in an airtight container.

. . . . . . . . . . . . . . . . . . . . . . . .

# Classic Pecan Roll

## Skill Level: Advanced

*This creamy, light-colored pecan-packed candy will certainly become a favorite with someone in your family, just as it did in mine.*

✳ MAKES ABOUT 2 POUNDS

    2¼ cups granulated sugar
    3 tablespoons light corn syrup
    1 cup half-and-half
    1 teaspoon vanilla extract
    1½ to 2 cups finely chopped pecans

In a heavy 3-quart saucepan over medium heat, bring the sugar, corn syrup, and half-and-

half to a boil, stirring until the sugar dissolves and the mixture begins to boil. Cover and cook 2 to 3 minutes to dissolve the sugar crystals on the sides of the pan. Remove the lid. Cook, stirring only a few times to prevent scorching, to the soft ball stage (234°F to 240°F, with 236°F recommended).

Remove from the heat. Cool about 10 minutes to reduce the beating time. Tear 2 large sheets of waxed paper.

Beat the candy by hand until it begins to stiffen and hold its shape. Stir in the vanilla and pecans. Divide the mixture into two parts, placing each half of the candy onto waxed paper. Form into 2 (about 2-inch-diameter) rolls and wrap in the waxed paper. Cool at room temperature. To store, wrap the candy rolls tightly in plastic wrap or foil and refrigerate, slicing as needed. If preferred, the sliced candy may be stored in an airtight container.

COOK'S NOTE: As an option, do not add the pecans to the candy. Form the candy into 2 long rolls and then roll the candy into the chopped pecans to coat.

. . . . . . . . . . . . . . . . . . . . . . . .

# Caramel Pecan Roll

## Skill Level: Expert

*This recipe requires a little extra effort, but in the end, you will have a beautiful and delicious candy that will impress the worst of critics.*

✳ MAKES ABOUT 2½ POUNDS

*Caramel*
½ cup granulated sugar
½ cup packed light brown sugar
½ cup light corn syrup
¼ cup butter
1 cup heavy cream, divided

*Cream Candy Filling*
2 cups granulated sugar
½ cup light corn syrup
½ cup milk
Dash salt
2 tablespoons butter
1 teaspoon vanilla extract

1¼ cups finely chopped pecans, for coating

Butter a 10 × 15-inch jelly roll pan or spray with nonstick spray. Spray a plate or platter with nonstick spray.

TO MAKE THE CARAMEL: In a heavy 2-quart saucepan over medium-low heat, bring the sugars, corn syrup, butter, and ½ cup of the cream to a boil, stirring until the sugars dissolve and the mixture begins to boil. Slowly stir in the remaining ½ cup cream. Cook, stirring occasionally to prevent scorching, to the firm ball stage (244°F to 248°F, with 248°F recommended).

Remove from the heat. Pour the caramel into the buttered pan, spreading in an even layer and making sure that it has straight cor-

ners and edges. (This is much easier to do than it sounds.) Cool at room temperature while making the filling.

TO MAKE THE FILLING: In a heavy 2-quart saucepan over medium heat, bring the sugar, corn syrup, milk, and salt to a boil, stirring until the sugar dissolves and the mixture begins to boil. Cook, stirring occasionally to prevent scorching, to the soft ball stage (234°F to 240°F, with 238°F recommended).

Remove from the heat. Add the butter and vanilla. Beat by hand until the candy begins to hold its shape. Pour onto the plate.

Divide the candy filling into four equal portions. As soon as the candy is cool enough to handle, take one portion and knead by hand until smooth and creamy. (The cooled candy may develop a hard crust and appear to be hopelessly ruined, but it will become creamy with just a few minutes of kneading.) Form the kneaded candy into a roll about 4 inches long.

TO ASSEMBLE: Cut the cooled caramel into 4 equal pieces by making a cut in the vertical center of the caramel, then a cut in the horizontal center of the caramel. Tear a sheet of waxed paper. Spread the pecans onto another sheet of waxed paper.

Place one piece of the caramel on the waxed paper. Place the kneaded candy roll at one end of caramel, patting the candy roll until it is about the same size of the caramel. Roll up jelly roll fashion, wrapping the caramel around the roll. If, after rolling, a thinner roll is desired, gently stretch the roll from the center outward until it is the desired size and shape.

Roll the caramel-wrapped roll in the pecans, pressing the nuts into the caramel coating. Wrap tightly in foil. If the pecans do not adhere to the caramel, sprinkle a few extra nuts

(*clockwise from top left*)
Carnival Candied Apples;
Potato Fondant; Mom's Divinity;
Elegant Sparkling Strawberries;
Aunt Bill's Brown Candy

*(left to right)*
**Old-Fashioned Caramel Apples;**
**Crazy Crunch; Marry Me Toffee**

*(clockwise from top left)*
**Sensational Orange–Mint Patties;
Buckeyes; Cathedral Cookies;
Aunt Mary's Turtles; Luscious
Raspberry Fudge Truffles and
Chocolate Dipped Strawberries**

into the foil used to wrap the roll; the nuts will then adhere.

Repeat with the remaining candy filling and caramel. Store wrapped tightly and covered in an airtight container. Slice as needed using a sharp knife and a sawing motion. The candy may be stored in the refrigerator if desired. Bring to room temperature before serving.

## Penuche Nut Roll

### Skill Level: Advanced

*This recipe found stashed in my mother's collection is just as delicious as I hoped it would be. With a rich, robust, brown sugar flavor and an ultracreamy texture, it instantly became a new favorite. Thank you, Barbara Y., for sharing your special recipe.*

✳ MAKES ABOUT 2½ POUNDS

2 cups granulated sugar
1 cup packed light brown sugar
½ cup light corn syrup
1 cup half-and-half or evaporated milk
1½ cups finely chopped pecans

In a heavy 3-quart saucepan over medium heat, bring the sugars, corn syrup, and half-and-half to a boil, stirring just until the sugar dissolves and the mixture begins to boil. Reduce the heat to low. Cover and cook 2 to 3 minutes to dissolve the sugar crystals on the sides of the pan. Remove the lid. Cook over low heat, without stirring, to the soft ball stage (234°F to 240°F, with 236°F recommended).

Remove from the heat. Cool to lukewarm (110°F), about 1 hour.

Spray a plate with nonstick spray. Beat the candy by hand until it is creamy and begins to hold its shape. Pour onto the plate. Spread the pecans onto a sheet of waxed paper.

Divide the candy into 2 to 6 equal portions. As soon as the candy is cool enough to handle, take one portion and knead by hand until the candy is smooth and creamy. (The cooled candy may develop a hard crust and appear to be hopelessly ruined, but it will become creamy with just a few minutes of kneading.) Form the candy into a roll about 1¼ inches in diameter. Roll the candy in the chopped pecans. Repeat until all the candy is kneaded, shaped, and rolled. Wrap each roll tightly in plastic wrap or foil, slicing as needed. The candy may be stored in the refrigerator if desired. Bring to room temperature before serving.

## Peanut Butter Cinnamon Roll

### Skill Level: Advanced

*Peanut butter fans will love this wonderful combination!*

✳ MAKES ABOUT 2 POUNDS

2 cups granulated sugar
¾ cup milk
About 1 tablespoon ground cinnamon for rolling, divided
¼ cup smooth peanut butter, or to taste
½ teaspoon vanilla extract

In a heavy 3-quart saucepan over medium-low to medium heat, bring the sugar and milk to a boil, stirring until the sugar dissolves and the mixture begins to boil. Cover and cook 2 to 3 minutes to dissolve the sugar crystals on the sides of the pan. Remove the lid. Cook, stirring occasionally to prevent scorching, to the soft ball stage (234°F to 240°F, with 236°F recommended).

Remove from the heat. Cool 20 minutes. Tear two large sheets of waxed paper. Sprinkle half of the cinnamon on each sheet of waxed paper.

Stir the peanut butter and vanilla into the candy. Beat by hand until the candy thickens and loses its gloss. Turn half of the mixture out of the pan onto another sheet of waxed paper. Knead by hand until smooth. Shape into a roll about 1½ inches in diameter; roll the log in cinnamon. Repeat with the remaining candy and cinnamon. Wrap the rolls tightly in plastic wrap or waxed paper. Store in an airtight container, slicing as needed.

COOK'S NOTES: This recipe can be made in a heavy 2-quart saucepan but may boil over the sides of the pan if not carefully watched.

The candy may appear very dry until it is kneaded. If it is still too dry after kneading, sprinkle a few drops of half-and-half or milk onto the roll and knead until well blended. If the candy is too sticky, add a little powdered sugar during kneading.

# Peanut Butter–Apricot Roll

## Skill Level: Advanced

*This unusual blend of peanut butter and apricots may remind you of another old-time favorite, peanut butter and jelly.*

\* MAKES ABOUT 3 POUNDS

   3 cups granulated sugar
   ½ cup peanut butter
   1 cup milk
   1 cup finely chopped dried apricots
   ½ teaspoon salt
   About ½ cup powdered sugar, for rolling
   2 teaspoons vanilla extract

In a heavy 3- or 4-quart saucepan over medium-low heat, bring the sugar, peanut butter, milk, apricots, and salt to a boil, stirring until the sugar dissolves and the mixture begins to boil. Cook, without stirring, to the soft ball stage (234°F to 240°F, with 236°F recommended).

Remove from the heat. Cool to lukewarm (110°F), about 1 hour. Cover a large countertop area with waxed paper; sprinkle lightly with powdered sugar.

Add the vanilla to the candy. Beat by hand until the candy loses its gloss and begins to hold its shape. Pour onto the sugared waxed paper. Form into 2 (about 1½-inch-diameter) rolls. Wrap tightly in waxed paper, plastic wrap, or foil. Let stand at room temperature until firm. Slice as needed. Store in an airtight container.

# Potato Candies

## Potato Fondant

### Skill Level: Novice, Super Simple

*Seniors often remember Potato Fondant with great fondness. One woman said that it was a common after-dinner treat when she was a young girl, just as it was when her mother was a child. Each child in the family took turns choosing what color the candy would be and decorating it in creative and unusual ways.*

✳ MAKES ABOUT 1 CUP

> 2 tablespoons unseasoned mashed potatoes
> Few grains salt
> Few drops vanilla extract or other extract
> 1 to 2 drops food coloring
> About 1½ cups sifted powdered sugar

In a small mixing bowl, combine the potatoes, salt, and vanilla. Tint the mixture with a small amount of food coloring if desired. Gradually add the powdered sugar, blending until the mixture has the consistency of fondant (similar to pie dough). Knead the candy by hand until smooth. Use this candy as a fondant for wafers or as a filling.

### VARIATIONS

*Rainbow Wafers:* Dust a sheet of waxed paper with powdered sugar. Place the Potato Fondant on the waxed paper; cover with another sheet of waxed paper. Roll the fondant to wafer thinness, about ¼ inch thick. Using a cookie cutter, cut the fondant into small, round wafers or into other shapes as desired. If desired, decorate the tops of each wafer with a whole almond, or pecan or walnut half. Let the wafers dry before storing in an airtight container. The wafers will become hard and somewhat brittle.

*Nut Creams:* Press a small ball of Potato Fondant between 2 pecan or walnut halves. Store in an airtight container.

*Stuffed Dates:* Remove the seeds from the dates by making a cut along the side. Fill the cavity of each date with a small amount of fondant. Roll the filled dates in granulated sugar. Store in an airtight container.

COOK'S NOTE: Omit the salt if using seasoned mashed potatoes leftover from a meal. If desired, a few tablespoons of finely chopped nuts or sweetened flaked coconut may be worked into the fondant.

# Potato Kisses

## Skill Level: Novice, Super Simple

*Filled with coconut, these candies are surprisingly delicious.*

✳ **MAKES ABOUT 18**

> ½ **cup unseasoned hot mashed potatoes**
> 1 **teaspoon butter or margarine**
> 1 **pound powdered sugar, sifted**
> ½ **teaspoon almond extract**
> 1 (3½-ounce) **can sweetened flaked coconut**

Cover a countertop area or a large baking sheet with waxed paper.

In a medium mixing bowl, combine the mashed potatoes and butter, mixing well. Gradually add the powdered sugar, blending until smooth. Stir in the almond extract and coconut. Drop by spoonfuls onto the waxed paper. Cool. Store in an airtight container.

### VARIATIONS

*Chocolate Spud Buds:* Omit the almond extract. Use ⅔ cup hot mashed potatoes and 2 teaspoons butter. Add 2½ tablespoons unsweetened cocoa powder with the powdered sugar. Stir in a pinch salt and 1 teaspoon vanilla extract with the coconut.

*Chocolate Tater Tots:* Substitute vanilla extract for the almond extract. Press the candy into a small buttered pan. When the candy has cooled, spread 2 to 3 ounces melted semisweet chocolate on top of the candy. Cover and refrigerate until the chocolate is firm. Cut into squares.

*Chocolate Mash:* Omit the almond extract and the coconut. Add 3 to 4 tablespoons unsweet-

ened cocoa powder with the powdered sugar. Stir in ½ teaspoon vanilla extract and 1 cup chopped nuts before dropping the candies onto the waxed paper.

# Potato Pinwheels

## Skill Level: Novice, Super Simple

*Peanut butter lovers will love the pinwheels cut from this fondant-wrapped candy roll.*

✳ **MAKES ABOUT 2 POUNDS**

> 1 **medium cooked potato, peeled, buttered, and mashed**
> 1 **pound powdered sugar, sifted**
> 1 **teaspoon vanilla extract**
> 1 (12-ounce) **jar smooth peanut butter**
> ½ **cup chopped pecans, walnuts, or peanuts**

In a medium mixing bowl, let the potato stand until cool. Gradually add the powdered sugar, blending with the potato until the mixture has

## Potato Candies

Once quite popular as an after-dinner treat with our grandparents and great-grandparents, potato candies are now somewhat of a novelty, with only a handful of lucky people knowing how delicious they can be. For another potato candy, try Wacky Potato Fudge (page 113).

a consistency similar to pie dough. Stir in the vanilla, blending well. Place the potato dough on a sheet of waxed paper; cover with another sheet of waxed paper. Roll the potato dough into a rectangle the thickness of pie dough, about ¼ inch thick.

Remove the top layer of the waxed paper. Spread the peanut butter on top of the potato. Sprinkle the nuts on top of the peanut butter layer, gently pressing them into the peanut butter. Beginning at the long side of the rectangle, roll the candy jelly roll fashion. Seal the waxed paper tightly and cover again in foil. Refrigerate overnight. To serve, slice into ¼-inch slices. Store tightly wrapped in the refrigerator.

# Taffies

## Peppermint Taffy

### Skill Level: Average

*Though not as soft as the taffy I loved as a child, this sticky, chewy candy is my favorite of the homemade taffy recipes.*

✳ **MAKES ABOUT 1½ POUNDS**

2 cups granulated sugar
1 cup water
1 cup light corn syrup
1 teaspoon salt
½ teaspoon glycerin
2 teaspoons butter or margarine
½ teaspoon peppermint extract
¼ to ½ teaspoon red food coloring, optional

Butter a large platter or a 10 × 15-inch jelly roll pan.

In a heavy 2-quart saucepan over medium heat, bring the sugar, water, corn syrup, salt, and glycerin to a boil, stirring until the sugar dissolves and the mixture begins to boil. Cook, without stirring, to the mid–hard ball stage, 258°F.

Remove from the heat. Add the butter, peppermint extract, and food coloring, stirring until the butter melts and the food coloring is well blended. Pour the hot candy onto the buttered baking sheet. Cool just until the taffy can be handled, 10 to 15 minutes. Do not allow the candy to cool too long or it will set in the pan.

With buttered hands, pull and stretch the taffy until the color lightens and the candy changes texture and becomes opaque. Stretch it into a long rope. Using kitchen shears or a sharp knife, cut the rope into small pieces. Wrap each piece of taffy in waxed paper. Store at room temperature.

COOK'S NOTES: Glycerin can be purchased in the pharmacy section of most large grocery stores and craft stores that sell cake and candy supplies.

Other extracts may be substituted for the peppermint extract, and other food colorings may be used in place of red. If preferred, the food coloring may be omitted entirely, leaving the taffy white.

Keep a glass or a bowl filled with cool water nearby while pulling the candy so that you can quickly dip your hands into the water if the hot candy sticks to your fingers.

## White Taffy

### Skill Level: Average

*Much like hard candy, this very old recipe produces a mild, vanilla-flavored hard taffy that is distinctively different from most commercially available taffies.*

✳ **MAKES ABOUT 1 POUND**

**2 cups granulated sugar**
**½ cup light corn syrup**
**⅔ cup water**
**1 teaspoon vanilla extract**

Butter a large platter or a 10 × 15-inch jelly roll pan.

In a 2-quart saucepan over medium heat, bring the sugar, corn syrup, and water to a boil, stirring until the sugar dissolves and the mixture begins to boil. Cook, without stirring, to the hard crack stage, 300°F.

Remove from the heat. Stir in the vanilla. Pour the candy onto the platter. Cool just until the taffy can be handled, 10 to 15 minutes. Do not allow the candy to cool too long or it will harden.

With buttered hands, pull and stretch the taffy until the candy changes texture and becomes opaque. Stretch the candy into a long rope, twisting the rope as you pull. Using kitchen shears or a sharp knife, cut the rope into small pieces, turning or twisting the rope again after each cut. Wrap each piece of taffy in waxed paper. Store at room temperature.

# Brown Sugar Taffy

## Skill Level: Average

*Those who like the robust flavor of brown sugar may prefer this recipe.*

✳ MAKES ABOUT ½ POUND

**1 cup packed light brown sugar**
**½ cup corn syrup**
**1½ tablespoons butter or margarine**
**1 tablespoon cider vinegar**

# Taffy

When it comes to pulling taffy, the more the merrier, for it is important to pull the taffy before the candy hardens and sets. Make a party of it, letting each set of hands take a small amount of candy to stretch, manipulate, and shape into a rope. Children can participate with adult supervision, but remember to use caution; hot taffy can burn fingers and hands very quickly.

Butter a large platter or a 10 × 15-inch jelly roll pan.

In a 1-quart saucepan over medium heat, bring the brown sugar, corn syrup, butter, and vinegar to a boil, stirring until the sugar dissolves and the mixture begins to boil. Cook, without stirring, to the hard ball stage, 260°F.

Remove from the heat. Pour the candy onto the platter. Cool just until the taffy can be handled, 10 to 15 minutes. Do not allow the candy to cool too long or it will harden.

With buttered hands, pull and stretch the taffy until the candy changes texture and becomes opaque. Stretch the candy into a long rope, twisting the rope as you pull. Using kitchen shears or a sharp knife, cut the rope into small pieces, turning or twisting the rope again after each cut. Wrap each piece of taffy in waxed paper. Store at room temperature.

# Molasses Foam Taffy

## Skill Level: Average

*This unusual old recipe does not require pulling the candy after it is cooked.*

✳ MAKES ABOUT ½ POUND

   **1 cup granulated sugar**
   **1 cup molasses**
   **2 tablespoons cider vinegar**
   **Butter the size of an egg (¼ cup)**
   **1 teaspoon baking soda**

Butter a large baking sheet.

In a 2-quart saucepan over medium heat, bring the sugar, molasses, vinegar, and butter to a boil, stirring until the sugar dissolves and the mixture begins to boil. Cook, without stirring, to the soft ball stage (234°F to 240°F, with 240°F recommended).

Remove from the heat. Add the baking soda. Beat by hand with a wire egg beater or a slotted spoon until the mixture is light and foamy.

Pour the mixture onto the buttered baking sheet. Refrigerate until firm. Turn the candy onto waxed paper and break into pieces with a hammer or a mallet. Wrap each piece of taffy in waxed paper. Store at room temperature.

# Old-Fashioned Taffy

## Skill Level: Average

*If you ever wondered what your grandparents or great-grandparents did on their first date, you can imagine that they may have held an old-fashioned taffy pull with a molasses-based recipe such as this one.*

✳ MAKES ABOUT 1 POUND

   **¾ cup granulated sugar**
   **1¼ cups light molasses**
   **1 tablespoon cider vinegar**
   **1 tablespoon butter or margarine**
   **⅛ teaspoon baking soda**
   **Dash salt**

Butter a large platter or a 10 × 15-inch jelly roll pan.

In a 1-quart saucepan, combine the sugar, molasses, and vinegar, stirring to mix. Let stand 10 to 20 minutes, stirring occasionally until the sugar dissolves. Bring to a boil over medium-low heat. Cook, without stirring, to 270°F.

Remove from the heat. Stir in the butter, baking soda, and salt. Pour into the buttered platter. Cool just until the taffy can be handled, 10 to 15 minutes. Do not allow the candy to cool too long or it will harden. With buttered hands, pull and stretch the taffy until the color lightens. Form into a long rope. Using kitchen shears or a sharp knife, cut the rope into small pieces. Wrap each piece of taffy in waxed paper. Store at room temperature.

Remove from the heat. Pour the candy onto the platter.

# The Taffy Pull

One day when I was about nine years old, I told my mother how much I loved the pink, blue, and white ribbon-striped taffy sold at the local swimming pool snack bar. A 12 × 3-inch package of taffy cost a nickel in those days, and the summer heat made the taffy just soft enough that I could tear off a piece and mold it into any shape I wanted before popping it into my mouth. As far as I was concerned, my nickel's worth of taffy was the perfect end to a carefree summer afternoon.

I do not recall what prompted me to tell my mother about my love for this taffy, but I clearly recall what happened next. My mother smiled, stood up from her chair, and enthusiastically said, "We don't have to *buy* taffy. We can *make* taffy!"

This was news to a nine-year-old kid, but soon I found myself in the kitchen watching my mother's magic. She placed her "candy pot" on the stove, carefully measured and added ingredients, and began that calming, lazy stirring motion that seems to define her personality.

Before long, our homemade taffy was ready to be pulled, stretched, and manipulated into a rope. As my mother and I stood facing each other with well-buttered hands and a string of hot candy draped between us, she began to tell of her childhood in Depression-ridden rural Arkansas and how families would gather for community taffy pulls as a way to pass the time. "This was in the day before electricity or television," she reminded me, "and we had to make our own fun."

In the end, Mom's stories were just as entertaining as the candy.

I was nearly forty years old before I realized that my mother taught me more about life that day than she taught me about taffy. Her message was not one of proper measuring, stirring, or technique, but one of self-reliance.

"Share your joy with others, child.

"Learn to make your own fun.

"Know that you do not have to depend on others but can depend upon yourself.

"And above all, never forget where you came from."

My mother's unspoken words are with me as I share my joy with you.

# Molasses Taffy

## Skill Level: Average

*The combination of brown sugar and molasses gives this old-fashioned taffy a robust flavor.*

✳ MAKES ABOUT 2 POUNDS

1 cup granulated sugar
¾ cup packed light brown sugar
2 cups light molasses
1 cup water
¼ cup butter or margarine
⅛ teaspoon baking soda
¼ teaspoon salt

Butter a 10 × 15-inch baking sheet.

In a 2-quart saucepan over medium heat, bring the sugars, molasses and water to a boil, stirring until the sugars dissolve and the mixture begins to boil. Cook to the soft crack stage, 272°F, stirring frequently to prevent scorching.

Remove from the heat. Add the butter, baking soda, and salt, stirring just enough to mix well. Pour into the buttered pan. Cool just until the candy can be handled.

With buttered hands, pull the taffy until it is firm and light yellow. Stretch it into a rope, twist, and cut into 1-inch lengths. Wrap each piece of taffy in waxed paper.

# Make Mine Fudge

One of the most celebrated romances in history is America's enduring love affair with sweet, creamy fudge. This extraordinary confection captured our hearts long ago, enticing us with its flawless silky texture and daring us to resist.

Our passion may be deep dark chocolate, German's sweet chocolate, or the luxurious taste of velvety white chocolate that so many of us adore. We dream of fudge rich with maple, peanut butter, butterscotch, or buttermilk, while others flirt with orange, lemon, or gorgeous flecks of tropical pineapple wrapped in thick white cream. We rendezvous with eggnog, spicy pumpkin, or brown sugar penuche to find our perfect match, indulging in our love for apricot, cranberry, and coffee along the way. We welcome the familiar and court the unusual, tossing in sweetened flaked coconut, bright red cherries, or freshly shelled pecans as we please, stacking layer upon layer and combining two favorites for those who cannot choose.

We recall the sweet times shared with America's favorite homemade candy, knowing that few other romances are as comforting as ours. We thank our grandmothers for their old-fashioned recipes and our mothers for the simpler versions made with marshmallow creme, scanning them all to find our favorite.

# Old-Fashioned Chocolate Fudges

## Aunt Erma's Legendary 'Til It's Done Fudge

### Skill Level: Advanced

*If you are born into a family overflowing with children, you must find a way to distinguish yourself lest you become lost in a sea of look-alike faces. For my aunt Erma, the eighth of my grandparents' ten children, fame came in the form of fudge. Aunts, uncles, and cousins alike declare that Erma's fudge was the best they ever tasted. Coming from a family that has produced several dozen outstanding cooks and twice as many critics, this is quite a compliment.*

*A few years ago, I called Erma's daughter in hopes of learning the secret behind this legendary fudge. This is what my cousin said.*

*"Take a skillet, put everything in it except the vanilla, and cook it."*

*"How long?" I asked.*

*"'Til it's done."*

*Some of us were born with internal timers that ding when fudge is ready. I did not inherit that gene.*

✳ MAKES ABOUT 1¼ POUNDS

2 cups granulated sugar
Scant ½ cup unsweetened cocoa powder
Scant ⅓ cup light corn syrup
1 cup half-and-half
1 tablespoon butter
1 teaspoon vanilla extract
½ cup chopped pecans or sweetened flaked coconut (optional)

Butter a plate or a 9 × 5-inch pan.

In a 10- to 12-inch heavy skillet over low heat, bring the sugar, cocoa, corn syrup, and half-and-half to a boil, stirring until the sugar dissolves and the mixture begins to boil. Cook at a slow, steady boil over low heat, without stirring, to the soft ball stage (234°F to 240°F, with 234°F recommended).

Remove from the heat. Add the butter and vanilla. Beat by hand until the candy begins to hold its shape and feels heavy. Add the pecans, if using. Pour into the buttered plate or pan. Cool and cut into pieces. Store in an airtight container.

COOK'S NOTE: This fudge has a very deep chocolate flavor. The amount of cocoa may be reduced if desired.

## Grace's Walnut Butter Fudge

### Skill Level: Advanced

*Grace's fudge is as legendary with hometown friends as Aunt Erma's fudge is with my family. This buttery, chocolate satin candy is worth every step.*

✳ MAKES ABOUT 1¼ POUNDS

2 cups granulated sugar

6 tablespoons unsweetened cocoa powder

¾ cup water

½ cup butter

1 teaspoon vanilla extract

½ to 1 cup chopped walnuts

Have a medium to large clean, dry mixing bowl available.

In a heavy 3-quart saucepan, combine the sugar and cocoa until well blended. Slowly stir in the water. Bring to a boil over low heat, stirring until the sugar dissolves and the mixture begins to boil. Cover and cook 3 minutes to dissolve the sugar crystals on the sides of the pan, lifting the lid a few times to prevent the mixture from boiling over the sides. Remove the lid. Add the butter without stirring. Cook at a slow, steady boil over low heat, without stirring, to the soft ball stage (234°F to 240°F, with 236°F recommended).

Remove from the heat. Pour into a clean, dry mixing bowl without scraping the sides of the saucepan. Cool to lukewarm (110°F), about 1 hour, without stirring the candy or moving the bowl. Butter a 9 × 5-inch loaf pan.

Add the vanilla. Beat by hand until the candy begins to thicken and lose its gloss. Immediately stir in the nuts and turn into the buttered pan. (This candy sets very quickly.) Cool and cut into squares. Store in an airtight container.

COOK'S NOTE: For a firmer fudge, cook to 238°F.

# Old-Fashioned Chocolate Fudges

These classic recipes represent candy making at its finest. Those who can turn out a perfect batch of sweet, creamy, old-fashioned fudge without timers or thermometers are at the top of their craft. Often the secret is slow cooking, plus experience, precision, and a great deal of skill. Fortunately, those of us who are fudge challenged can also be experts if we cheat and use a candy thermometer.

# Private Collection Fudge

## Skill Level: Advanced

*This extrasweet, extracreamy prizewinner from the 1972* Ponca City News *recipe contest miraculously finds its way to the back of my refrigerator where only I can find it. If you are willing to share, the kneaded chocolate rolls make a wonderful gift.*

✳ MAKES ABOUT 2 POUNDS

1 cup milk

2 ounces unsweetened baking chocolate, finely chopped

3 cups granulated sugar

¼ cup light corn syrup

⅛ teaspoon salt

1 teaspoon cider vinegar

2 tablespoons butter

1 teaspoon vanilla extract

½ to 1 cup chopped walnuts or pecans

In a heavy 3-quart saucepan over low heat, combine the milk and chocolate, stirring constantly until the milk is hot and the chocolate is completely melted.

Remove from the heat temporarily. Stir in the sugar, corn syrup, and salt. Place over medium heat and bring to a boil, stirring just until the sugar dissolves. Reduce the heat to medium low. Cover and cook 2 to 3 minutes to dissolve the sugar crystals on the sides of the pan. Remove the lid. Cook at a slow, steady boil over low or medium-low heat, without stirring, to the soft ball stage (234°F to 240°F, with 238°F recommended).

Remove from the heat. Gently stir in the vinegar. Add the butter without stirring. Cool to lukewarm (110°F), about 1 hour. Butter a large platter.

Add the vanilla. Beat by hand until the candy begins to thicken and hold its shape. Stir in the nuts. Pour onto the buttered platter. Cool 20 to 30 minutes or until the candy can be handled without sticking to your hands, and then knead by hand for 5 minutes.

Shape the candy into 2 (1½-inch-diameter) rolls or logs. Wrap tightly in plastic wrap. Store, covered, in a cool, dry place or in the refrigerator until ready to serve. To serve, cut into thin slices.

- - - - - - - - - - - - - - - - - - - -

# Granny's Best Fudge

## Skill Level: Advanced

*Sweet, creamy, and loaded with chocolate, this recipe from our great-grandmothers comes with an old-fashioned hug.*

✳ MAKES ABOUT 2 POUNDS

3 cups granulated sugar

1 cup milk

3 ounces unsweetened baking chocolate, finely chopped

½ cup light corn syrup

¼ cup butter

1 teaspoon vanilla extract

1 cup pecans in large pieces

Butter an 8-inch square pan.

In a heavy 3-quart saucepan over medium-low heat, bring the sugar, milk, chocolate, and corn syrup to a boil, stirring until the sugar dissolves and the mixture begins to boil. Cover and cook 2 to 3 minutes to dissolve the sugar crystals on the sides of the pan. Cook, without stirring, to the soft ball stage (234°F to 240°F, with 238°F recommended).

Remove from the heat. Add the butter without stirring. Cool 20 minutes. Add the vanilla. Beat by hand until the candy thickens and holds its shape. Stir in the pecans. Pour into the buttered pan. Cool and cut into squares. Store in an airtight container.

COOK'S NOTE: For a firmer fudge, cook to 240°F.

- - - - - - - - - - - - - - - - - - - -

# Jolly Good Fudge

## Skill Level: Advanced

*Sometimes a name says it all, and this one is no exception. This soft, medium chocolate fudge is one of my favorites.*

✳ MAKES 1½ POUNDS

⅔ cup milk

1 ounce unsweetened baking chocolate, finely chopped

2 cups granulated sugar

1 tablespoon light corn syrup

Dash salt

2 tablespoons butter

1 teaspoon vanilla extract

1 cup pecans or walnuts in large pieces
   (optional)

In a heavy 2-quart saucepan, combine the milk and chocolate over low heat, stirring constantly, until the chocolate is completely melted. Stir in the sugar, corn syrup, and salt. Bring to a boil over low heat, stirring until the sugar dissolves and the mixture begins to boil. Cover and cook 2 to 3 minutes to dissolve the sugar crystals on the sides of the pan. Remove the lid. Cook at a slow, steady boil over low heat, without stirring, to the soft ball stage (234°F to 240°F, with 236°F recommended).

Remove from the heat. Add the butter without stirring. Cool 20 minutes. Butter a 9 × 5-inch loaf pan.

Add the vanilla. Beat by hand until the candy thickens, loses its gloss, and begins to hold its shape. Stir in the nuts. Pour into the buttered pan. Cool and cut into squares. Store in an airtight container.

COOK'S NOTES: For a darker chocolate fudge, use up to 2 ounces of unsweetened baking chocolate.

If preferred, 3 to 4 tablespoons unsweetened cocoa powder may be substituted for the unsweetened baking chocolate. Combine the sugar and cocoa in the saucepan until well blended, and then stir in the milk, corn syrup, and salt. Cook as directed.

. . . . . . . . . . . . . . . . . . . . . . . . .

# Old-Time Cocoa Fudge

## Skill Level: Advanced

*If you like traditional fudge with a moderate amount of chocolate flavor, try this classic combination.*

✳ MAKES ABOUT 1½ POUNDS

2 cups granulated sugar

¼ cup unsweetened cocoa powder

¼ cup light corn syrup

1 cup milk

3 tablespoons butter

1 teaspoon vanilla extract

In a heavy 2-quart saucepan, combine the sugar and cocoa until well blended. Stir in the corn syrup and milk. Bring to a boil over low heat, stirring until the sugar dissolves and the mixture begins to boil. Cover and cook 2 to 3 minutes to dissolve the sugar crystals on the sides of the pan. Remove the lid. Cook at a slow, steady boil over low heat, without stirring, to the soft ball stage (234°F to 240°F, with 238°F recommended).

Remove from the heat. Add the butter without stirring. Cool to lukewarm (110°F), 45 minutes to 1 hour. Butter a 9 × 5-inch loaf pan.

Add the vanilla. Beat by hand until the candy thickens, loses its gloss, and begins to hold its shape. Pour into the buttered pan. Cool and cut into squares. Store in an airtight container.

. . . . . . . . . . . . . . . . . . . . . . . . .

# Bullet Fudge

## Skill Level: Advanced

*This 1950s-style fudge recipe from Oklahoma State University has a lot in common with a horse named Bullet; both are fast, both are dark, and both are loved by Cowboys.*

✳ **MAKES ABOUT 1¾ POUNDS**

2¼ cups granulated sugar
5 tablespoons unsweetened cocoa powder
1½ tablespoons light corn syrup
½ cup milk
6 tablespoons butter or margarine
1 teaspoon vanilla extract
½ cup pecans in large pieces

Butter a 9 × 5-inch loaf pan.

In a heavy 2-quart saucepan, combine the sugar and cocoa until well blended. Stir in the corn syrup, milk, and butter. Bring to a boil over medium heat, stirring until the sugar dissolves and the mixture begins to boil. Continue to boil, stirring occasionally to prevent scorching, to the soft ball stage (234°F to 240°F, with 236°F recommended), 4 to 5 minutes.

Remove from the heat. Cool 20 to 30 minutes. Add the vanilla and pecans. Beat by hand until the candy thickens, loses its gloss, and begins to hold its shape. Pour into the buttered pan. Cool and cut into squares. Store in an airtight container.

COOK'S NOTE: While this candy may not seem "fast" to some, it cooks much more quickly than most old-fashioned fudges. The original recipe called for boiling the candy mixture rapidly for only 1 minute, but the time may vary depending on the heat source and the saucepan

used. It is best to rely on the candy thermometer rather than the timing method.

- - - - - - - - - - - - - - - - - - - - - - -

# Sweet Milk Fudge

## Skill Level: Advanced

*Few ingredients hint at a recipe's age quite like "sweet milk," meaning the fresh, unspoiled milk that we now take for granted. Even in the 1940s, electricity was not available in many parts of rural America, making fresh milk somewhat rare. Women like my grandmother routinely cooked with buttermilk, canned milk, or soured clabber milk, saving precious sweet milk for their children to drink. Only the most special of recipes might be honored with fresh, sweet milk, because it usually involved trudging to a barn and milking an unfriendly cow named Bessie.*

*One bite of this light chocolate fudge may explain why women were once willing to fend off rain, hail, sleet, and snow to make this spectacular candy. The soft, smooth texture is nothing short of divine.*

✳ **MAKES ABOUT 1½ POUNDS**

1 cup granulated sugar
1 cup packed light brown sugar
1½ tablespoons unsweetened cocoa powder
Pinch salt
½ cup light corn syrup
½ cup milk
2 tablespoons butter
1 teaspoon vanilla extract
1 cup pecans in large pieces

Butter a 9 × 5-inch loaf pan.

In a heavy 2-quart saucepan over medium heat, bring the sugars, cocoa, salt, corn syrup, milk, and butter to a boil, stirring until the sugars dissolve and the mixture begins to boil. Reduce the heat to low or medium low. Cover and cook 2 to 3 minutes to dissolve the sugar crystals on the sides of the pan, lifting the lid a few times to prevent the mixture from boiling over. Remove the lid. Cook at a slow, steady boil over low or medium-low heat, without stirring, to the soft ball stage (234°F to 240°F, with 236°F recommended).

Remove from the heat. Add the vanilla. Beat by hand until the candy thickens and begins to hold its shape. Stir in the pecans. Pour into the buttered pan. Cool and cut into squares. Store in an airtight container.

# Extra-Chocolaty Brown Sugar Fudge

## Skill Level: Advanced

*The combination of brown sugar and an extra dose of chocolate gives this candy a different flavor from many old-fashioned fudges.*

✳ MAKES ABOUT 4 POUNDS

2 cups granulated sugar
2 cups packed light brown sugar
1½ cups milk
¼ cup light corn syrup
4 ounces unsweetened baking chocolate, finely chopped
6 tablespoons butter
2 teaspoons vanilla extract
1½ cups pecans in large pieces

In a heavy 5-quart kettle over medium heat, bring the sugars, milk, corn syrup, and choco-

late to a boil, stirring until the sugars dissolve and the mixture begins to boil. Reduce the heat to medium low. Cover and cook 2 to 3 minutes to dissolve the sugar crystals on the sides of the pan. Remove the lid. Cook, stirring only as needed to prevent scorching, at a slow, steady boil over medium-low heat to the soft ball stage (234°F to 240°F, with 238°F recommended).

Remove from the heat. Add the butter without stirring. Cool to lukewarm (110°F), about 1 hour. Butter a 9 × 13-inch pan.

Add the vanilla. Beat by hand until the candy thickens and begins to hold its shape. Stir in the nuts. Pour into the buttered pan. Cool and cut into squares. Store in an airtight container.

COOK'S NOTE: To make a smaller amount of candy, cut the ingredients in half and cook the candy in a 3-quart pan.

# Marshmallow and Marshmallow-Creme Chocolate Fudges

## Charlotte's Extra-Good, Extra-Wicked Fudge

### Skill Level: Average

*When I first began writing this book, I asked people to sample different recipes I planned to include. As one man bit into this extradelicious, extracreamy light chocolate confection, I said, "This is one of my favorite recipes. I got it from my hometown friend Charlotte. She calls it Extra-Good Fudge."*

*The man quickly shot back, "You should call it extra wicked."*

✳ **MAKES ABOUT 7 POUNDS**

4½ cups granulated sugar
1 (12-ounce) can evaporated milk
½ cup butter or margarine
1 (12-ounce) package semisweet chocolate chips
18 ounces Hershey's milk chocolate bars (about 12 [1.55-ounce] bars)
1 (13-ounce) jar marshmallow creme
3 cups coarsely chopped walnuts or pecans
1 teaspoon vanilla extract

Butter a 9 × 13-inch pan and an 8-inch square pan.

In a heavy 5-quart kettle over medium heat, bring the sugar, milk, and butter to a rolling boil, stirring until the sugar dissolves and the mixture begins to boil. Continue to boil rapidly, stirring constantly to prevent scorching, until the mixture reaches the soft ball stage (234°F to 240°F, with 236°F recommended), about 10 minutes.

Remove from the heat. Stir in the chocolate chips and milk chocolate until nearly melted. Add the marshmallow creme and stir until the chocolate is completely melted and the mixture is smooth and well blended. If desired, use an

## Marshmallow Chocolate Fudges

Until about the early 1940s, old-fashioned slow-cooked fudge was the only kind of fudge that most people knew to make. Today we have a wonderful selection of quick marshmallow and marshmallow creme–based chocolate fudge recipes that can be made in a matter of minutes. I love to tell friends that I can produce 6 to 7 pounds of melt-in-your-mouth fudge faster than they can bake two dozen cookies.

electric mixer on medium speed to beat the candy in the kettle 1 to 2 minutes to thoroughly blend the ingredients. Stir in the nuts and vanilla. Pour into the buttered pans. Cool and cut into squares. Store in an airtight container.

COOK'S NOTE: This is a soft fudge and often cuts best if slightly chilled first. This candy will stay moist and delicious for at least 4 weeks if stored in an airtight container in the refrigerator.

# Jo-Joe's Million-Dollar Fudge

## Skill Level: Average

*One advantage to being from a huge family is that you have an endless supply of cousins willing to share fabulous recipes. This extracreamy medium chocolate fudge is a favorite with cousins Jo and Joe of Winthrop, Arkansas.*

✳ MAKES ABOUT 6 POUNDS

  1 (12-ounce) package semisweet chocolate chips
  1 (4-ounce) package German's sweet chocolate, coarsely chopped
  1 (7-ounce) jar marshmallow creme
  5 cups granulated sugar
  1 (12-ounce) can evaporated milk
  ½ cup butter or margarine
  3 cups pecans in large pieces
  1 teaspoon vanilla extract (optional)

Butter a 9 × 13-inch pan and an 8-inch square pan.

In a large mixing bowl, combine the choco-late chips, sweet chocolate, and marshmallow creme; set aside.

In a heavy 5-quart kettle over medium heat, bring the sugar and milk to a rolling boil, stirring until the sugar dissolves and the mixture begins to boil. Continue to boil rapidly, stirring constantly to prevent scorching, 5 minutes, or until the mixture reaches the soft ball stage (234°F to 240°F, with 234°F to 236°F recommended).

Remove from the heat. Stir in the butter until melted. Pour the hot mixture over the chocolate and marshmallow creme mixture. Stir until the chocolates and marshmallow creme are melted and the mixture is smooth and well blended. Stir in the pecans and vanilla, if desired. Pour into the buttered pans. Cool and cut into squares. Store in an airtight container.

# Aunt Mary's Favorite Fudge

## Skill Level: Average

*My mother recalls this as the very first recipe for marshmallow creme fudge to appear in her kitchen. Her sister Mary came across it while living in California during World War II, saying that it was the best fudge she ever tasted. Aunt Mary treated her family to this candy for the next 45 years.*

✳ MAKES ABOUT 5 POUNDS

  18 ounces (3 cups) semisweet chocolate chips
  1 (7-ounce) jar marshmallow creme
  1 cup butter or margarine
  1 teaspoon vanilla extract
  4½ cups granulated sugar
  1 (12-ounce) can evaporated milk
  2 cups pecans in large pieces

Butter a 9 × 13-inch pan.

In a large mixing bowl, combine the chocolate chips, marshmallow creme, butter, and vanilla; set aside.

In a heavy 5-quart kettle over medium heat, bring the sugar and milk to a rolling boil, stirring until the sugar dissolves and the mixture begins to boil. Continue to boil rapidly, stirring constantly to prevent scorching, 6 minutes, or until the mixture reaches the soft ball stage (234°F to 240°F, with 234°F recommended).

Pour the hot mixture into the bowl over the chocolate and marshmallow creme mixture. Beat 2 minutes with an electric mixer. Stir in the pecans and pour into the buttered pan. Cool and cut into squares. Store in an airtight container.

### VARIATION

*Ozark Mountain Fudge:* For a lighter chocolate fudge, substitute 1 (13-ounce) jar marshmallow creme for the 7-ounce jar. Add an additional 1 cup pecans.

. . . . . . . . . . . . . . . . . . . .

# Margaret's Double Fantasy Fudge

## Skill Level: Average

*My cousin Margaret keeps plenty of this medium chocolate fudge on hand to feed her Louisiana friends and neighbors during the holidays.*

✳ MAKES ABOUT 7 POUNDS

6 cups granulated sugar
1⅓ cups evaporated milk
1½ cups butter or margarine
2 (12-ounce) packages semisweet chocolate
   chips

1 (13-ounce) jar marshmallow creme
2 cups pecans in large pieces, or more to taste
2 teaspoons vanilla extract

Butter 2 (9 × 13-inch) pans.

In a heavy 5-quart kettle over medium heat, bring the sugar, milk, and butter to a rolling boil, stirring until the sugar dissolves and the mixture begins to boil. Continue to boil rapidly, stirring constantly to prevent scorching, 5 minutes, or until the mixture reaches the soft ball stage (234°F to 240°F, with 234°F recommended).

Remove from the heat. Stir in the chocolate chips until melted. Add the marshmallow creme and stir until the mixture is smooth and well blended. Stir in the pecans and vanilla. Pour into the buttered pans. Cool and cut into squares. Store in an airtight container in refrigerator or at room temperature.

. . . . . . . . . . . . . . . . . . . .

# Hall of Fame Chocolate Fudge

## Skill Level: Average

*An instant hit with friends and family this wonderfully smooth, deep chocolate fudge is destined for the chocolate lover's hall of fame. Thanks to my cousin Margaret, all of us can now enjoy her friend Ruby's special recipe.*

✳ MAKES ABOUT 6 POUNDS

4½ cups granulated sugar
1 (12-ounce) can evaporated milk
¼ cup butter
Pinch salt
1 (12-ounce) package semisweet chocolate
   chips

3 (4-ounce) packages German's sweet
   chocolate, coarsely chopped
1 (7-ounce) jar marshmallow creme
2 cups pecans or walnuts in large pieces
1 teaspoon vanilla extract (optional)

Butter a 9 × 13-inch pan and an 8-inch square pan.

In a heavy 5-quart kettle over medium heat, bring the sugar, milk, butter, and salt to a rolling boil, stirring until the sugar dissolves and the mixture begins to boil. Continue to boil rapidly, stirring constantly to prevent scorching, 6 minutes, or until the mixture reaches the soft ball stage (234°F to 240°F, with 236°F recommended).

Remove from the heat. Stir in the chocolate and marshmallow creme until melted and well blended. Add the nuts and vanilla, if desired. Pour into the buttered pans. Cool and cut into squares. Store in an airtight container.

. . . . . . . . . . . . . . . . . . . . . . .

## Famous Fudge

### Skill Level: Average

*With a deeper chocolate flavor than many marsh-mallow creme fudges, it is no wonder this version is such a winner. Just for fun, try substituting almond extract for the vanilla extract and ¾ cup sliced toasted almonds for the pecans or walnuts.*
✳ MAKES 2½ TO 3 POUNDS

3 cups granulated sugar
1 cup evaporated milk
½ cup margarine
1 (12-ounce) package semisweet chocolate
   chips

1 cup marshmallow creme
1 teaspoon vanilla extract
1 cup pecans or walnuts in large pieces
   (optional)

Butter a 9 × 13-inch or a 9-inch square pan.

In a heavy 5-quart kettle over medium heat, bring the sugar, milk, and margarine to a rolling boil, stirring until the sugar dissolves and the mixture begins to boil. Cook, stirring constantly to prevent scorching, to the soft ball stage (234°F to 240°F, with 236°F recommended).

Remove from the heat. Stir in the chocolate chips and marshmallow creme until melted and well blended. Add the vanilla and the nuts, if desired. Pour into the buttered pan. Cool and cut into squares. Store in an airtight container.

. . . . . . . . . . . . . . . . . . . . . . .

## Five-Minute Fudge

### Skill Level: Average

*This simple, medium chocolate fudge can be made using a kitchen timer. Depending on the chips you choose, it can be either chocolate or butterscotch.*
✳ MAKES ABOUT 2 POUNDS

1⅔ cups granulated sugar
⅔ cup evaporated milk
½ teaspoon salt
1 cup (6 ounces) semisweet chocolate chips or
   butterscotch chips
1½ cups miniature marshmallows
1 teaspoon vanilla extract

Butter an 8-inch square pan or a slightly smaller pan if one is available.

In a heavy 3-quart saucepan over medium

heat, bring the sugar, milk, and salt to a rolling boil, stirring until the sugar dissolves and the mixture begins to boil. Continue to boil rapidly, stirring constantly to prevent scorching, 5 minutes. (If using a candy thermometer, the temperature should be approximately 226°F, which is below the soft ball range.)

Remove from the heat. Stir in the chocolate chips until melted. Add the marshmallows and stir until the marshmallows melt and the mixture is smooth and well blended. Stir in the vanilla. Pour into the buttered pan. Cool and cut into squares. Store in an airtight container.

## Christmas Fudge

### Skill Level: Average

*By using marshmallows rather than marshmallow creme, this medium chocolate fudge puts one more spin on a classic recipe.*

✳ MAKES ABOUT 1½ POUNDS

2 cups granulated sugar
⅔ cup evaporated milk
1 cup (6 ounces) semisweet chocolate chips
10 large marshmallows, quartered
½ cup margarine or butter
1 teaspoon vanilla extract
1 cup pecans or walnuts in large pieces (optional)

Butter an 8-inch square pan.

In a heavy 3-quart saucepan over medium-low heat, bring the sugar and milk to a rolling boil, stirring until the sugar dissolves and the mixture begins to boil. Continue to boil rapidly, stirring constantly to prevent scorching, 6

minutes, or until the mixture reaches the soft ball stage (234°F to 240°F, with 234°F recommended).

Remove from the heat. Stir in the chocolate chips until melted. Add the marshmallows, butter, and vanilla and stir until the marshmallows melt and the mixture is smooth and well blended. Stir in the nuts, if desired. Pour into the buttered pan. Cool and cut into squares. Store in an airtight container.

## Extra-Firm Fudge

### Skill Level: Average

*Extrachocolaty and extrafirm, this recipe adds the marshmallows during cooking.*

✳ MAKES ABOUT 2 POUNDS

2¼ cups granulated sugar
1 cup evaporated milk
¼ cup butter or margarine
16 large marshmallows
¼ teaspoon salt
1 cup (6 ounces) semisweet chocolate chips
1 teaspoon vanilla extract

Butter an 8-inch square pan.

In a heavy 5-quart kettle over medium heat, bring the sugar, milk, butter, marshmallows, and salt to a rolling boil, stirring until the sugar dissolves and the mixture begins to boil. Cook, stirring constantly to prevent scorching, to the soft ball stage (234°F to 240°F, with 234°F recommended).

Remove from the heat. Add the chocolate chips and vanilla and stir until the chocolate is melted and the mixture is smooth and well blended. Pour into the buttered pan. Cool and cut into squares. Store in an airtight container.

COOK'S NOTE: This fudge is very firm when cooked to 234°F. For a slightly softer version, cook to 232°F or add a few more marshmallows.

. . . . . . . . . . . . . . . . . . . .

# Marshmallow Cocoa Fudge

## Skill Level: Advanced

*This intriguing recipe combines elements of old-fashioned fudge with marshmallow creme, producing a soft, light chocolate candy that is quite sweet and creamy.*

✳ MAKES ABOUT 1½ POUNDS

    2 cups granulated sugar
    2 tablespoons unsweetened cocoa powder
    1 cup milk
    2 tablespoons marshmallow creme
    1 teaspoon vanilla extract
    ½ cup coarsely chopped pecans or walnuts

Butter a 9 × 5-inch loaf pan.

In a heavy 3-quart saucepan over medium heat, combine the sugar and cocoa, stirring until well blended. Stir in the milk. Bring to a rolling boil, stirring until the sugar dissolves and the mixture begins to boil. Cook, stirring frequently to prevent scorching, to the soft ball stage (234°F to 240°F, with 234°F recommended).

Remove from the heat. Add the marshmallow creme and vanilla without stirring. Let cool slightly, about 5 minutes, to reduce the beating time. Beat by hand until the candy thickens, loses its gloss, and begins to hold its

shape. Stir in the nuts. Pour into the buttered pan. Cool and cut into squares. Store in an airtight container.

. . . . . . . . . . . . . . . . . . . .

# Rocky Road Fudge

## Skill Level: Average

*Chunks of marshmallows coated in chocolate make this fudge a real kid pleaser.*

✳ MAKES ABOUT 3 POUNDS

    40 large marshmallows, divided
    4 cups granulated sugar
    1½ cups evaporated milk
    1 (12-ounce) package semisweet chocolate
        chips
    ¼ cup butter or margarine
    1½ cups pecans or walnuts in large pieces
    1 teaspoon vanilla extract

Using kitchen shears, cut 20 of the marshmallows into quarters. Cover the marshmallows and freeze 1 hour or more. When ready to make the candy, cut the remaining marshmallows in half. Butter a 9 × 13-inch pan or 9-inch square pan.

In a heavy 5-quart kettle over medium heat, bring the sugar and milk to a rolling boil, stirring until the sugar dissolves and the mixture begins to boil. Cook, stirring constantly to prevent scorching, to the soft ball stage (234°F to 240°F, with 234°F recommended).

Remove from the heat. Add the chocolate chips, butter, and the room temperature marshmallow halves. Stir until the chocolate chips and marshmallows are melted and the mixture is well blended and slightly thickened.

Stir in the nuts, vanilla, and frozen quartered marshmallows. Pour into the buttered pan. Cool in the refrigerator 30 minutes to 1 hour. Cut into squares. Store in an airtight container.

* * * * * * * * * * * * *

# Microwave Rocky Road Fudge

## Skill Level: Novice, Super Simple

*My cousin Margaret's 5-minute recipe is almost too good to be true. Even the busiest people can find time to make this candy.*
✳ MAKES ABOUT 2½ POUNDS

16 ounces chocolate almond bark or semisweet chocolate baking squares
1 (14-ounce) can sweetened condensed milk
2 teaspoons vanilla extract
2 cups miniature marshmallows
1 cup pecans in large pieces

Line an 8-inch square pan with foil.

In a large microwave-proof bowl, combine the chocolate and the sweetened condensed milk. Microwave on High, uncovered, 1 to 1½ minutes. Stir. Microwave 1 to 1½ minutes, or until the chocolate is almost melted.

Remove the bowl from the microwave. Stir until the chocolate is completely melted and the mixture is smooth. Stir in the vanilla, marshmallows, and pecans, mixing until the marshmallows and nuts are well coated. Spread into the prepared pan. Refrigerate 2 hours, or until firm. Lift the candy from the pan and peel off the foil lining. Cut into squares. Store in an airtight container.

COOK'S NOTE: The texture of the chocolate almond bark version is smoother than the semisweet baking chocolate one.

* * * * * * * * * * * * *

# Microwave Fudge

## Skill Level: Novice, Easy

*Busy chocoholics will love this quick and easy fudge recipe.*
✳ MAKES ABOUT 3 POUNDS

3 cups granulated sugar
¾ cup butter or margarine
⅔ cup evaporated milk
1 (12-ounce) package semisweet chocolate chips
1 (7-ounce) jar marshmallow creme
1 teaspoon vanilla extract
2 cups pecans or walnuts in large pieces

Butter a 9 × 13-inch pan.

In a 3-quart microwave-proof bowl, combine the sugar, butter, and milk. Microwave on High, uncovered, 5 to 6 minutes, or until the mixture comes to a rolling boil, stirring twice during cooking. Microwave on High 3 minutes, stirring once or twice to prevent the mixture from boiling over the sides of the bowl.

Remove the bowl from the microwave. Stir in the chocolate chips until melted. Blend in the marshmallow creme and vanilla, mixing until smooth. Stir in the nuts. Pour into the buttered pan. Cool and cut into squares. Store in an airtight container.

# Other Chocolate Fudges

## Katie's Perfect Fudge

### Skill Level: Average

*A longtime favorite with my friend Katie, this quick fudge recipe is unlike any other I have seen, cooking much like a marshmallow-based fudge, yet without the marshmallows. If made as directed, this extra-chocolaty, extracreamy fudge will be perfect every time.*

✳ MAKES ABOUT 5 POUNDS

18 ounces (3 cups) semisweet chocolate chips
1 cup butter or margarine, thinly sliced
4½ cups granulated sugar
1 (12-ounce) can evaporated milk
1 teaspoon vanilla extract
3 cups broken pecans or walnuts

In a large mixing bowl, combine the chocolate chips and butter. Butter a 9 × 13-inch pan.

In a heavy 5-quart kettle over medium heat, bring the sugar and milk to a rolling boil, stirring until the sugar dissolves and the mixture begins to boil. Boil rapidly, stirring constantly to prevent scorching, exactly 8½ minutes.

Remove from the heat. Pour the hot mixture over the chocolate chips and butter. Stir until the chocolate and butter are melted and the candy is smooth and creamy. Stir in the vanilla and nuts. Pour into the buttered pan. Refrigerate overnight or until firm. Cut into squares. Store in an airtight container.

### VARIATIONS

*Katie's Chocolate Mint Fudge:* Substitute 18 ounces (3 cups) mint chocolate chips for the semisweet chocolate chips. Omit the nuts, if desired.

*Katie's Peanut Butter Fudge:* Substitute 18 ounces (3 cups) peanut butter chips for the semisweet chocolate chips.

## Chocolate Cream Cheese Fudge

### Skill Level: Novice, Easy

*A friend's mother has received so much fame with this buttery, creamy fudge that she keeps the recipe hidden from friends and family in hopes that no one else will learn how to make it.*

✳ MAKES ABOUT 1 POUND

2 (3-ounce) packages cream cheese, softened
1 (1-pound) package powdered sugar, sifted
4 ounces unsweetened baking chocolate, melted
½ to 1 teaspoon vanilla extract, to taste
Dash salt (optional)

Butter a small pan or dish.

In a small mixing bowl, beat the cream

cheese by hand or with an electric mixer until it is soft and smooth. Slowly blend in the powdered sugar. Add the chocolate, mixing well. Stir in the vanilla and salt, if desired.

Press the candy into the buttered pan. Refrigerate until firm, about 15 minutes. Cut into squares. Store in airtight container.

COOK'S NOTE: If preferred, the cream cheese can be melted in the top of a double boiler over hot but not boiling water. The powdered sugar, melted chocolate, salt, and vanilla can then be stirred into the mixture, blending until smooth.

### VARIATION

*Cream Cheese Pecan Fudge:* Omit the chocolate. Make as directed, stirring in 1 cup pecans in large pieces before pressing the candy into the pan.

# Creamy Two-Chocolate Fudge

## Skill Level: Average

*Treat your taste buds to an ultracreamy sensation with this simple 5-minute recipe.*
* MAKES ABOUT 2 POUNDS

> 1 (12-ounce) package semisweet chocolate chips
> 1 (6-ounce) package milk chocolate chips
> 1 (14-ounce) can sweetened condensed milk
> 1 to 2 teaspoons vanilla extract, or to taste
> 1 cup pecans or walnuts in large pieces

Line an 8-inch square pan with foil.

In a heavy 2-quart saucepan over low heat, combine the chocolate chips and sweetened condensed milk. Cook over low heat, stirring constantly, just until the chocolate is melted and the mixture is smooth.

Remove from the heat. Stir in the vanilla and nuts. Spread into the lined pan. Refrigerate until firm, about 2 hours. Lift the candy from the pan. Peel off the foil lining and cut into squares. Store in an airtight container in the refrigerator.

# French Fudge

## Skill Level: Novice, Super Simple

*Ooh la la! For those who love the taste of rich dark chocolate, nothing could be easier.*
* MAKES ABOUT ¾ POUND

> 1 cup (6 ounces) semisweet chocolate chips
> ⅓ cup plus 1 tablespoon sweetened condensed milk
> Pinch salt
> ½ cup sweetened flaked coconut or pecans or walnuts in large pieces

Line a plate or a small baking sheet with waxed paper.

In the top pan of a double boiler over hot but not boiling water, melt the chocolate chips, stirring until smooth.

Remove from the heat. Blend in the milk and salt, stirring until smooth. Stir in the coconut. Pour onto the waxed paper and pat to the desired thickness using the back of a spoon or a flat spatula. Refrigerate about 20 minutes, or until firm. Cover and slice as needed, or cut into pieces and store in an airtight container in the refrigerator.

. . . . . . . . . . . . . . . . . . . . . . .

# Wacky Potato Fudge

## Skill Level: Novice, Easy

*As bizarre as it may sound, this old-time favorite is quite tasty, reminding some of thick chocolate buttercream frosting. Children love watching the potatoes turn to liquid as the sugar is added, so save some leftover potatoes and entertain your kids.*

✳ **MAKES ABOUT 1¼ POUNDS**

> 3 tablespoons butter or margarine
> 3 tablespoons unsweetened cocoa powder
> ⅓ cup unseasoned cold mashed potatoes
> ⅛ teaspoon salt
> 1 teaspoon vanilla extract
> About 4 cups powdered sugar, sifted
> ½ cup pecans in large pieces (optional)

Butter a 9 × 5-inch loaf pan.

In a medium microwave-proof bowl, heat the butter and cocoa in the microwave until the butter is melted, about 45 seconds. Stir to blend. Add the potatoes, salt, and vanilla, mixing thoroughly. Blend in the powdered sugar a little at a time until the mixture is thick and reaches the desired consistency. If necessary, knead by hand until the candy is smooth. Add the nuts, if desired.

Press the candy into the buttered pan. Refrigerate about 20 minutes or until set. Cut into squares. Store in an airtight container.

**COOK'S NOTE:** If unseasoned, leftover cooked potatoes are not available, bake a large potato in the microwave. Scoop out half of the cooked potato and place it into a small bowl. Mash the potato with a fork, adding a few drops of milk and ½ tablespoon butter. One-half of a large potato will yield about ⅓ cup mashed potatoes.

. . . . . . . . . . . . . . . . . . . . . . .

# Chocolate Velvet Fudge

## Skill Level: Novice, Easy

*When I got the recipe for Wacky Potato Fudge (at left), I thought I had seen it all, but then I met a woman who makes fudge with Velveeta cheese spread. Later I learned that this recipe has been floating around in my family for years and that I just had not seen it. This unusually creamy fudge may not be for everyone, but many people think it is delicious. For the best flavor, let it stand overnight before serving.*

✳ **MAKES ABOUT 1¼ POUNDS**

> 1 to 1¼ pounds powdered sugar, sifted
> ¼ cup unsweetened cocoa powder
> ¼ pound Velveeta processed cheese spread
> ½ cup butter or margarine (preferably butter)
> ½ teaspoon vanilla extract
> ½ cup pecans or walnuts in large pieces
> (optional)

In a medium bowl, stir together 1 pound of the powdered sugar and the cocoa until well blended. Butter a 9 × 5-inch loaf pan or a plate.

In the top pan of a double boiler over hot but not boiling water, melt the cheese spread and the butter, stirring until smooth. Gradually add the cheese mixture to the powdered sugar mixture, blending well. Stir in the vanilla. If desired, blend on low speed with an electric mixer until the candy is smooth and creamy. If the candy is too soft, gradually add more powdered sugar until it reaches the desired consistency.

Stir in the nuts, if using. Pour into the buttered pan or plate. Cool 1 hour or more before cutting into squares. Store in an airtight container in the refrigerator.

# Emergency Chocolate Fudge

### Skill Level: Novice, Easy

*While this may seem unbelievable to anyone born after about 1970, baby boomers can remember the days when grocery stores closed for the night sometime near the dinner hour. Our mothers and grandmothers often kept a box of instant nonfat dry milk on hand for emergencies, as milk was a staple in every household. No doubt, this old recipe was prob-ably invented by someone who found herself craving chocolate at 8:00 P.M. and was unable to quell her sweet tooth until morning.*

✳ **MAKES ABOUT 1¼ POUNDS**

¼ **cup butter or margarine**
¼ **cup water**
3 **cups powdered sugar, sifted**
½ **cup instant dry nonfat dry milk**
½ **cup unsweetened cocoa powder**
⅛ **teaspoon salt**
1 **teaspoon vanilla extract**
½ **cup pecans (optional)**

Butter a 9 × 5-inch loaf pan.

In a 1½-quart saucepan, heat the butter and water together until the butter melts.

In a medium bowl, mix the powdered sugar, dry milk, cocoa, and salt. Gradually add the butter mixture to the dry ingredients, stirring in about ¼ cup of the butter mixture at a time. Beat the candy until smooth after each addition of the butter. Stir in the vanilla and nuts, if desired. Pour into the buttered pan. Cover and refrigerate until firm, about 30 minutes. Cut into squares. Store in an airtight container.

# Peanut Butter Fudges

## Traditional Peanut Butter Fudge

### Skill Level: Advanced

*Nothing beats the old-fashioned goodness of this peanut butter fudge.*

❋ MAKES ABOUT 1½ POUNDS

- 2 cups granulated sugar
- 1 cup evaporated milk
- 1 teaspoon vanilla extract
- 3 to 4 tablespoons smooth or crunchy peanut butter, or to taste

Butter a 9 × 5-inch loaf pan.

In a heavy 3-quart saucepan over medium-low heat, bring the sugar and milk to a boil, stirring until the sugar dissolves and the mixture begins to boil. Cover and cook 2 to 3 minutes to dissolve the sugar crystals on the sides of the pan. Remove the lid. Cook, stirring occasionally to prevent scorching, to the soft ball stage (234°F to 240°F, with 238°F recommended).

Remove from the heat. Add the vanilla and peanut butter. Beat by hand until the candy thickens and loses its gloss. Pour into the buttered pan. Cool and cut into squares. Store in an airtight container.

### VARIATION

*Old-Time Peanut Butter Fudge:* Use ¾ cup milk and ¼ cup peanut butter.

## One Sharp Peanut Butter Fudge

### Skill Level: Advanced

*Without a doubt, this creamy version of old-fashioned peanut butter fudge is one sharp candy, especially since it is a favorite with my Sharp family cousins.*

❋ MAKES ABOUT 1 POUND

- 2 cups granulated sugar
- 1 cup milk
- 2 tablespoons light corn syrup
- 3 heaping tablespoons smooth peanut butter

Butter a plate or a 9 × 5-inch loaf pan.

In a heavy 3-quart saucepan over medium-low heat, bring the sugar, milk, and corn syrup to a boil, stirring until the sugar dissolves and the mixture begins to boil. Cook, stirring to prevent scorching, to the soft ball stage (234°F to 240°F, with 234°F recommended).

Remove from the heat. Stir in the peanut butter. Beat by hand until the candy loses its gloss and begins to hold its shape. Pour onto the buttered plate. Cool and cut into squares. Store in an airtight container.

### VARIATION

*Pioneer Peanut Butter Fudge:* Use ⅔ cup milk and ½ cup smooth peanut butter. Add ¼ teaspoon salt to the sugar, corn syrup, and milk mixture.

Cook in a heavy 2-quart saucepan to 236°F. Stir in 1 teaspoon vanilla while beating the candy.

. . . . . . . . . . . . . . . . . . . . . . . . . .

# Peanut Smoothies

## Skill Level: Advanced

*With a medium peanut butter flavor, this pudding-smooth candy is perfect every time.*

✳ MAKES ABOUT 1¼ POUNDS

> 1 cup granulated sugar
> ½ cup evaporated milk
> 1 tablespoon butter
> 1 (3-ounce) package vanilla pudding mix (not instant)
> ½ cup crunchy peanut butter
> ½ teaspoon vanilla extract

Butter a 9 × 5-inch loaf pan.

In a heavy 2-quart saucepan over medium heat, bring the sugar, milk, butter, and pudding mix to a boil, stirring until the sugar dissolves and the mixture begins to boil. Cook, stirring constantly to prevent scorching, to the soft ball stage (234°F to 240°F, with 234°F recommended).

Remove from the heat. Stir in the peanut butter until melted. Add the vanilla. Beat by hand until the candy begins to thicken slightly. Pour into the buttered pan. Cool and cut into squares. Store in an airtight container.

### VARIATION

*Peanut-Pecan Smoothies:* Smooth peanut butter may be substituted for the crunchy peanut butter. Add ½ cup chopped pecans before pouring the candy into the pan.

# Lindsay's Light and Luscious Peanut Butter Fudge

## Skill Level: Average

*My niece Lindsay and I fell in love with this light and creamy peanut butter fudge when she was just a young child. Twenty years later, her eyes still sparkle as we share our favorite holiday tradition.*

✳ MAKES ABOUT 3½ POUNDS

> 3 cups granulated sugar
> 1 (5-ounce) can evaporated milk
> ¾ cup butter or margarine
> 1 (10-ounce) package peanut butter chips
> 1 (7-ounce) jar marshmallow creme
> 1½ cups pecans in large pieces
> 1 teaspoon vanilla extract

Butter a 9 × 13-inch pan.

In a heavy 5-quart kettle over medium heat, bring the sugar, milk, and butter to a boil, stirring until the sugar dissolves and the mixture begins to boil. Cook, stirring constantly to prevent scorching, to the soft ball stage (234°F to 240°F, with 234°F recommended), about 5 minutes.

Remove from the heat. Stir in the peanut butter chips until melted. Add the marshmallow creme and stir until smooth. Stir in the pecans and vanilla. Pour into the buttered pan. Cool and cut into squares. Store in an airtight container.

COOK'S NOTE: Peanut butter chips are often slow to melt. If desired, place an electric mixer directly into the kettle and beat for 1 to 2 minutes to blend the chips with the other ingredients.

# Peanut Cremes

## Skill Level: Average

*Extrasmooth and extrascrumptious, this very lightly flavored peanut butter candy is so popular that the recipe often comes with slightly different variations. For a double dose of decadence, try dipping chilled squares of this candy into luscious, melted chocolate.*

✳ MAKES ABOUT 2 POUNDS

2 cups granulated sugar
1 (5-ounce) can (⅔ cup) evaporated milk
1 (7-ounce) jar marshmallow creme
1 cup crunchy peanut butter
1 teaspoon vanilla extract (optional)

Butter an 8-inch square pan

In a heavy 3-quart saucepan over medium heat, bring the sugar and milk to a boil, stirring until the sugar dissolves and the mixture begins to boil. Cook, stirring constantly to prevent scorching, to the soft ball stage (234°F to 240°F, with 236°F recommended)

Remove from the heat. Add the marshmallow creme and peanut butter, stirring until the candy is smooth and well blended. Stir in the vanilla if desired. Pour into the buttered pan. Cool and cut into squares. Store in an airtight container.

### VARIATION

*Double Peanut Cremes:* For a stronger peanut butter flavor, use 2 cups crunchy peanut butter.

# Super Peanut Butter Fudge

## Skill Level: Average

*Extra peanut butter gives either of these two candies a strong peanut butter flavor and a semifirm texture.*

✳ MAKES ABOUT 1½ POUNDS

2 cups granulated sugar
3 tablespoons butter or margarine
1 cup evaporated milk
1 cup miniature marshmallows
1 (12-ounce) jar smooth peanut butter

Butter a 9 × 5-inch loaf pan.

In a heavy 2-quart saucepan over medium heat, bring the sugar, butter, and milk to a boil, stirring until the sugar dissolves and the mixture begins to boil. Cook, stirring constantly, to the soft ball stage (234°F).

Remove from the heat. Add the marshmallows and peanut butter. Blend well. Pour into the buttered pan. Cool and cut into squares. Store in an airtight container.

### VARIATION

*Brown Sugar Peanut Butter Fudge:* Substitute 1 cup packed light brown sugar for 1 cup of the granulated sugar. Reduce the butter to 2 tablespoons and the evaporated milk to ½ cup. Add a dash salt to the milk mixture. Reduce the peanut butter to ½ to 1 cup. Add 1 teaspoon vanilla with the marshmallows and peanut butter.

COOK'S NOTE: If made with only ½ cup peanut butter, the fudge will have a medium peanut butter flavor.

# Two Flavor Fudges

## Classic Combo Fudge

### Skill Level: Average

*With the same, unforgettable flavor as the enormously popular chocolate-peanut butter no-bake cookies, this candy is destined to become a family classic.*

✳ MAKES ABOUT 2½ POUNDS

4 cups granulated sugar
6 tablespoons unsweetened cocoa powder
Dash salt
2 cups milk
1 cup smooth peanut butter
17 large marshmallows
1 teaspoon vanilla extract
1 cup chopped peanuts, pecans or walnuts (optional)

Butter a 9-inch-square pan.

In a heavy 5-quart kettle, combine the sugar, cocoa, and salt until well blended. Stir in the milk. Bring to a boil over medium-low heat, stirring until the sugar dissolves and the mixture begins to boil. Cover and cook 2 to 3 minutes to dissolve the sugar crystals on the sides of the pan. Remove the lid. Cook, stirring frequently to prevent scorching, to the soft ball stage (234°F to 240°F, with 236°F recommended).

Remove from the heat. Add the peanut butter, marshmallows, and vanilla. Stir until the candy is smooth and well blended. Stir in the nuts, if desired. Pour into the buttered pan. Cool and cut into squares. Store in an airtight container.

. . . . . . . . . . . . . . . . . . . . . . .

## Fancy Chocolate Fudge

### Skill Level: Advanced

*Those who prefer old-fashioned fudge to marshmallow fudge will enjoy the hint of peanut butter in this two-flavor chocolate candy.*

✳ MAKES ABOUT 2 POUNDS

1 cup milk
2 ounces unsweetened baking chocolate, finely chopped
3 cups granulated sugar
3 tablespoons light corn syrup
⅛ teaspoon salt
1 teaspoon vanilla extract
½ cup smooth peanut butter
¾ cup walnuts or pecans in large pieces (optional)

In a heavy 3-quart saucepan, combine the milk and chocolate over low heat, stirring constantly until the milk is hot and the chocolate is completely melted.

Remove from the heat temporarily. Stir in the sugar, corn syrup, and salt. Bring to a boil over medium-low heat, stirring until the sugar dissolves and the mixture begins to boil. Cover and cook 2 to 3 minutes to dissolve the sugar crystals on the sides of the pan. Remove the lid. Cook, stirring only as needed to prevent scorching, to the soft ball stage (234°F to 240°F, with 236°F recommended).

Remove from the heat. Add the vanilla without stirring. Cool to lukewarm (110°F), about 1 hour. Butter an 8-inch square pan.

Stir in the peanut butter. Beat by hand until the candy begins to thicken and lose its gloss. Stir in the nuts, if desired. Pour into the buttered pan. Cool and cut into squares. Store in an airtight container.

. . . . . . . . . . . . . . . . . . . . . . . . .

# Twice-as-Tempting Two-Tone Fudge

## Skill Level: Average

*My uncle John, a renowned candy connoisseur and the official family taste tester for all recipes containing sugar, chose this layered fudge as his favorite of all the candies he sampled. Declared "absolutely delicious" by more than one taster, this recipe combines two old favorites, chocolate and peanut butter, to create a doubly tempting treat for the taste buds.*

✳ **MAKES ABOUT 4 POUNDS**

½ cup butter or margarine, divided
¼ cup unsweetened cocoa powder
1 (10-ounce) package peanut butter chips
4½ cups granulated sugar
1 (12-ounce) can evaporated milk
1 (7-ounce) jar marshmallow creme
1 teaspoon vanilla extract

Butter a 9 × 13-inch pan.

In a small bowl, melt ¼ cup of butter in the microwave. Blend in the cocoa, stirring until smooth; set aside. Using a food processor, chop the peanut butter chips into small pieces; set aside.

In a heavy 5-quart kettle over medium heat, bring the sugar, milk, and remaining ¼ cup butter to a boil, stirring until the sugar dissolves and the mixture begins to boil. Cook, stirring constantly to prevent scorching, to the soft ball stage (234°F to 240°F, with 234°F recommended).

Remove from the heat. Stir in the peanut butter chips until melted. Add the marshmallow creme and vanilla and stir until the candy is smooth and well blended.

Pour half of the candy mixture into the buttered pan, spreading evenly. Add the cocoa and butter mixture to the remaining candy mixture in the kettle. Stir until the candy is thoroughly blended. Pour on top of the peanut butter layer in the pan, spreading evenly. Cool and cut into squares. Store in an airtight container.

COOK'S NOTE: Chopping the peanut butter chips in the food processor helps them melt more quickly.

. . . . . . . . . . . . . . . . . . . . . . . . .

# Blissful Butterscotch-Chocolate Fudge

## Skill Level: Average

*Delight the butterscotch lovers in your life with this ultrasmooth blend of two beloved flavors, chocolate and butterscotch.*

✳ **MAKES ABOUT 3 POUNDS**

2 cups packed light brown sugar

1 cup granulated sugar

1 cup evaporated milk

½ cup butter or margarine

1 cup (6 ounces) butterscotch chips

1 cup (6 ounces) semisweet chocolate chips

1 (7-ounce) jar marshmallow creme

1 teaspoon vanilla extract

1 cup pecans or walnuts in large pieces
(optional)

5 to 6 ounces semisweet baking chocolate,
coarsely chopped

2 cups granulated sugar

¾ cup sour cream

½ cup butter or margarine

Dash salt

4 ounces white baking chocolate, coarsely
chopped

1 (7-ounce) jar marshmallow creme,
divided

1 teaspoon vanilla extract,
divided

Butter a 9 × 13-inch pan.

In a heavy 5-quart kettle over medium heat, bring the sugars, milk, and butter to a boil, stirring until the sugars dissolve and the mixture begins to boil. Cook, stirring constantly to prevent scorching, to the soft ball stage (234°F to 240°F, with 236°F recommended).

Remove from the heat. Stir in the butterscotch chips and chocolate chips until melted. Add the marshmallow creme and vanilla. Stir until the candy is smooth and well blended. Stir in the nuts, if desired. Pour into the buttered pan. Cool and cut into squares. Store in an airtight container.

Butter an 8-inch square pan. Place the chopped semisweet chocolate into a medium mixing bowl.

In a heavy 2-quart saucepan over medium heat, bring the sugar, sour cream, butter, and salt to a boil, stirring until the sugar dissolves and the mixture begins to boil. Cook, stirring occasionally to prevent scorching, to the soft ball stage (234°F to 240°F, with 238°F recommended).

Remove from the heat. Pour half of the hot mixture over the semisweet chocolate in the bowl. Add the white chocolate to the remaining hot mixture to melt.

Add half of the marshmallow creme and ½ teaspoon of the vanilla to the semisweet chocolate mixture and stir until the chocolate is melted and the mixture is smooth and well blended. Pour into the buttered pan, spreading evenly.

Add the remaining marshmallow creme and ½ teaspoon vanilla to the white chocolate mixture and stir until the white chocolate is melted and the mixture is smooth and well blended. Pour the white chocolate mixture on top of the semisweet chocolate layer in the pan, spreading evenly. Cool and cut into squares. Store in an airtight container.

# Double-Duty Fudge

## Skill Level: Average

*This gorgeous "snowcapped" candy pulls double duty, pleasing both the white chocolate lovers and the dark chocolate lovers with one simple recipe. For a truly dazzling treat, try adding chopped nuts to the dark chocolate layer and chopped candied cherries to the white chocolate layer; see the variation below.*

✳ **MAKES ABOUT 2¼ POUNDS**

## VARIATION

Evenly divide ¾ to 1 cup chopped candied cherries, walnuts, or pecans between the two mixtures just before they are poured into the pan. If preferred, one layer can contain ½ cup chopped cherries, with the other layer containing ½ cup chopped walnuts or pecans. As another option, crushed peppermint candies may be sprinkled on top of the white layer, or be creative and use your own combinations.

COOK'S NOTE: This fudge can be cut into neat squares if slightly chilled first.

. . . . . . . . . . . . . . . . . . . . . . . .

# Tuxedo Fudge

## Skill Level: Advanced

*Make a date with this black and white old-fashioned fudge, combining coconut, pecans, and chocolate into one layered candy.*

✳ MAKES ABOUT 3½ POUNDS

*Coconut Layer*
**2 cups granulated sugar**
**Dash salt**
**½ cup butter or margarine**
**¼ cup light corn syrup**
**½ cup milk**
**1 teaspoon vanilla extract**
**½ cup sweetened flaked coconut**

*Chocolate Layer*
**2 cups granulated sugar**
**2 tablespoons unsweetened cocoa powder**
**Dash salt**
**½ cup butter or margarine**
**¼ cup light corn syrup**

**½ cup milk**
**1 teaspoon vanilla extract**
**½ cup pecans in large pieces (optional)**

TO MAKE THE COCONUT LAYER: In a heavy 2-quart saucepan over low to medium-low heat, bring the sugar, salt, butter, corn syrup, and milk to a boil, stirring until the sugar dissolves and the mixture begins to boil. Cover and cook 2 to 3 minutes to dissolve the sugar crystals on the sides of the pan. Remove the lid. Cook, stirring only as needed to prevent scorching, to the soft ball stage (234°F to 240°F, with 236°F recommended).

Remove from the heat. Cool slightly, about 10 minutes. Butter an 8- or 9-inch square pan. Add the vanilla. Beat by hand until the candy begins to thicken and lose its gloss. Stir in the coconut. Spread the candy into the buttered pan. Cool at room temperature while making the chocolate layer.

TO MAKE THE CHOCOLATE LAYER: In a heavy 2-quart saucepan, combine the sugar and cocoa until well blended. Add the salt, butter, corn syrup, and milk. Bring to a boil over low to medium-low heat, stirring until the sugar dissolves and the mixture begins to boil. Cover and cook 2 to 3 minutes to dissolve the sugar crystals on the sides of the pan. Remove the lid. Cook, stirring only as needed to prevent scorching, to the soft ball stage (234°F to 240°F, with 236°F recommended).

Remove from the heat. Cool slightly, about 10 minutes. Add the vanilla. Beat by hand until the candy begins to thicken and lose its gloss. Stir in the pecans if desired. Spread the chocolate layer over the coconut layer in the pan. Cool and cut into squares. Store in an airtight container.

. . . . . . . . . . . . . . . . . . . . . . . .

# Penuches

## Panache Penuche

### Skill Level: Advanced

*Personalize this creamy, fudgelike candy by adding your choice of lemon peel, cherries, orange zest, raisins, or nuts. This versatile 1950s-style recipe will accommodate a range of tastes.*

✴ **MAKES ABOUT 1½ POUNDS**

1½ cups granulated sugar
1 cup packed light brown sugar
¾ cup half-and-half
¼ teaspoon salt
2 tablespoons butter or margarine
1 teaspoon vanilla extract
1 teaspoon freshly grated lemon zest
⅓ cup raisins or pecans in large pieces

Butter an 8-inch square pan.

In a heavy 2-quart saucepan over low to medium-low heat, bring the sugars, half-and-half, and salt to a boil, stirring until the sugars dissolve and the mixture begins to boil. Cover and cook 2 to 3 minutes to dissolve the sugar crystals on the sides of the pan. Remove the lid. Cook, without stirring, to the soft ball stage (234°F to 240°F with 238°F recommended).

Add the butter without stirring. Cool to lukewarm (110°F), about 1 hour.

Add the vanilla. Beat by hand until the candy becomes creamy. Stir in the zest and raisins. Continue beating until the candy begins to lose its gloss. Quickly spread into the buttered pan. Cool and cut into squares. Store in an airtight container.

### VARIATIONS

This recipe can also be made using ⅓ cup half-and-half and ⅓ cup milk.

*Cherry-Nut Penuche:* Omit the lemon zest. Use ⅓ cup nuts instead of the raisins. Add ⅓ cup well-drained, finely cut maraschino cherries when adding the nuts.

*Orange Penuche:* Substitute 2 teaspoons freshly grated orange zest for the lemon zest.

*Raisin-Nut Penuche:* Omit the lemon zest. Use ⅓ cup raisins and ⅓ cup pecans.

*Panache Panocha Fudge:* Omit the salt and lemon zest. Use ⅓ cup half-and-half and ⅓ cup milk. Cook to 236°F. Substitute 1 cup coarsely chopped pecans for the ⅓ cup raisins or nuts.

## Brown Sugar Panocha

### Skill Level: Advanced

*Made with all brown sugar rather than a mixture of brown and white sugars, this version of penuche has a robust flavor.*

✴ **MAKES ABOUT 1½ POUNDS**

2½ cups packed light brown sugar
¾ cup milk
1 tablespoon butter or margarine
1 tablespoon light corn syrup
Dash salt
1 teaspoon vanilla extract
½ cup walnuts or pecans in large pieces

Butter a 9 × 5-inch loaf pan.

In a heavy 2-quart saucepan over low to medium-low heat, bring the sugar, milk, butter, corn syrup, and salt to a boil, stirring until the sugar dissolves and the mixture begins to boil. Cook, stirring very gently (never vigorously) a few times to prevent scorching, to the soft ball stage (234°F to 240°F, with 238°F recommended).

Remove from the heat. Cool to lukewarm (110°F), about 1 hour.

Add the vanilla. Beat by hand until the candy begins to hold its shape. Add the nuts. Quickly spread in the buttered pan. Cool and cut into squares. Store in an airtight container.

## What's in a Name?

Amaze your friends with a bit of candy trivia by citing the different spellings for penuche, a fudgelike candy usually made with brown sugar, cream or milk, butter, and nuts. The various spellings are penuche, penuchi, panocha, panoche, pinoche, or pinochi.

**VARIATION**

*Brown Sugar Penuche:* Omit the corn syrup and the salt. Substitute half-and-half for the milk. Cook as directed to 236°F.

COOK'S NOTE: This recipe can be made without the corn syrup if desired, though corn syrup does help make candies creamier.

# Quick Walnut Penuche

## Skill Level: Novice, Easy

*For the flavor of penuche without the hand beating, this quick recipe is an excellent choice.*

✳ MAKES ABOUT ½ POUND

½ cup butter or margarine
1 cup packed light brown sugar
¼ cup milk
1¾ to 2 cups powdered sugar, sifted
1 cup walnuts in large pieces

Butter a plate.

In a heavy 1-quart saucepan over medium-low heat, melt the butter. Stir in the brown sugar. Cook, stirring constantly, 2 minutes. Add the milk and bring to a boil, stirring constantly.

Remove from the heat. Cool to room temperature, 30 to 45 minutes. Gradually add the powdered sugar, stirring until well blended and the mixture has the consistency of fudge. Stir in the walnuts. Pour onto the buttered plate. Cool and cut into squares. Store in an airtight container in the refrigerator.

# Other Fudges

## Banana Fudge

### Skill Level: Advanced

*This recipe may not be for everyone, but those who love banana-flavored sweets will find this an interesting and unusual treat.*

✳ MAKES ABOUT 1¼ POUNDS

    2 cups granulated sugar
    2 tablespoons light corn syrup
    ⅔ cup milk
    2 ripe bananas, mashed
    2 tablespoons butter or margarine
    ½ teaspoon vanilla extract
    ¾ cup pecans in large pieces (optional)

In a heavy 2-quart saucepan over medium-low heat, bring the sugar, corn syrup, milk, and bananas to a boil, stirring until the sugar dissolves and the mixture begins to boil. Cook, stirring occasionally to prevent scorching, to the soft ball stage (234°F to 240°F, with 236°F recommended).

Remove from the heat. Stir in the butter, vanilla, and pecans, if using. Set the saucepan in a pan of cool water about 20 minutes to allow the candy to cool. Butter a 9 × 5-inch loaf pan.

Beat by hand until the candy changes texture, lightens in color, and becomes smooth. Pour into the buttered pan. Cool and cut into squares. Store in an airtight container.

COOK'S NOTE: This candy is more likely to need stirring during the last few minutes of cooking.

· · · · · · · · · · · · · · · · · · · ·

## Extra-Buttery Buttermilk Fudge

### Skill Level: Advanced

*Adding the butter and the pecans before cooking gives this blonde creamy candy a rich, nutty flavor.*

✳ MAKES ABOUT 1½ POUNDS

    2 cups granulated sugar
    1 cup buttermilk
    Pinch salt
    ½ cup butter or margarine
    ½ cup pecans in large pieces
    1 tablespoon vanilla extract

In a heavy 3-quart saucepan over medium heat, bring the sugar, buttermilk, and salt to a boil, stirring until the sugar dissolves and the mixture begins to boil. Reduce the heat to low. Stir in the butter. Cook slowly over low heat, stirring only if needed to prevent scorching, 5 minutes. Stir in the pecans. Cook, gently stirring a few times to prevent scorching, to the soft ball stage (234°F to 240°F, with 238°F recommended).

Remove from the heat. Cool 20 minutes. Butter a 9 × 5-inch loaf pan.

Add the vanilla. Beat by hand until the candy thickens and loses its gloss. Pour into the buttered pan. Cool and cut into squares. Store in an airtight container.

COOK'S NOTE: For a very soft fudge, cook to 236°F.

# Sinfully Rich Buttermilk Fudge

## Skill Level: Advanced

*Caramel colored, pecan packed, and absolutely yummy, this ultrarich candy is sometimes slightly grainy but is so delicious no one will care.*

✳ MAKES ABOUT 1½ POUNDS

1 teaspoon baking soda
1 cup buttermilk
2 cups granulated sugar
2 tablespoons light corn syrup
2 tablespoons butter or margarine
1 teaspoon vanilla extract
¾ to 1 cup pecans in large pieces

In a heavy 5-quart kettle, dissolve the baking soda in the buttermilk, stirring until well blended. Stir in the sugar and corn syrup. Bring to a boil over low heat, stirring until the sugar dissolves and the mixture begins to boil. Cover and cook 2 to 3 minutes to dissolve the sugar crystals on the sides of the pan, lifting the lid a few times so the candy will not boil over. Re-

move the lid. Cook slowly over low heat, stirring occasionally to prevent scorching, to the soft ball stage (234°F to 240°F, with 238°F recommended).

Remove from the heat. Add the butter without stirring. Cool 15 to 20 minutes. Butter a 9 × 5-inch loaf pan.

Add the vanilla. Beat by hand until the candy thickens and loses its gloss. Quickly stir in the pecans. Pour into the buttered pan. Cool and cut into squares. Store in an airtight container.

### VARIATION

*Sweet and Creamy Buttermilk Fudge:* For a creamy, buttery-yellow fudge that retains the mild flavor of buttermilk, omit the baking soda. Cook in a heavy 2-quart saucepan as described above. Add 1 additional tablespoon butter or margarine after removing the candy from the heat.

COOK'S NOTES: Slow cooking will make this candy creamier.

For a candy similar to Sinfully Rich Buttermilk Fudge, see Fresh Buttermilk Candy (page 31).

For a candy with a flavor similar to Sweet and Creamy Buttermilk Fudge, see Sweet Buttermilk Candy (page 31).

# Coffee Fudge

## Skill Level: Advanced

*Even those who do not like coffee-flavored desserts will be impressed with the sophisticated blend of chocolate and coffee in this candy. Give your dinner guests a few pieces to take home with them.*

✳ **MAKES ABOUT 2½ POUNDS**

3 cups granulated sugar
1 cup milk
½ cup half-and-half
⅓ cup light corn syrup
2 tablespoons instant coffee granules
3 tablespoons butter
½ cup semisweet chocolate chips
1 teaspoon vanilla extract
½ cup coarsely chopped pecans, walnuts, or
    hazelnuts (optional)

In a heavy 3-quart saucepan over medium heat, bring the sugar, milk, half-and-half, corn syrup, and coffee to a boil, stirring until the sugar dissolves and the mixture begins to boil. Cover and cook 2 to 3 minutes to remove the sugar crystals from the sides of the pan. Remove the lid. Cook, stirring occasionally to prevent scorching, to the soft ball stage (234°F to 240°F, with 236°F recommended).

Remove from the heat. Add the butter and chocolate chips without stirring. Cool slightly, about 10 minutes, or until the chocolate is partially melted. Butter an 8-inch square pan.

Add the vanilla. Beat by hand until the candy begins to thicken, hold its shape, and lose its gloss. Stir in the nuts, if desired. Pour into the buttered pan. Cool and cut into squares. Store in an airtight container.

**COOK'S NOTE:** The amount of coffee used is a matter of personal preference. This candy has a distinct coffee flavoring that is loved by some, but not by all. The coffee may be reduced or omitted entirely.

. . . . . . . . . . . . . . . . . . . . . . . .

# Light Mocha Fudge

## Skill Level: Average

*With just a hint of coffee flavoring, this white chocolate–marshmallow fudge will entice the coffee lovers in your family.*

✳ **MAKES ABOUT 2 POUNDS**

2 cups granulated sugar
⅔ cup evaporated milk
½ cup butter or margarine
½ tablespoon instant coffee granules
6 ounces white baking chocolate, coarsely
    chopped
16 large marshmallows
1 teaspoon vanilla extract
1 cup pecans or walnuts in large pieces
    (optional)

Butter an 8-inch square pan.

In a heavy 3-quart saucepan over medium heat, bring the sugar, milk, butter, and coffee to a boil, stirring until the sugar dissolves and the mixture begins to boil. Cook, stirring frequently to prevent scorching, to the soft ball stage (234°F to 240°F, with 234°F recommended).

Remove from the heat. Add the white chocolate, stirring until melted. Add the marshmallows. Let the marshmallows stand 1 to 2 minutes to soften. Stir the candy until it is smooth and well blended. Stir in the vanilla and nuts, if using. Pour into the buttered pan. Cool and cut into squares. Store in an airtight container.

### VARIATION

*Dark Mocha Fudge:* Substitute 1 cup (6 ounces) semisweet chocolate for the white baking chocolate.

COOK'S NOTES: The amount of coffee used is a matter of personal preference. This candy has a light coffee flavor. The coffee can be doubled or omitted entirely if preferred.

This recipe produces semifirm fudge. To soften it a bit, add a few more marshmallows.

# Out-of-This-World Maple Fudge

## Skill Level: Advanced

*Deserving of its name, this exceptionally smooth and creamy fudge will definitely be a favorite with maple lovers everywhere. My thanks go to the* Ponca City News *for allowing me to reprint this old gem.*

✳ MAKES ABOUT 2½ POUNDS

3 cups granulated sugar
1 cup sour cream
1 tablespoon light corn syrup
½ cup butter or margarine
¼ teaspoon butter flavoring
¼ teaspoon cream of tartar

¼ teaspoon salt
1 teaspoon maple extract
1 cup coarsely chopped walnuts

In a heavy 3-quart saucepan over medium-low heat, bring the sugar, sour cream, corn syrup, butter, butter flavoring, cream of tartar, and salt to a boil, stirring until the sugar dissolves and the mixture begins to boil. Cover and cook 2 to 3 minutes to dissolve the sugar crystals on the sides of the pan. Remove the lid. Cook very slowly over low to medium-low heat, without stirring, to the soft ball stage (234°F to 240°F, with 238°F recommended for soft fudge or 240°F for firmer fudge.)

Remove from the heat. Cool to lukewarm (110°F), 45 minutes to 1 hour. Butter an 8-inch square pan.

Beat by hand until the candy begins to hold its shape. Stir in the maple extract and walnuts. Pour into the buttered pan. Cool and cut into squares. Store in an airtight container.

COOK'S NOTE: This recipe is an excellent example of how candy ingredients interact to produce smooth and creamy candies. For further explanation, see The Science of Candy Making (page 11).

# Wildcat Maple Sugar Fudge

## Skill Level: Advanced

*Smooth, creamy, and rich in maple flavor, this recipe from a 1942 cookbook published by Kansas State University will leave maple fans roaring for more.*

✳ MAKES ABOUT 1½ POUNDS

1 cup granulated sugar
1 cup maple sugar
1 cup milk or ¾ cup evaporated milk and
   ½ cup water
2 tablespoons light corn syrup
Dash salt
2 tablespoons butter or margarine
1 teaspoon vanilla extract

In a heavy 3-quart saucepan over low to medium-low heat, bring the sugars, milk, corn syrup, and salt to a boil, stirring until the sugars dissolve and the mixture begins to boil. Cover and cook 2 to 3 minutes to dissolve the sugar crystals on the sides of the pan. Remove the lid. Cook, without stirring, to the soft ball stage (234°F to 240°F, with 236°F recommended for soft fudge or 238°F for firm fudge).

Remove from the heat. Add the butter without stirring. Cool to lukewarm (110°F), 45 minutes to 1 hour. Butter a 9 × 5-inch loaf pan.

Add the vanilla. Beat by hand until the candy is thick and creamy. (The candy may retain some of its gloss.) Pour into the buttered pan. Cool and cut into squares. Store in an airtight container.

### VARIATION

*Wildcat Brown Sugar Fudge:* Substitute 1 cup packed light brown sugar for the maple sugar.

COOK'S NOTE: Maple sugar can be purchased via the Internet from companies and farms that produce high-quality maple syrups.

# Norway
# Black Walnut Fudge

## Skill Level: Advanced

*This version of an interesting old recipe from the* Ponca City News *is surprisingly delicious, with black walnuts and dates giving the candy a unique flavor and charm. The original recipe called for a piece of butter the size of an egg.*

✳ MAKES ABOUT 4 POUNDS

3 cups granulated sugar
3 cups packed light brown sugar
2 cups half-and-half
2 tablespoons light corn syrup
Butter the size of an egg (¼ cup butter)
1 cup coarsely chopped black walnuts
1 cup chopped dates (with no sugar additives;
   optional)
1 teaspoon vanilla extract

In a heavy 5-quart kettle over medium heat, bring the sugars, half-and-half, and corn syrup to a boil, stirring until the sugars dissolve and the mixture begins to boil. Reduce the heat to medium low. Cover and cook 2 to 3 minutes to dissolve the sugar crystals on the sides of the pan. Remove the lid. Cook slowly, stirring only as needed to prevent scorching, to the soft ball stage (234°F to 240°F, with 234°F recommended).

Remove from the heat. Add the butter, walnuts, and dates, if using, without stirring or shaking the pan. Cool to lukewarm (110°F), about 1 hour. Butter a 9 × 13-inch pan.

Add the vanilla. Beat by hand until the candy begins to thicken and lose its gloss. Pour into the buttered pan. Cool and cut into squares. Store in an airtight container.

COOK'S NOTES: Before starting this recipe, read the package label to be certain the dates contain no sugar additives such as dextrose. These additives will spark a chain reaction, causing sugar crystals to form and the candy to sugar in the pan.

This recipe may be reduced by half, cooked in a heavy 3-quart saucepan, and poured into a buttered 8-inch square pan.

. . . . . . . . . . . . . . . . . . . . . . . . .

# Creamy Orange Fudge

## Skill Level: Advanced

*Perfect for a springtime luncheon or Mother's Day celebration, this enchanting orange delicacy is a nice change of pace from the usual chocolate fudges.*

✳ MAKES ABOUT 1½ POUNDS

2¼ cups granulated sugar
¾ cup half-and-half
1 tablespoon butter
2 tablespoons freshly grated orange zest
6 tablespoons orange juice
1 teaspoon lemon juice
¼ teaspoon cream of tartar
1 cup pecans or walnuts in large pieces
   (optional)

In a heavy 2-quart saucepan over low to medium-low heat, bring the sugar, half-and-half, butter, orange zest, orange juice, lemon juice, and cream of tartar to a boil, stirring until the sugar dissolves and the mixture begins to boil. Cover and cook 2 to 3 minutes to dissolve the sugar crystals on the sides of the pan. Remove the lid. Cook over low heat, stirring only as needed to prevent scorching, to the soft

ball stage (234°F to 240°F, with 238°F recommended).

Remove from the heat. Cool to lukewarm (110°F), 45 minutes to 1 hour. Butter a 9 × 5-inch loaf pan.

Beat by hand until the candy begins to thicken and lose its gloss. Quickly stir in the nuts, if using. Pour into the buttered pan. Cool and cut into squares. Store in an airtight container.

. . . . . . . . . . . . . . . . . . . . . . . . .

# Pineapple Sherbet Fudge

## Skill Level: Advanced

*Long recognized as a sign of hospitality, fresh pineapples once adorned the tables of the wealthy as a special greeting to guests. With just a hint of lemon, this creamy white, pineapple-speckled fudge will help you welcome friends with style.*

✳ MAKES ABOUT 2¼ POUNDS

3 cups granulated sugar
1 cup half-and-half
3 tablespoons light corn syrup
1 (8-ounce) can crushed pineapple, drained
2 teaspoons lemon juice
¼ teaspoon cream of tartar
¼ cup butter
¼ teaspoon pure lemon extract
¾ cup coarsely chopped walnuts
   (optional)

Butter an 8-inch square pan.

In a heavy 3-quart saucepan over medium heat, bring the sugar, half-and-half, corn syrup, pineapple, lemon juice, and cream of tartar to a boil, stirring until the sugar dissolves and the mixture begins to boil. Reduce the heat to low or medium low. Cover and cook 2 to 3 minutes to dissolve the sugar crystals on the sides of the pan. Remove the lid. Cook, without stirring, to the soft ball stage (234°F to 240°F, with 236°F recommended).

Remove from the heat. Add the butter and lemon extract. Beat by hand until the candy begins to thicken and hold its shape. Stir in the walnuts, if desired. Pour into the buttered pan. Cool and cut into squares. Store in an airtight container.

cook's notes: If preferred, ½ teaspoon vanilla extract may be substituted for the lemon extract.

Although most candies are cooled before beating, this candy must be beaten while still hot.

. . . . . . . . . . . . . . . . . . . . . . . .

# Hawaiian Fudge

## Skill Level: Advanced

*A hint of ginger adds interest to this unusual pineapple-flavored prizewinner from the 1964* Ponca City News *recipe contest.*

✳ MAKES ABOUT 2 POUNDS

   2 cups granulated sugar
   1 cup packed light brown sugar
   1 cup crushed pineapple, drained
   ½ cup half-and-half or evaporated milk
   1 teaspoon ground ginger
   2 tablespoons butter or margarine
   2 teaspoons vanilla extract
   1 cup pecans in large pieces

In a heavy 3-quart saucepan over medium-low heat, bring the sugars, pineapple, half-and-half, and ginger to a boil, stirring until the sugars dissolve and the mixture begins to boil. Cover and cook 2 to 3 minutes to remove the sugar crystals from the sides of the pan. Remove the lid. Cook, stirring occasionally to prevent scorching, to the soft ball stage (234°F to 240°F, with 234°F recommended).

Remove from the heat. Add the butter without stirring. Cool to lukewarm (110°F), 45 minutes to 1 hour. Butter a 9 × 5-inch loaf pan.

Add the vanilla and pecans. Beat by hand until the candy is thick and creamy. Pour into the buttered pan. Cool and cut into squares. Store in an airtight container.

. . . . . . . . . . . . . . . . . . . . . . . .

# The Preacher's Pineapple Fudge

## Skill Level: Advanced

*A retired minister friend chose this dense, light brown fudge as his favorite of all the candies he tasted.*

✳ MAKES ABOUT 2 POUNDS

   3 cups granulated sugar
   1 cup evaporated milk
   2 tablespoons butter or margarine
   1 cup crushed pineapple, drained
   2 teaspoons lemon juice

In a heavy 2-quart saucepan over medium-low heat, bring the sugar, milk, and butter to a boil, stirring until the sugar dissolves and the mixture begins to boil. Stir in the pineapple. Cover and cook 2 to 3 minutes to dissolve the sugar crystals on the sides of the pan. Remove the lid. Cook over low heat to medium-low heat, stirring occasionally to prevent scorching, to the soft ball stage (234°F to 240°F, with 236°F recommended).

Remove from the heat. Cool to lukewarm (110°F), 45 minutes to 1 hour. Butter an 8-inch square pan.

Add the lemon juice. Beat by hand until the candy loses its gloss and begins to thicken and hold its shape. Pour into the buttered pan. Cool and cut into squares. Store in an airtight container.

. . . . . . . . . . . . . . . . . . . . . . . . .

# Pumpkin Fudge

## Skill Level: Average

*Do not be surprised if pumpkin-loving friends say that this is the best pumpkin-flavored food they have ever tasted.*

✳ MAKES 2½ TO 3 POUNDS

    3 cups granulated sugar
    ½ cup butter or margarine
    1 cup half-and-half
    ½ cup canned pumpkin
    ½ teaspoon ground cinnamon
    ¼ teaspoon ground nutmeg
    Dash ground cloves
    1 (12-ounce) package butterscotch chips
    1 (7-ounce) jar marshmallow creme
    1 teaspoon vanilla extract
    1½ cups coarsely chopped pecans or walnuts
        (optional)

Butter an 8-inch or 9-inch square pan.

In a heavy 5-quart kettle over medium-low to medium heat, bring the sugar, butter, half-and-half, pumpkin, cinnamon, nutmeg, and cloves to a boil, stirring until the sugar dissolves and the mixture begins to boil. Cook, stirring constantly to prevent scorching, to the soft ball stage (234°F to 240°F, with 234°F recommended).

Remove from the heat. Stir in the butterscotch chips until melted. Stir in the marshmallow creme until blended. Add the vanilla and walnuts, if using. Pour into the buttered pan. Cool and cut into squares. Store in an airtight container.

### VARIATION

*Light Pumpkin Fudge:* For a lighter flavor, substitute vanilla-flavored baking chips for the butterscotch chips.

COOK'S NOTE: Though this is a popular combination of spices, the particular spices used and the amount used may be adjusted for personal tastes. For example, ground ginger can be substituted for the nutmeg. Look at your favorite pumpkin pie recipe for ideas.

. . . . . . . . . . . . . . . . . . . . . . . . .

# Creamy Blonde Fudge

## Skill Level: Advanced

*Additional cream and butter make this candy richer than its cousin, Creamy White Fudge (page 132). Both candies have a creamy, but slightly sticky texture due to the ingredients.*

✳ MAKES ABOUT 2½ POUNDS

3 cups granulated sugar
1 cup half-and-half
½ cup milk
¼ cup light corn syrup
2 tablespoons butter or margarine
1½ teaspoons vanilla extract
1 cup pecans or walnuts in large pieces

In a heavy 5-quart kettle over medium heat, bring the sugar, half-and-half, milk, corn syrup, and butter to a boil, stirring until the sugar dissolves and the mixture begins to boil. Cook, stirring occasionally to prevent scorching, to the soft ball stage (234°F to 240°F, with 238°F recommended).

Remove from the heat. Cool to lukewarm (110°F), 45 minutes to 1 hour. Butter an 8-inch square pan.

Add the vanilla. Beat by hand until the mixture begins to thicken and lose its gloss. Stir in the nuts. Quickly spread the candy into the buttered pan. Cool and cut into squares. Store in an airtight container.

. . . . . . . . . . . . . . . . . . . . . . . . . .

# Creamy White Fudge

## Skill Level: Advanced

*With less cream and no butter, this candy is not quite as rich as its cousin, Creamy Blonde Fudge (page 131). Both candies have a creamy, but slightly sticky texture due to the ingredients.*
✳ MAKES ABOUT 2½ POUNDS

3 cups granulated sugar
½ cup half-and-half or milk
1 cup light corn syrup

1 teaspoon vanilla extract
1 cup coarsely chopped pecans or walnuts

In a heavy 5-quart kettle over medium heat, bring the sugar, half-and-half, and corn syrup to a boil, stirring until the sugar dissolves and the mixture begins to boil. Reduce the heat to medium low. Cover and cook 2 to 3 minutes to dissolve the sugar crystals on the sides of the pan. Remove the lid. Cook, stirring occasionally, to the soft ball stage (234°F to 240°F, with 238°F recommended).

Remove from the heat. Cool 20 minutes without stirring. Butter an 8-inch square pan.

Add the vanilla. Beat by hand until the candy thickens and loses its gloss. Stir in the nuts. Pour into the buttered pan. Cool and cut into squares. Store in an airtight container.

. . . . . . . . . . . . . . . . . . . . . . . . . .

# Coconut Fudge

## Skill Level: Advanced

*Bright red candied cherries make this light brown coconut fudge particularly fun and festive.*
✳ MAKES ABOUT 2½ POUNDS

3 cups granulated sugar
1 cup half-and-half
1 cup light corn syrup
1 tablespoon vanilla extract
½ cup sweetened flaked coconut
1 cup coarsely chopped pecans (optional)
½ to 1 cup chopped candied cherries (optional)
½ cup chopped candied pineapple (optional)

In a heavy 5-quart kettle over medium-low heat, bring the sugar, half-and-half, and corn syrup to a boil, stirring until the sugar dissolves and the mixture begins to boil. Reduce the heat to low. Cook slowly, gently stirring only a few times to prevent scorching, to the soft ball stage (234°F to 240°F, with 240°F recommended).

Remove from the heat. Cool 20 minutes. Butter an 8-inch square pan.

Add the vanilla. Beat by hand until the candy thickens and begins to hold its shape. (The candy will retain some of its gloss.) Stir in the coconut and the pecans, cherries, and pineapple, if using. Pour into the buttered pan. Cool and cut into squares. Store in an airtight container.

COOK'S NOTE: The quantity and combination of coconut, pecans, cherries, and pineapple used is a matter of personal preference. Adjust to taste.

. . . . . . . . . . . . . . . . . .

# White Cherry Fudge

## Skill Level: Advanced

*A bite of this colorful, ultrasweet, and creamy fudge is just the thing to put me into a festive holiday mood. I often include a few pieces in gift tins to add a bit of color and cheer.*

✳ MAKES ABOUT 1½ POUNDS

2¼ cups granulated sugar
½ cup sour cream
¼ cup milk
2 tablespoons butter or margarine

1 tablespoon light corn syrup
¼ teaspoon salt
2 teaspoons vanilla extract
1 cup walnuts in large pieces
⅓ cup chopped candied cherries

In a heavy 2-quart saucepan over medium-low to medium heat, bring the sugar, sour cream, milk, butter, corn syrup, and salt to a boil, stirring until the sugar dissolves and the mixture begins to boil. Cook, stirring constantly to prevent scorching, to the soft ball stage (234°F to 240°F, with 238°F recommended).

Remove from the heat. Cool to lukewarm (110°F), 45 minutes to 1 hour. Butter an 8-inch square pan.

Add the vanilla. Beat by hand just until the candy begins to lose its gloss and hold its shape. Quickly stir in the walnuts and cherries. Immediately turn into the buttered pan. (Note: The candy can set up very rapidly once it begins to cool, so it is important to work quickly.) Cool and cut into squares. Store in an airtight container.

COOK'S NOTES: This fudge is not very thick when poured into an 8-inch square pan. If preferred, pour the candy into a smaller pan or double the recipe, cooking the candy in a heavy 3- to 4-quart saucepan.

If the humidity is high, cook the candy to 240°F.

. . . . . . . . . . . . . . . . . .

# Royal Eggnog Fudge

## Skill Level: Average

*Spice up your holidays with this unusual combination of white chocolate, cinnamon, nutmeg, and cloves.*

✳ **MAKES ABOUT 2½ POUNDS**

2 cups granulated sugar
¼ teaspoon ground cinnamon
⅛ teaspoon ground nutmeg
⅛ teaspoon ground cloves
1 cup commercially prepared eggnog (no
    alcohol added)
¼ cup butter or margarine
8 ounces white chocolate baking squares,
    coarsely chopped
1 (7-ounce) jar marshmallow creme
1 teaspoon vanilla extract
1 cup pecans or walnuts in large pieces

Butter an 8-inch or 9-inch square pan.

In a heavy 2- to 3-quart saucepan, combine the sugar, cinnamon, nutmeg, and cloves, stirring until well blended. Add the eggnog and butter. Bring to a boil over medium heat, stirring constantly. Cook, stirring constantly to prevent scorching, to the soft ball stage (234°F to 240°F, with 238°F recommended).

Remove from the heat. Stir in the chocolate until melted. Add the marshmallow creme and vanilla and stir until smooth and well blended. Add the nuts. Pour into the buttered pan. Cool and cut into squares. Store in an airtight container.

### VARIATION

*Cherry Eggnog Fudge:* Omit the cinnamon, nutmeg, and cloves. Stir in ½ to ¾ cup chopped candied cherries when adding the nuts.

**COOK'S NOTE:** The amount of spices needed may depend upon both personal taste and the brand of eggnog used in the candy. If highly spiced eggnog is used, additional nutmeg may not be necessary. Taste the eggnog before making the candy and then adjust the spices as desired. The cinnamon, nutmeg, and cloves may be omitted entirely if preferred.

# Lemon–White Chocolate Fudge

## Skill Level: Average

*Fun to make and fun to eat, this versatile recipe contains just enough white chocolate to capture attention, but not enough to overwhelm. Though the lemon version is perhaps the most unusual and the most popular, other variations have equally enthusiastic fans.*

✳ **MAKES ABOUT 2¼ POUNDS**

2 cups granulated sugar
¾ cup sour cream
½ cup butter or margarine
Dash salt
Freshly grated zest of 2 lemons
8 ounces white baking chocolate, coarsely
    chopped
1 (7-ounce) jar marshmallow creme
1 to 1½ teaspoons pure lemon extract
1 to 2 drops yellow food coloring (optional)

Butter an 8-inch square pan.

In a heavy 2-quart saucepan over medium heat, bring the sugar, sour cream, butter, salt, and lemon zest to a boil, stirring until the sugar dissolves and the mixture begins to boil. Cook, stirring occasionally to prevent scorching, to the soft ball stage (234°F to 240°F, with 238°F recommended).

Remove from the heat. Stir in the chocolate until melted. Add the marshmallow creme and lemon extract. Stir until the candy is smooth and well blended. Stir in the food coloring, if using. Pour into the buttered pan. Cool to room temperature, chill, and cut into squares. Store in an airtight container.

## VARIATIONS

*Apricot–White Chocolate Fudge:* Omit the lemon zest and the yellow food coloring. Substitute 1 teaspoon vanilla extract or pure almond extract for the lemon extract. Add ¾ cup chopped dried apricots before pouring the candy into the pan. Add ¾ cup coarsely chopped walnuts or pecans, or sliced, toasted almonds (optional).

*Cherry–White Chocolate Fudge:* Omit the lemon zest and the yellow food coloring. Substitute 1 teaspoon cherry extract for the lemon extract. Add ¾ cup chopped dried cherries, chopped candied cherries, or drained and chopped maraschino cherries before pouring the candy into the pan. Add ¾ cup coarsely chopped walnuts or pecans, or sliced, toasted almonds (optional).

*Cranberry–White Chocolate Fudge:* Omit the lemon zest and the yellow food coloring. Substitute 1 teaspoon vanilla extract for the lemon extract. Add ¾ cup chopped dried cranberries before pouring the candy into the pan. Add ¾ cup coarsely chopped walnuts or pecans, or sliced, toasted almonds (optional).

*Orange–White Chocolate Fudge:* Substitute the freshly grated zest of 1 orange for the lemon zest. Substitute 1 teaspoon orange extract for the lemon extract. Omit the yellow food coloring.

*Rum Raisin–White Chocolate Fudge:* Omit the lemon zest and the yellow food coloring. Substitute 1 teaspoon imitation Jamaica rum flavoring or rum extract for the lemon extract. Add ¾ cup golden raisins or raisins before pouring the candy into the pan.

*Rum Nut–White Chocolate Fudge:* Omit the lemon zest and the yellow food coloring. Substitute 1 teaspoon imitation Jamaica rum flavoring or rum extract for the lemon extract. Add ¾ cup coarsely chopped walnuts or pecans before pouring the candy into the pan.

*White Chocolate Fudge:* Omit the lemon zest and the yellow food coloring. Substitute 1 teaspoon vanilla extract for the lemon extract. Add ¾ cup coarsely chopped walnuts, black walnuts, or pecans (optional) before pouring the candy into the pan.

*Chocolate Fudge:* Omit the lemon zest and the yellow food coloring. Substitute 1 teaspoon vanilla extract for the lemon extract. Substitute 8 to 10 ounces semisweet chocolate for the white chocolate. If desired, add ¾ cup coarsely chopped walnuts, black walnuts, or pecans before pouring the candy into the pan. Chopped candied cherries or drained and chopped maraschino cherries may be used in place of the nuts.

COOK'S NOTE: For a stronger white chocolate flavor, increase the amount of white chocolate up to 12 ounces.

# Dreamy White Christmas Fudge

### Skill Level: Average

*You will be dreaming of a different kind of white Christmas once you taste my cousin Margaret's special recipe. The incredible blend of white chocolate, toasted almonds, and fruit all in one luscious fudge, what could possibly be better?*

※ MAKES ABOUT 1½ POUNDS

2½ cups powdered sugar

⅔ cup milk

¼ cup butter or margarine

12 ounces white chocolate, coarsely chopped

½ teaspoon almond extract

¾ cup coarsely chopped dried apricots, cherries, or cranberries

¾ cup sliced almonds, toasted

Line an 8-inch square pan with foil. Butter the foil lining.

In a heavy 3-quart saucepan over medium heat, bring the sugar, milk, and butter to a boil, stirring until the sugar dissolves and the mixture begins to boil. Reduce the heat slightly. Cook at a steady boil, without stirring, for 5 minutes. (If using a candy thermometer, the mixture will reach approximately 222°F.)

Remove from the heat. Add the white chocolate and stir until melted and smooth. Add the almond extract, fruit, and almonds. Pour into the prepared pan. Refrigerate 2 hours. Invert the pan and remove the foil lining. Cut into squares. Store in an airtight container in the refrigerator.

COOK'S NOTE: This fudge is very soft and best served cold. Do not try cooking this candy to a soft ball stage (234°F to 240°F). For a slightly firmer fudge, boil the candy mixture about 1 minute longer.

# Designer Delights

One of the great pleasures of being a candy maker is adding our own personal signature to the candies we make. Many of the recipes in Designer Delights inspire this creativity, letting us shape, mold, and decorate a candy just to our liking.

Those of us who love chocolate-coated candies know that a minor change in the type of chocolate we choose allows us to customize a coating to our personal tastes. A simple white chocolate drizzle often adds a touch of elegance to a favorite dark chocolate–coated candy, signaling to others that this special creation deserves to be noticed. Nut-loving candy makers may prefer to sprinkle freshly dipped candies with toasted pecans, walnuts, hazelnuts, or almonds, while others may add a bit of artistry by topping their candies with white or dark chocolate shavings or decorator sprinkles.

Fondants are the most versatile confections on earth, with fondant recipes providing us with basic instructions and then letting us choose the flavorings, colorings, shapes, and ingredients that will create the candies that we crave. A fondant can become the maple cream center in a box of Forrest Gump's chocolates or the delicate pastel wafer we serve with a cup of hot tea. Though we often think of fondants as the filling for bonbons, nothing says that our fondant-based candies must always be round. When candy makers dream of oval pink Easter eggs coated in fluffy white coconut, they simply turn to their fondant recipes and let their imaginations soar.

Nothing gives us that pampered feeling quite like the taste of a silky smooth, light, and fluffy truffle. Considered the ultimate luxury candy, truffles are much easier to make than most people think, usually requiring more time than talent. Once again, many basic truffle recipes can be flavored, coated, and decorated any way a budding gourmet desires. And remember, truffles do not have to be perfectly shaped to taste good. Sometimes handmade imperfections only add charm to this divine and thoughtful hand-fashioned gift.

# Balls and Shaped Candies

## Chocolate Cherry Creams

### Skill Level: Novice, Easy

*Anyone who loves chocolate-covered cherries will adore these pretty little chocolate snowballs, especially when cherry extract is added.*
✳ MAKES ABOUT 30

> 1 cup (6 ounces) semisweet chocolate chips
> 1/3 cup evaporated milk
> 1 1/2 cups powdered sugar, sifted
> 1/3 cup finely chopped pecans or walnuts
> 1/3 cup maraschino cherries, chopped and
>     well-drained
> 1/2 teaspoon cherry extract (optional)
> 1 1/4 cups sweetened flaked coconut

In a heavy 2-quart saucepan over low heat, heat the chocolate chips and milk together until the chocolate melts, stirring until smooth.

Remove from the heat. Stir in the powdered sugar, nuts, cherries, and cherry extract, if using, blending well. Cover and refrigerate until the mixture is cool enough to handle, about 1 hour.

Shape the mixture into balls 1 inch in diameter. Roll the balls in the coconut. Store in an airtight container in the refrigerator.

### VARIATION
*Almond Cherry Creams:* Substitute 1/4 to 1/2 teaspoon pure almond extract for the cherry extract. Substitute finely chopped toasted almonds for the pecans or walnuts.

COOK'S NOTE: If the mixture is too soft to hold its shape, stir in additional powdered sugar, a spoonful at a time, until it reaches the desired consistency. If the mixture is too thick, stir in additional milk, a few drops at a time, until it is the desired consistency.

## Chocolate Angel Sweets

### Skill Level: Novice, Easy

*In just a few minutes, you can be eating these yummy little fudge candies.*
✳ MAKES ABOUT 36

> 1 cup (6 ounces) semisweet chocolate chips
> 2 tablespoons butter or margarine
> 1 cup sifted powdered sugar
> 1 to 2 tablespoons evaporated milk
> 1 cup chopped walnuts or pecans
> 2 cups miniature marshmallows
> 1 (3.5-ounce) can sweetened flaked coconut

Cover 2 large baking sheets with waxed paper.

In a heavy 1-quart saucepan, heat the chocolate chips and butter together over low heat until melted, stirring to prevent scorching.

Remove from the heat. Blend in the powdered sugar and 1 tablespoon milk. Stir in the nuts and marshmallows, blending well. (The marshmallows will only partially melt.) If the mixture is too thick to handle, stir in additional milk, a few drops at a time, until the mixture reaches the desired consistency.

Cool slightly, about 5 minutes. Shape the mixture into balls 1 inch in diameter. Roll the balls in the coconut. Place on the lined baking sheet. Refrigerate until firm, about 30 minutes. Store in an airtight container in the refrigerator.

### VARIATION

*Butterscotch Angel Sweets:* Substitute 1 cup butterscotch chips for the semisweet chocolate chips.

· · · · · · · · · · · · · · · · · · · ·

# Festive Chocolate Nut Balls

### Skill Level: Novice, Super Simple

*Just change the extract in this good and simple recipe, and you have a new candy flavor.*
✳ MAKES ABOUT 30

**1 cup very fine vanilla wafer crumbs**
**1 cup powdered sugar**
**2 tablespoons unsweetened cocoa powder**
**2 tablespoons light corn syrup**
**2 tablespoons half-and-half**
**1 teaspoon vanilla, almond, or rum extract**
**¾ cup finely chopped pecans or walnuts**
**¾ cup sweetened flaked coconut**
**About 1½ cups ground pecans or walnuts, or**
 **flaked coconut, for rolling**

Cover a large countertop area or a large baking sheet with waxed paper.

Pour the crumbs into a medium mixing bowl. Add the powdered sugar and cocoa, mixing well. Blend in the corn syrup, half-

and-half, and vanilla. Stir in the nuts and coconut.

Shape the mixture into balls 1 inch in diameter. Roll the balls in the ground nuts, coconut, or a combination of both as desired. Place on the lined baking sheet to dry, about 15 minutes. Store in an airtight container.

· · · · · · · · · · · · · · · · · · · ·

# Creamy Apricot Balls

### Skill Level: Novice, Super Simple

*A few of these creamy apricot candies make a wonderful addition to a holiday gift tin.*
✳ MAKES ABOUT 35

**1½ cups ground dried apricots**
**2 cups sweetened flaked coconut**
**⅔ cup sweetened condensed milk**
**About ¾ cup powdered sugar, for rolling**

Cover a large countertop area or a large baking sheet with waxed paper.

In a large mixing bowl, mix together the apricots and coconut. Stir in the milk, blending well. Shape the mixture into balls 1 inch in diameter. Roll in powdered sugar. Place on the waxed paper. Let stand, uncovered, until firm. Store in an airtight container.

· · · · · · · · · · · · · · · · · · · ·

# Zesty Apricot Nut Balls

## Skill Level: Novice, Super Simple

*Flavored with coconut, lemon, and orange, Zesty Apricot Nut Balls are a delightful combination, especially for a spring or summer event.*

❋ MAKES ABOUT 18

 ¾ cup dried apricots
 ½ cup pecans or walnut halves or pieces
 1 cup sweetened flaked coconut
 2 tablespoons powdered sugar
 1 teaspoon freshly grated lemon zest
 1 teaspoon lemon juice
 1 teaspoon freshly grated orange zest
 1 tablespoon orange juice
 About ½ cup powdered sugar, for rolling

Cover a large countertop area or a large baking sheet with waxed paper.

Steam the apricots over boiling water for 10 minutes. Finely chop the apricots and the nuts by hand or in a food processor. Transfer the apricots and nuts to a medium mixing bowl. Add the coconut, powdered sugar, lemon zest, lemon juice, orange zest, and orange juice and stir until well blended. Shape the mixture into balls ¾ inch in diameter. Roll in the powdered sugar. Place on the waxed paper until dry. Store in an airtight container.

# Apricot Nuggets

## Skill Level: Novice, Super Simple

*With a flavor somewhat like apricot buttercream frosting, these nut-coated candies only get better with age.*

❋ MAKES ABOUT 70

 1 (1-pound) package powdered sugar
 6 tablespoons butter or margarine, softened
 2 tablespoons orange juice
 1 teaspoon vanilla extract
 11 ounces dried apricots, finely ground (about 1½ cups)
 1½ cups finely chopped pecans, for rolling

In a large mixing bowl, combine the powdered sugar, butter, orange juice, and vanilla until thoroughly blended. Stir in the apricots. Knead the mixture by hand until well mixed. Shape the mixture into balls 1 inch in diameter. Roll in the chopped pecans. Store in an airtight container in the refrigerator. These candies taste best after 1 to 2 days in the refrigerator.

# Apricot Tea Balls

## Skill Level: Novice, Super Simple

*In the 1950s, candies made of apricots and oranges were extremely popular, with fruit-flavored balls such as these often appearing at ladies' teas. A food grinder was used to grind the apricots and orange in the '50s, but today's cook can use a food processor.*

❋ MAKES ABOUT 40

20 ounces dried apricots, finely ground
1 peeled, chopped orange, finely ground
2 cups granulated sugar, plus ¾ cup for rolling
½ cup finely chopped pecans

In a medium mixing bowl, combine the apricots, orange, and sugar. Cover and let stand at room temperature 2 to 3 hours. Stir in the pecans. Shape the mixture into balls 1 inch in diameter. Roll the balls in granulated sugar. Store in an airtight container.

# Orange-Nut Tea Balls

### Skill Level: Novice, Super Simple

*Served in small fluted paper cups, these moist and delicious orange balls make a wonderful addition to any dessert table.*
✳MAKES ABOUT 50

12 ounces vanilla wafers
1 (1-pound) package powdered sugar
1 (6-ounce) can frozen orange juice
   concentrate, thawed
½ cup butter or margarine, melted
3 cups finely chopped walnuts or pecans,
   divided

Using a food processor, chop the vanilla wafers until they are very fine crumbs. Transfer the wafer crumbs to a large mixing bowl. Add the powdered sugar, orange juice concentrate, and butter, stirring until blended. Stir in 1 cup of the nuts. Cover and refrigerate until firm enough to handle, 30 minutes to 1 hour.

Working with half the mixture at a time to prevent drying, shape the mixture into balls 1 inch in diameter. Roll each ball in the remaining chopped nuts. Place in an airtight container, separating each layer with waxed paper. Store in the refrigerator up to 1 week or in the freezer up to 1 month. These candies taste best when served cold.

### VARIATIONS
The balls may be rolled in sweetened flaked coconut if preferred. The walnuts or pecans may also be lightly toasted. The butter may be reduced by up to half, though the balls will not be quite as moist.

# Elegant Sparkling Strawberries

### Skill Level: Novice, Easy

*Let your creativity flow with these elegant, sparkling red strawberries. Perfect as a garnish or as a special event candy, these beauties are guaranteed to brighten up any tray.*
✳MAKES ABOUT 40 STRAWBERRIES

1 (14-ounce) can sweetened condensed milk
1 (3-ounce) package strawberry-flavored
   gelatin
2 cups sweetened flaked coconut
1½ to 2 cups finely chopped walnuts or pecans
40 blanched, slivered almonds (about 3.5
   ounces)
2 to 3 drops green food coloring
About ½ cup red decorator sugar, for rolling
About ¼ cup green decorator sugar, for rolling

In a large mixing bowl, combine the milk and strawberry gelatin, stirring until well blended. Stir in the coconut and chopped nuts, blending well. Cover and refrigerate 30 minutes to make the mixture easier to handle.

Place the almonds into a small plastic bag. Add the green food coloring to the bag. Seal tightly and shake until the almonds are tinted to resemble green stems. Remove the almonds from the bag and place them on paper towels to dry.

Pour the red decorator sugar into a small custard cup. Pour the green decorator sugar into another small custard cup. Line a large baking sheet or a 10 × 15-inch jelly roll pan with waxed paper.

Shape the milk mixture into small balls about ¾ inch to 1 inch in diameter. Pinch one end of the ball between the thumb and index finger until it resembles a strawberry. Roll the bottom two-thirds of the strawberry in red decorator sugar. Dip the top end of the strawberry in green decorator sugar. Place a green almond into the green end of the strawberry to resemble a stem. Place on waxed paper. Repeat until all strawberries are shaped. Store in an airtight container in the refrigerator, separating each layer with a sheet of waxed paper. These candies may be frozen for up to 1 month.

COOK'S NOTES: Other versions of this recipe contain varying amounts of coconut and nuts, with most recipes using two to three times as much strawberry gelatin. A few versions also add about 2 tablespoons granulated sugar to the mixture. While I prefer the lighter strawberry flavor that this recipe offers, the ingredients may be adjusted as desired as long as the mixture is thick enough to hold its shape when formed into a strawberry. If needed, a small amount of powdered sugar can be added to the mixture to help it hold its shape.

It is often easier to work with a few strawberries at a time. Dip about 12 shaped strawberries into the red decorator sugar and place them on the waxed paper. When all 12 are coated in red, dip the ends in the green sugar, insert the stems, and place them on the waxed paper again. Repeat until all the mixture is used.

# Cinnamon Walnut Balls

## Skill Level: Novice, Super Simple

*Busy hosts and hostesses will love these moist little cinnamon cakelike balls almost as much as their guests do. With the option to coat the balls in powdered sugar or to leave the cherries peeking out from the walnut-cinnamon mixture, these candies make a grand statement at any gathering.*

✳ MAKES ABOUT 36

> 2 cups very fine vanilla wafer crumbs
> ½ cup finely chopped maraschino cherries
> 1 cup finely chopped walnuts
> ⅓ cup granulated sugar
> ½ teaspoon ground cinnamon
> 1 teaspoon lemon juice
> ⅔ cup sweetened condensed milk
> About ½ cup powdered sugar, for rolling
>   (optional)

Place the crumbs in a large mixing bowl. Add the cherries and walnuts to the crumbs. Stir in the sugar, cinnamon, lemon juice, and milk, blending well.

Shape the mixture into balls 1 inch in diameter. If desired, roll the balls in powdered sugar to decorate. Store in an airtight container in the refrigerator or freezer. Serve slightly chilled or at room temperature.

. . . . . . . . . . . . . . . . . . . . . . . . . . . . .

# Cream Cheese Bonbons

## Skill Level: Novice, Super Simple

*Perfect for a bridal shower or a springtime luncheon, these attractive cream cheese candies can be tinted to match any party theme.*
✳ MAKES ABOUT 24

    1 (3-ounce) package cream cheese, softened
    2½ cups powdered sugar, sifted
    ¼ teaspoon vanilla extract
    Dash salt
    Few drops food coloring
    ½ to 1 cup sweetened flaked coconut, for
       rolling

In a medium bowl, beat the cream cheese by hand or with an electric mixer until smooth. Gradually add the powdered sugar, blending thoroughly. Add the vanilla, salt, and food coloring as desired. Cover and refrigerate 1 hour.

Line a large baking sheet with waxed paper. Shape the mixture into balls ¾ inch in diameter. Roll the balls in the coconut, flattening the tops of the balls slightly if desired. Place on the baking sheet. Cover and refrigerate 1 hour or until firm. Store in an airtight container in the refrigerator.

COOK'S NOTE: If preferred, the coconut used for rolling can also be tinted as desired. To tint the coconut, place the coconut in a small plastic bag and sprinkle lightly with water. Add a few drops of food coloring to the bag. Seal the bag and shake well.

. . . . . . . . . . . . . . . . . . . . . . . . . . . . .

# Date-Nut Balls

## Skill Level: Novice, Easy

*Coated in delicious coconut, these crunchy date balls are an old-time favorite.*
✳ MAKES ABOUT 50

    2 eggs, lightly beaten
    1 cup granulated sugar
    1½ cups chopped pitted dates
    1 teaspoon vanilla extract
    1 tablespoon butter or margarine
    1 cup crisp rice cereal
    1 cup finely chopped pecans
    About 1½ cups sweetened flaked coconut, for
       rolling

Cover a large countertop area or a large baking sheet with waxed paper.

In a heavy 2-quart saucepan over medium-low to medium heat, combine the eggs, sugar, and dates. Cook until thick, about 10 minutes, stirring constantly.

Remove from the heat. Stir in the vanilla and butter. Cool. Stir in the cereal and pecans. Shape the mixture into balls 1 inch in diameter. Roll the balls in the coconut. Place on the lined baking sheet. Let stand until firm. Store in an airtight container.

COOK'S NOTE: For similar recipes, see Humdinger Date Balls (page 144), Frying Pan Cookies (page 232), and Skillet Cookies (page 233).

# Humdinger Date Balls

## Skill Level: Novice, Easy

*Someone should write a self-help book about how to overcome an addiction to these crunchy little candies.*

❋ MAKES ABOUT 50

½ cup butter or margarine
1 cup granulated sugar
8 ounces pitted dates, chopped
1 cup finely chopped pecans
1 teaspoon vanilla extract
1½ cups crisp rice cereal
About 1½ cups powdered sugar,
    for rolling

Cover a large countertop area or a large baking sheet with waxed paper.

In a heavy 2-quart saucepan over medium-low to medium heat, melt the butter. Stir in the sugar, dates, and pecans. Cook, stirring until the sugar melts and the ingredients are thoroughly mixed, thick and well blended, 8 to 10 minutes.

Remove from the heat. Stir in the vanilla and cereal. Cool slightly, about 3 minutes. Shape the mixture into balls 1 inch in diameter. Roll the balls in the powdered sugar. Place on the lined baking sheet to cool. Store in an airtight container.

### VARIATION

*Snowballs:* Add 1 beaten egg to the butter, sugar, and date mixture. Bring to a boil, stirring. Boil, stirring constantly, 4 minutes. Remove from the heat. Stir in the vanilla and 2 cups cereal. Complete as described above, rolling the balls in about 1½ cups sweetened flaked coconut instead of powdered sugar.

COOK'S NOTE: For similar recipes, see Date-Nut Balls (page 143), Frying Pan Cookies (page 232), and Skillet Cookies (page 233).

# Caramel-Raisin Balls

## Skill Level: Novice, Easy

*Filled with chewy raisins and covered in coconut, these little candies are a fruit lover's delight.*

❋ MAKES ABOUT 24

½ cup packed light brown sugar
2 tablespoons butter or margarine
2 tablespoons water
½ teaspoon vanilla extract
¼ cup raisins, chopped
¾ to 1 cup nonfat dry milk
¼ cup sweetened flaked coconut, for rolling

Cover a large countertop area or a large baking sheet with waxed paper.

In a very small saucepan over medium heat, bring the brown sugar, butter, and water to a boil, stirring until the sugar dissolves and the mixture begins to boil. Boil 1 minute.

Remove from the heat. Add the vanilla and raisins. Gradually stir in the milk, mixing well after each addition. Add enough milk that the candy has the consistency of mashed potatoes.

Shape the mixture into balls 1 inch in diameter. Roll each ball in the coconut. Place the balls on waxed paper until firm. Store in an airtight container.

# Marzipan Potatoes

## Skill Level: Novice, Super Simple

*Shaped like miniature potatoes, these rum-flavored, nut-filled candies will be the talk of your next cocktail party.*
✳ MAKES 18 TO 20

1¼ cups finely ground almonds or hazelnuts
1 cup powdered sugar
1 egg yolk, preferably pasteurized, or equivalent egg substitute (see Cook's Note below)
1 tablespoon butter, melted
1 tablespoon rum or cognac
Unsweetened cocoa powder, for dusting

In a medium mixing bowl, combine the nuts, powdered sugar, egg yolk, butter, and rum, stirring to blend. Knead by hand until well blended. Form into a ball. Pinch off small pieces about the size of a walnut and shape into oval-shaped balls that resemble small potatoes. Using a toothpick, poke a few holes into the marzipan potatoes to resemble the eyes on potatoes. Dust generously with cocoa. Place in an airtight container and refrigerate until ready to serve.

COOK'S NOTES: Since this recipe contains a raw egg yolk or egg substitute, these candies should be eaten within 2 days.

Uncooked eggs should not be eaten by young children, the elderly, or anyone with a compromised immune system because they may contain salmonella bacteria that can cause serious illness.

Pasteurized eggs are available in many markets and are safe to eat raw in dishes that are not cooked.

# Bourbon Balls

## Skill Level: Novice, Super Simple

*Anything made with chocolate syrup cannot possibly be bad for you.*
✳ MAKES ABOUT 48

2½ cups very fine vanilla wafer or graham cracker crumbs
1 cup powdered sugar, plus about ¾ cup for rolling
1 cup finely chopped pecans or walnuts
1 tablespoon Hershey's chocolate syrup
3 tablespoons light corn syrup
¼ cup bourbon

Pour the crumbs into a medium mixing bowl. Add the powdered sugar and nuts, stirring until well blended. Stir in the chocolate syrup, corn syrup, and bourbon, mixing thoroughly.

Shape the mixture into balls 1 inch in diameter. Roll the balls in the powdered sugar. Refrigerate in an airtight container until ready to serve.

# Risky Whiskey
# Rumba Balls

## Skill Level: Novice, Super Simple

*This two-timing recipe has two times the flavor.*
✳ MAKES ABOUT 48

> 1 pound vanilla wafers
> 2 cups pecan halves
> 2 cups powdered sugar, plus about ¾ cup for rolling
> 3 tablespoons light corn syrup
> 3 jiggers bourbon or rum (slightly more than ½ cup)

Using a food processor, chop the vanilla wafers until they are very fine crumbs. Transfer the crumbs to a medium mixing bowl. Using a food processor, chop the pecans until they are finely ground. Add the pecans to the crumbs. Stir in the powdered sugar, blending thoroughly.

In a small bowl, combine the corn syrup and bourbon, mixing well. Pour the liquor mixture over the crumb mixture. Blend together thoroughly. Shape the mixture into balls 1 inch in diameter. Roll the balls in the powdered sugar. Refrigerate in an airtight container for 1 week before serving.

# Chocolate Cocktails

## Skill Level: Novice, Super Simple

*These chocolate rum balls give new meaning to the term "happy hour."*
✳ MAKES ABOUT 48

> 3½ cups very fine vanilla wafer crumbs
> 1 cup finely chopped pecans or walnuts
> 1 cup powdered sugar, plus about ¾ cup for rolling
> 3 tablespoons unsweetened cocoa powder
> ⅓ cup light or dark rum
> ⅓ cup light or dark corn syrup

Pour the crumbs into a medium mixing bowl. Stir in the nuts, powdered sugar, and cocoa until well blended. Stir in the rum and corn syrup, mixing well. Shape the mixture into balls 1 inch in diameter. Roll the balls in the powdered sugar. Store in an airtight container.

### VARIATION
*Chocolate Bourbon Balls:* Substitute ⅓ cup bourbon for the rum.

# Dipsy Doodles

## Skill Level: Novice, Super Simple

*Chocolate and Kahlua make an intoxicating combination.*
✳ MAKES ABOUT 48

> 1 pound chocolate wafers
> 1 cup powdered sugar
> 2½ cups finely chopped pecans, divided

⅓ **cup Kahlua coffee liqueur**
⅓ **cup light corn syrup**
**2 teaspoons vanilla extract**

Using a food processor, chop the chocolate wafers until they are very fine crumbs. Transfer to a medium mixing bowl. Add the powdered sugar and 1½ cups of the pecans, stirring until well blended. Stir in the Kahlua and corn syrup, a little at a time, until the mixture is the consistency of cookie dough. Do not let the mixture become too soft. Stir in the vanilla, mixing well.

Using the food processor, chop the remaining 1 cup pecans until they are almost a fine powder. Shape the Kahlua mixture into balls 1 inch in diameter. Roll the balls in the ground pecans. Store in an airtight container.

# Chocolate-Coated Candies

## Coconut Bonbons

### Skill Level: Novice, Easy

*One of my favorite childhood memories is of standing on my tiptoes watching my mother dip her delicious Coconut Bonbons in mouthwatering melted chocolate. This recipe is as popular today as it was decades ago, finding new fans in generation after generation of family and friends.*

✳ **MAKES 100 TO 110 PIECES**

> ½ cup butter or margarine, softened
> 1 (14-ounce) can sweetened condensed milk
> 1½ pounds powdered sugar, sifted
> 1 (7-ounce) package sweetened flaked coconut
> 1 to 2 cups finely chopped pecans
> 14 ounces dark chocolate candy coating
> 4 ounces baking chocolate or semisweet chocolate chips

In a large mixing bowl, combine the butter and milk by hand or with an electric mixer. Gradually add the powdered sugar, blending until smooth. Stir in the coconut and pecans. Cover and chill 2 hours or until firm.

Line 2 large baking sheets with waxed paper. Shape the coconut mixture into balls ¾ inch in diameter. Place the balls on the lined baking sheets. Cover and chill 1 hour or more.

Cover a large countertop area or two large baking sheets with waxed paper.

In the top pan of a double boiler over hot but not boiling water, melt the candy coating and chocolate together, stirring until smooth. Using a toothpick, fork, or specially designed dipping tool, dip the balls into the melted chocolate until coated. Drop the balls onto waxed paper. Let stand until the chocolate is firm. Store in an airtight container.

### VARIATION

*Margaret's Coconut Bonbons:* Use 2 pounds powdered sugar and 4 cups finely chopped pecans, adding ¼ teaspoon salt and 1 teaspoon vanilla to the bonbon mixture. Have an additional 6 ounces semisweet chocolate chips or baking squares and another 1½ tablespoons shortening on hand in case additional chocolate coating is needed. Margaret, my cousin, prefers to make this candy approximately 1 week in advance of serving to allow the flavors to blend.

COOK'S NOTE: For helpful tips, see Dipping Candies in Chocolate (page 23). For alternate chocolate coating recipes, see Chocolate Coatings (page 151).

# Martha Washingtons

## Skill Level: Novice, Easy

*George Washington probably regretted cutting down the cherry tree once he tasted Martha's cherry-filled candy.*

✳ **MAKES ABOUT 150 PIECES**

1 cup butter or margarine, softened
1 (14-ounce) can sweetened condensed milk
2 (1-pound) packages powdered sugar
1 (3.5-ounce) can sweetened flaked coconut
4 cups finely chopped pecans
1 (6-ounce) jar maraschino cherries, well drained and finely chopped
20 ounces dark chocolate candy coating
4 ounces baking chocolate or semisweet chocolate chips

In a large mixing bowl, combine the butter and milk by hand or with an electric mixer. Gradually add the powdered sugar, blending until smooth. Stir in the coconut, pecans, and cherries. Cover and chill 2 hours, or until firm.

Line 2 large baking sheets with waxed paper. Shape the mixture into balls ¾ inch in diameter. Place the balls on the lined baking sheet. Cover and chill 1 hour or more.

Cover a large countertop area or 2 large baking sheets with waxed paper.

In the top pan of a double boiler over hot but not boiling water, melt the candy coating and chocolate together, stirring until smooth. Using a toothpick, fork, or specially designed dipping tool, dip each ball into the melted chocolate until coated. Drop onto the waxed paper. Let stand until the chocolate is firm. Store in an airtight container.

**COOK'S NOTE:** For helpful tips, see Dipping Candies in Chocolate (page 23). For alternate chocolate coating recipes, see Chocolate Coatings (page 151).

# Chocolate Cherry Coconut Drops

## Skill Level: Novice, Easy

*Martha Washingtons (at left) are a very similar candy. This one has less sugar and pecans but more coconut. With two versions to try, surely one of these candies will find its way to your next holiday celebration.*

✳ **MAKES ABOUT 150 PIECES**

½ cup butter or margarine, softened
1 cup sweetened condensed milk
1 (1-pound) package powdered sugar
2 (7-ounce) cans sweetened flaked coconut
2 cups finely chopped pecans
1 cup maraschino cherries, well drained and finely chopped
20 ounces dark chocolate candy coating
4 ounces baking chocolate or semisweet chocolate chips

In a large mixing bowl, combine the butter and milk by hand or with an electric mixer. Gradually add the powdered sugar, blending until smooth. Stir in the coconut, pecans, and cherries. Cover and chill 2 hours, or until firm.

Line 2 large baking sheets with waxed paper. Shape the mixture into balls ¾ inch in di-

# Chocolate Coatings

The combination of products used for chocolate candy coatings is often a matter of personal preference and product availability. Old-fashioned candies were dipped in a fairly common recipe of 12 ounces semisweet chocolate melted with 2 ounces of paraffin wax, which produces a shiny, medium-firm coating, but paraffin wax is no longer approved for use in candies and other foods.

Another of the older methods is to use melted chocolate-flavored almond bark. A few people mix chocolate almond bark with semisweet chips, letting the almond bark substitute for the paraffin wax. I have only seen this combination used in a few recipes and personally prefer other options.

Most new or updated candy recipes rely on premixed candy coating products that include both chocolate and a firming agent. These products require no decision making whatsoever. Just melt the chocolate and dip. Most of these coatings dry in a matter of minutes, if not seconds, making them very convenient to use.

Chocolate candy–coating products have been on grocery store shelves in some cities for several years but are just now reaching the heartland. Coating products are available in dark chocolate, milk chocolate, and white chocolate, as well as imitation chocolate. Some of the brand names are Baker's, Ghirardelli, Nestle's, Bakel's, a Swedish product usually available only in specialty stores, and Merckens, available on the Internet.

Some candy-coating products produce a very thin, crisp outer shell that is loved by some but not by all. When used for truffles, very thin coatings can sometimes crack as they cool, most likely because the truffle centers are still frozen when dropped into the chocolate. If this occurs, let the melted chocolate cool slightly before dipping more candies. Be aware that the cooler the chocolate, the thicker the chocolate shell will be.

Some coating products can become quite hard or brittle when refrigerated and are best served at room temperature, creating a slight dilemma for those of us who like our candies served cold. To create a softer, less crunchy coating, I often combine approximately 10 ounces of dark chocolate candy-coating pieces with 2 to 4 ounces of semisweet baking chocolate. Of course, the more baking chocolate added, the softer the coating becomes.

When creating a custom blend, test a few candies before dipping the entire batch. If needed, add more candy coating chips to make the chocolate firmer, or add slightly more baking chocolate or chocolate chips to make it softer.

White chocolate lovers should be aware that white chocolate chips are nearly impossible to melt into a smooth liquid form. If a white chocolate coating is desired, use white chocolate candy coating (preferred) or a combination of white chocolate baking squares melted with solid vegetable shortening.

The recipes on the following page will cover approximately sixty candies. The exact number of candies that can be covered may vary, depending upon the size of the candies and the thickness or temperature of the chocolate. Most experienced candy makers will say that it is always a good idea to have a little extra chocolate on hand in case your candies need slightly more coating than a recipe indicates.

These are just a few of the coating combinations that have appeared in candy recipes I have gathered over time. These examples can serve as a starting point for helping new candy makers develop their own special blend for chocolate coatings. Adventurous candy makers may want to experiment with the more expensive gourmet chocolates after researching a method known as tempering (not covered in this cookbook).

Remember that all chocolate should be melted slowly over low heat, preferably in the top pan of a double boiler over hot but not boiling water. It may also be melted in the microwave if carefully watched. The firmness of candy-coating products may vary with individual brands.

For more information, see Dipping Candies in Chocolate (page 23).

# Chocolate Coatings

### SUPERFIRM CANDY COATING

* 12 ounces chocolate candy coating squares or chips

### FIRM CANDY COATING

* 10 ounces chocolate candy coating squares or chips
* 2 ounces semisweet chocolate chips or baking squares

### SEMIFIRM CANDY COATING

* 8 ounces chocolate candy coating squares or chips
* 4 ounces semisweet chocolate chips or baking squares

### SOFT SEMISWEET COATING
#### (requires refrigeration)

* 12 ounces semisweet chocolate chips or baking squares
* 2 tablespoons plus 2 teaspoons
* 1 tablespoon solid vegetable shortening

### ALMOND BARK COATING

* 12 ounces chocolate almond bark

### SWEET CHOCOLATE COATING

* 3 (4-ounce) packages German's sweet chocolate

### BUTTERY CHOCOLATE COATING
#### (requires refrigeration)

* 10 ounces bittersweet chocolate
* 8 tablespoons butter

### JANE'S SEMIFIRM CUSTOM COATING

* 2 to 3 handfuls Bakel's dark chocolate coating chips
* 1 handful Nestle's milk chocolate coating chips
* 1 to 2 ounces semisweet baking chocolate

### LYNDA'S FIRM CUSTOM COATING

* 6 ounces Bakel's dark chocolate coating chips
* 6 ounces Ghirardelli Double Chocolate Candy Making & Dipping Bar

### WHITE CHOCOLATE DECORATIVE DRIZZLE
#### (see Luscious Raspberry-Fudge Truffles [page 177])

* 3 ounces white baking chocolate
* 1 tablespoon solid vegetable shortening

ameter. Place the balls on the lined baking sheet. Cover and chill 1 hour or more.

Cover a large countertop area or 2 large baking sheets with waxed paper.

In the top pan of a double boiler over hot but not boiling water, melt the candy coating and chocolate together, stirring until smooth. Using a toothpick, fork, or specially designed dipping tool, dip each ball into the melted chocolate until coated. Drop onto the waxed paper. Let stand until the chocolate is firm. Store in an airtight container.

COOK'S NOTE: For helpful tips, see Dipping Candies in Chocolate (page 23). For alternate chocolate coating recipes, see Chocolate Coatings (page 151).

. . . . . . . . . . . . . . . . . . . . . . . .

# Cheery Cherry Date Balls

## Skill Level: Novice, Easy

*This recipe puts a new twist on Martha Washingtons (page 149) by adding dates and candied cherries rather than coconut and maraschino cherries.*

✳ MAKES ABOUT 150 PIECES

   1 cup butter or margarine, softened
   1 (14-ounce) can sweetened condensed milk
   2 (1-pound) packages powdered sugar
   1 teaspoon vanilla extract
   2 cups finely chopped pecans
   1 pound pitted dates, finely chopped
   6 ounces candied cherries, finely chopped
   20 ounces dark chocolate candy coating
   4 ounces baking chocolate or semisweet
      chocolate chips

In a large mixing bowl, combine the butter and milk by hand or with an electric mixer. Gradually add the powdered sugar, blending until smooth. Stir in the vanilla, pecans, dates, and cherries. Cover and chill 2 hours, or until firm.

Line 2 large baking sheets with waxed paper. Shape the mixture into balls ¾ inch in diameter. Place the balls on the baking sheet. Cover and chill 1 hour or more.

Cover a large countertop area or 2 large baking sheets with waxed paper.

In the top pan of a double boiler over hot but not boiling water, melt the candy coating and chocolate together, stirring until smooth. Using a toothpick, fork, or specially designed dipping tool, dip the balls into the melted chocolate until coated. Drop onto the waxed paper. Let stand until the chocolate is firm. Store in an airtight container.

COOK'S NOTE: For helpful tips, see Dipping Candies in Chocolate (page 23). For alternate chocolate coating recipes, see Chocolate Coatings (page 151).

. . . . . . . . . . . . . . . . . . . . . . . .

# Chocolate Fudge Drops

## Skill Level: Novice, Easy

*The only thing better than chocolate coated in chocolate is chocolate and nuts coated in chocolate.*

✳ MAKES ABOUT 50 PIECES

   1 (1-pound) package powdered sugar
   ¼ cup unsweetened cocoa powder
   ½ cup butter or margarine, softened
   1 (14-ounce) can sweetened condensed milk

1 teaspoon vanilla extract

1½ cups finely chopped pecans or walnuts

1 10-ounce package dark chocolate candy coating

2 ounces baking chocolate or semisweet chocolate chips

In a medium bowl, combine the powdered sugar and cocoa, stirring to blend.

In a large mixing bowl, combine the butter and milk by hand or with an electric mixer. Gradually add the powdered sugar mixture, blending until smooth. Stir in the vanilla and nuts. Cover and chill 2 hours or until firm.

Line 2 large baking sheets with waxed paper. Shape the mixture into balls ¾ to 1 inch in diameter. Place the balls on the lined baking sheets. Cover and chill 1 hour or more.

Cover a large countertop area or 2 large baking sheets with waxed paper.

In the top pan of a double boiler over hot but not boiling water, melt the candy coating and chocolate together, stirring until smooth. Using a toothpick, fork, or specially designed dipping tool, dip each ball into the melted chocolate. Drop onto the waxed paper. Let stand until the chocolate is firm. Store in an airtight container.

### VARIATION

*Chocolate-Nut Drops:* Omit the unsweetened cocoa powder. Use only 1 cup sweetened condensed milk.

COOK'S NOTES: For a slightly firmer filling, add an additional ½ cup to ¾ cup powdered sugar to the filling mixture or use only 1 cup sweetened condensed milk.

If desired, an additional 1 tablespoon unsweetened cocoa powder may be added to give the candy a deeper chocolate flavor.

For helpful tips, see Dipping Candies in Chocolate (page 23). For alternate chocolate coating recipes, see Chocolate Coatings (page 151).

# Crispy Peanut Butter Balls

## Skill Level: Novice, Easy

*Something about these crunchy little nuggets is just too good to resist. Make an extra-large batch, because these old favorites have a way of disappearing quickly.*

✳ MAKES ABOUT 70 PIECES

2 cups creamy or crunchy peanut butter

½ cup butter or margarine, softened

1 (1-pound) package powdered sugar

1 teaspoon vanilla extract

2 cups crisp rice cereal

10 ounces dark chocolate candy coating

2 ounces baking chocolate or semisweet chocolate chips

Line a large baking sheet with waxed paper.

In a large mixing bowl, combine the peanut butter and butter by hand or with an electric mixer. Gradually add the powdered sugar and vanilla, blending until smooth. If the mixture appears dry and crumbly, knead by hand until smooth. Stir in the cereal. Shape into balls 1 inch in diameter. Place the balls on the lined baking sheet. Freeze 10 to 20 minutes or while preparing the chocolate coating.

Cover a large area of the countertop or 2 large baking sheets with waxed paper.

In the top pan of a double boiler over hot

but not boiling water, melt the candy coating and chocolate together, stirring until smooth. Using a toothpick, fork, or specially designed dipping tool, dip the chilled balls in the melted chocolate until coated. Drop onto the waxed paper. Let stand until the chocolate is firm. Store in an airtight container.

### VARIATION

*Crispy Hazelnut Balls:* Substitute Nutella hazelnut spread for the peanut butter. Omit the vanilla extract.

COOK'S NOTE: For helpful tips, see Dipping Candies in Chocolate (page 23). For alternate chocolate coating recipes, see Chocolate Coatings (page 151).

# Buckeyes

## Skill Level: Novice, Easy

*A much-loved favorite, these deliciously smooth "peanut butter eyeballs" are the perfect treat for little ghosts and goblins.*

✳ MAKES ABOUT 38 PIECES

 1 cup creamy peanut butter
 ¼ cup butter or margarine, softened
 1 teaspoon vanilla extract
 2½ to 3 cups powdered sugar
 5 ounces dark chocolate candy coating
 1 ounce baking chocolate or semisweet
    chocolate chips

Line a large baking sheet with waxed paper.

In a large mixing bowl, combine the peanut butter, butter, and vanilla by hand or with an electric mixer. Gradually add the powdered sugar, blending until smooth and mixture can be shaped into balls. Shape into balls ¾ to 1 inch in diameter. Place the balls on the lined baking sheet. Cover and chill or freeze 20 minutes or longer.

Cover a large countertop area or a large baking sheet with waxed paper.

In the top pan of a double boiler over hot but not boiling water, melt the candy coating and chocolate together, stirring until smooth. Insert a toothpick into the top of each ball and dip the bottom two-thirds of each ball into the melted chocolate, leaving the top one-third uncoated. (If preferred, the entire ball may be coated in chocolate.) Carefully slide the balls onto waxed paper so the undipped portion is pointed upwards. Remove the toothpick. Using a knife or metal spatula, smooth over the hole left by the toothpick. Let stand until the chocolate is firm. Store in an airtight container.

COOK'S NOTES: The peanut butter filling is very soft. For a firmer filling, add more powdered sugar.

For helpful tips, see Dipping Candies in Chocolate (page 23). For alternate chocolate coating recipes, see Chocolate Coatings (page 151).

# Golf Balls

## Skill Level: Novice, Easy

*These nutty peanut butter candies may remind you of one of your favorite candy bars.*

✳ MAKES ABOUT 60 PIECES

1 cup creamy peanut butter
1 cup butter or margarine, softened
2⅓ cups graham cracker crumbs
1 (1-pound) package powdered sugar
1½ cups chopped salted roasted peanuts
10 ounces dark chocolate candy coating
2 ounce baking chocolate or semisweet
    chocolate chips

Line a large baking sheet with waxed paper.

In a large mixing bowl, combine the peanut butter and butter by hand or with an electric mixer. Gradually add the crumbs and powdered sugar, blending until smooth. Stir in the peanuts. Shape into balls 1 inch in diameter. Place the balls on the lined baking sheet. Cover and freeze 1 hour or more.

Cover a large countertop area or a large baking sheet with waxed paper.

In the top pan of a double boiler over hot but not boiling water, melt the candy coating and chocolate together, stirring until smooth. Using a toothpick, fork, or specially designed dipping tool, dip the frozen balls into the melted chocolate until coated. Drop onto the lined baking sheet. Let stand until the chocolate is firm. Store in an airtight container.

COOK'S NOTE: For helpful tips, see Dipping Candies in Chocolate (page 23). For alternate chocolate coating recipes, see Chocolate Coatings (page 151).

# Peanut Butter-Date Balls

## Skill Level: Novice, Easy

*The unusual combination of peanut butter, dates, and pecans is a real treat for date lovers.*

✳ MAKES ABOUT 36 PIECES

1 cup creamy peanut butter
1 tablespoon butter or margarine, softened
1 cup powdered sugar
2 teaspoons vanilla extract
1½ cups chopped pitted dates
½ cup finely chopped pecans
8 ounces dark chocolate candy coating
2 ounces baking chocolate or semisweet
    chocolate chips

Line a large baking sheet with waxed paper.

In a large mixing bowl, combine the peanut butter and butter by hand or with an electric mixer. Gradually add the powdered sugar, blending until smooth. Stir in the vanilla, dates, and pecans. Shape into balls ¾ to 1 inch in diameter. Place the balls on the lined baking sheet. Cover and chill 30 minutes or more.

Cover a large countertop area or a large baking sheet with waxed paper.

In the top pan of a double boiler over hot but not boiling water, melt the candy coating and chocolate together, stirring until smooth. Using a toothpick, fork, or specially designed dipping tool, dip each ball into the melted chocolate until coated. Drop onto the lined baking sheet. Let stand until the chocolate is firm. Store in an airtight container.

COOK'S NOTE: For helpful tips, see Dipping Candies in Chocolate (page 23). For alternate chocolate coating recipes, see Chocolate Coatings (page 151).

# Toasted Coconut Chocolate Drops

## Skill Level: Novice, Easy

*The combination of soft, fluffy marshmallow filling mixed with crispy, toasted coconut gives this candy an interesting contrast in textures.*

✳ **MAKES ABOUT 45 PIECES**

> 1 (3.5-ounce) can sweetened flaked coconut
> ½ (7-ounce) jar marshmallow creme (1 cup)
> ½ teaspoon vanilla extract
> Dash of salt
> 10 ounces dark chocolate candy coating
> 2 ounces baking chocolate or semisweet chocolate chips

Preheat the oven to 350°F. Spread the coconut across the bottom of a shallow pan. Toast the coconut about 8 minutes or until golden brown, watching carefully and stirring halfway through cooking. Cool.

In a large mixing bowl, combine the marshmallow creme, vanilla, salt, and coconut, stirring until well blended. Cover and chill 30 minutes or more (see Cook's Notes).

Line a large baking sheet with waxed paper. With lightly buttered hands, form the marshmallow mixture into balls ¾ inch in diameter. Cover and chill or freeze 30 minutes or more.

Cover a large countertop area or a large baking sheet with waxed paper.

In the top pan of a double boiler over hot but not boiling water, melt the candy coating and chocolate together, stirring until smooth. Using a toothpick, fork, or specially designed dipping tool, dip the chilled balls into the melted chocolate until coated. Drop onto the waxed paper. Let stand until the chocolate is firm. Store in an airtight container.

COOK'S NOTES: The marshmallow creme mixture remains very soft and can be difficult to shape into balls. As an alternative, drop small amounts of the mixture onto the lined baking sheet from the tip of a buttered spoon. Cover and freeze about 30 minutes. The frozen mixture can then be rolled into a ball more easily.

For helpful tips, see Dipping Candies in Chocolate (page 23). For alternate chocolate coating recipes, see Chocolate Coatings (page 151).

# Chocolate-Covered Haystacks

## Skill Level: Average

*Extra coconut and granulated sugar instead of brown, give these chocolate-covered haystacks a different taste and texture than Coconut Haystacks (page 66).*

✳ **MAKES ABOUT 24**

> ⅔ cup granulated sugar
> 3 tablespoons water
> 1 cup plus 1 tablespoon light corn syrup
> 4 cups sweetened flaked coconut
> 1½ cups (9 ounces) semisweet chocolate chips

Cover a large countertop area or a large baking sheet with waxed paper.

In a heavy 1-quart saucepan over medium heat, bring the sugar, water, and corn syrup to a boil, stirring until the sugar dissolves and the mixture begins to boil. Cook, without stirring, to the soft ball stage (234°F to 240°F, with 236°F recommended).

Remove from the heat. Stir in the coconut until well blended. Quickly drop by spoonfuls onto the waxed paper. To create the haystacks, dip your fingers into cold water and shape the candy into cones 1½ inches high while the candy is still warm. In the top pan of a double boiler over hot but not boiling water, melt the chocolate chips, stirring until smooth.

Spoon the melted chocolate over the top of candies. Let stand until the chocolate is firm. Cool. Store in an airtight container.

. . . . . . . . . . . . . . . . . . . . . . . . .

# Kentucky Bourbon Balls

## Skill Level: Novice, Easy

*Perfect for a New Year's Eve or Derby Day celebration, these chocolate-coated, nut-filled candies have just the right amount of bourbon flavor.*

✳ MAKES ABOUT 50 PIECES

    **1 cup finely chopped pecans or walnuts**
    **½ cup bourbon**
    **½ cup butter, softened**
    **1 (1-pound) package powdered sugar**
    **½ teaspoon vanilla extract**
    **10 ounces dark chocolate candy coating**
    **2 ounces baking chocolate or semisweet**
        **chocolate chips**

In a small bowl, combine the nuts and bourbon. Cover and let stand at room temperature at least 2 hours, preferably 8 hours, so the nuts can absorb the bourbon.

In a large mixing bowl, combine the butter, powdered sugar, and vanilla by hand or with an electric mixer. Stir in the pecans and bourbon. Cover and freeze 1 hour or more.

Line a large baking sheet with waxed paper. Shape the mixture into balls ¾ inch in diameter. Place the balls on the lined baking sheet. Cover and freeze 1 hour or until firm.

Cover a large countertop area or a baking sheet with waxed paper.

In the top pan of a double boiler over hot but not boiling water, melt the candy coating and chocolate together, stirring until smooth. Using a toothpick, fork, or specially designed dipping tool, dip the frozen balls into the melted chocolate until coated. Drop onto the lined baking sheet. Let stand until the chocolate is firm. Store in an airtight container.

COOK'S NOTE: For helpful tips, see Dipping Candies in Chocolate (page 23). For alternate chocolate coating recipes, see Chocolate Coatings (page 151).

. . . . . . . . . . . . . . . . . . . . . . . . .

# Almond Coffee Walnuts

## Skill Level: Novice, Easy

*Perfect for entertaining, these elegant dipped walnuts are a favorite dessert with Aunt Shirley, a legendary hostess and seasoned gourmet.*

✳ MAKES 36

    **⅔ cup almond paste**
    **2 tablespoons coffee liqueur**
    **1 tablespoon instant espresso powder**
    **72 walnut halves, toasted**
    **1½ cups (9 ounces) semisweet baking**
        **chocolate, coarsely chopped**

In a small bowl, combine the almond paste, liqueur, and espresso, blending until smooth. Spread about ½ teaspoon of the mixture onto the flat side of one walnut half. Place another walnut half on top of the filling, pressing lightly so that the filling holds the two halves together. Repeat until all the walnut halves are used.

Cover a large countertop area or a large baking sheet with waxed paper.

In the top pan of a double boiler over hot but not boiling water, melt the chocolate, stirring until smooth. Dip one half of the filled walnuts into the melted chocolate. Place on the waxed paper. Let stand until the chocolate is firm. Store in an airtight container in the refrigerator up to 1 week.

. . . . . . . . . . . . . . . . . . . . . . . . . . . .

# Chocolate-Dipped Strawberries

## Skill Level: Novice, Super Simple

*So easy, so romantic, and so delectable, this recipe is too good not to share. These delightful strawberries are the perfect ending to a candlelit dinner for two. This recipe is especially delicious when made with Triple Sec or Grand Marnier.*

✳ MAKES 8 TO 10 STRAWBERRIES

**8 to 10 fresh medium strawberries**
**1 ounce semisweet chocolate baking square**
**1 tablespoon evaporated milk**
**1 teaspoon orange or almond liqueur or**
    **⅛ teaspoon vanilla extract**

Leaving the green stems intact, wash, drain, and completely dry the strawberries by patting with a paper towel. Line a small or medium baking sheet with waxed paper.

In the top pan of a double boiler over hot but not boiling water, melt the chocolate, milk, and liqueur together, stirring until smooth. Insert a toothpick into the stem end of the strawberries and dip the lower two-thirds of the berries into the chocolate. Drop the berries onto the lined baking sheet. Let stand until the chocolate is firm. Serve immediately or lightly cover and refrigerate until ready to serve, storing no more than 4 to 8 hours. The berries can be refrigerated for up to 2 days but may lose their eye appeal when stored more than a few hours.

COOK'S NOTES: Work very quickly if doubling the recipe. The chocolate will become grainy if it is heated too long or held at too high a temperature.

Instead of using a large double boiler to melt the chocolate, create a small double boiler by placing a small glass dish into a pan of hot water. This method often makes dipping easier when working with small amounts of chocolate. Do not allow the water to seep into the chocolate mixture.

To make white chocolate–dipped strawberries, substitute white chocolate or white chocolate coating for the semisweet chocolate.

To keep the berries from having a flat side, turn a plastic colander upside down and place the toothpicks holding the dipped berries into the holes of the colander. Place the colander filled with berries into the refrigerator until ready to serve.

. . . . . . . . . . . . . . . . . . . . . . . . . . . .

# Chocolate-Covered Cherries

## Skill Level: Novice, Easy

*Just a few of these fondant-coated cherries will brighten up anyone's day.*
✳ MAKES ABOUT 40 CHERRIES

> 1 (16-ounce) jar maraschino cherries with stems
> 3 tablespoons butter, softened
> 3 tablespoons light corn syrup
> ¼ teaspoon salt
> 2 cups powdered sugar
> 10 ounces dark chocolate candy coating
> 2 ounces baking chocolate or semisweet chocolate chips

Leaving the stems intact, wash, drain, and completely dry the cherries by patting with a paper towel. Line a large baking sheet with waxed paper.

In a medium bowl, combine the butter, corn syrup, and salt. Gradually add the powdered sugar, stirring until smooth. Knead by hand until the fondant is smooth and creamy. Pinch off a small amount and shape around each cherry. Place on the lined baking sheet. Cover and chill 1 hour or until firm.

Cover a large countertop area or a large baking sheet with waxed paper.

In the top pan of a double boiler over hot but not boiling water, melt the candy coating and chocolate together, stirring until smooth. Hold each cherry by the stem and dip into the melted chocolate until coated. Place on the lined baking sheet. Let stand until the chocolate is firm. Store in an airtight container. The cherries will keep up to 1 week in the refrigerator.

## VARIATION

*Stuffed Cherries:* Rinse and dry the cherries as directed, removing the stems. Using the tip of a sharp knife or kitchen shears, carefully cut a small X in the top of each cherry. Pinch off a small amount of the fondant and stuff it into the center cavity of each cherry. Roll the cherries in granulated sugar or red decorator's sugar if desired. Store in an airtight container. Serve within 1 to 2 days.

COOK'S NOTES: This recipe can be reduced to make just a few cherries at a time using the melted chocolate left over from another chocolate-dipped candy recipe.

For helpful tips, see Dipping Candies in Chocolate (page 23). For alternate chocolate coating recipes, see Chocolate Coatings (page 151).

# Aunt Mary's Turtles

## Skill Level: Novice, Easy

*Hardly a Father's Day passed without one of us kids buying my father a box of his favorite chocolate-covered turtles, but only because we did not have my aunt Mary's recipe. If my father were here today, he would undoubtedly prefer to have this homemade version.*
✳ MAKES ABOUT 30 PIECES

> 1 (14-ounce) package caramels
> 3 tablespoons evaporated milk
> 2 cups pecans in large pieces
> 14 ounces dark chocolate candy coating
> 3 ounces baking chocolate or semisweet chocolate chips

Generously butter a large baking sheet.

Unwrap the caramels. In a heavy 2-quart saucepan, melt the caramels and milk together over low heat, stirring until smooth. Stir in the pecans until well coated. Drop the caramel-nut mixture by spoonfuls onto the buttered baking sheet. (Do not drop the uncoated caramel centers onto waxed paper. The waxed paper will adhere to the caramel and be very difficult to remove.) Chill until set, about 30 minutes to 1 hour.

Cover a large countertop area or a large baking sheet with waxed paper.

In the top pan of a double boiler over hot but not boiling water, melt the chocolate and shortening together, stirring until smooth. Using a toothpick, fork, or specially designed dipping tool, dip the chilled caramel-nut centers into the melted chocolate until coated. Drop onto the waxed paper. Let stand until the chocolate is firm. Store in an airtight container.

### VARIATION

*Margaret's Turtles:* Substitute 4 teaspoons whole milk for the evaporated milk.

COOK'S NOTES: Use a large metal spatula to remove the chilled caramel centers from the baking sheet.

For helpful tips, see Dipping Candies in Chocolate (page 23). For alternate chocolate coating recipes, see Chocolate Coatings (page 151).

# Blue Ribbon Turtles

### Skill Level: Novice, Easy

*Simple and delicious, these turtles took first prize honors in the 1970* Ponca City News *recipe contest.*
✳ MAKES 18 PIECES

**72 pecan halves**
**36 caramels, unwrapped**
**2 to 4 ounces semisweet chocolate baking squares**

Line a large baking sheet with aluminum foil; butter the foil. Preheat the oven to 325°F.

Place the pecans on the foil-lined baking sheet, arranging the pecan halves in X-shaped groups of four. Press the caramels by hand until slightly flattened. Place 2 caramels on top of each cluster, lightly pressing the caramels into the pecans. Heat the clusters in the oven 5 to 8 minutes or until the caramels soften. Remove from the oven and place the baking sheet on a wire rack. If needed, use a buttered spatula to spread the softened caramels over the pecans. Cool.

Cover a large countertop area with waxed paper. Remove the clusters from the baking sheet and place on the waxed paper.

In the top pan of a double boiler over hot but not boiling water, melt the chocolate, stirring until smooth. Brush the tops of the clusters with the melted chocolate. Let stand until the chocolate is firm. Store in an airtight container.

### VARIATION

*Caramel Pecan Clusters:* Use 24 caramels in place of 36 caramels. Arrange the pecan halves in clusters of three. Lightly press one caramel into the center of each pecan cluster. Complete the recipe as described above. Makes 24 candies.

COOK'S NOTE: The chocolate may be melted in the microwave if preferred.

# Gordon's Christmas Caramels

## Skill Level: Novice, Easy

*This fun recipe was invented when a family member casually dropped a few leftover caramels in some leftover melted chocolate and then tossed a few decorator sprinkles on top to add a little pizzazz. Gordon's invention was so popular that these caramels became a holiday tradition to be shared with family and friends throughout Louisiana. Let the kids have a turn and see how creative they can be.*

✳ MAKES ABOUT 52 PIECES

1 (14-ounce) package caramels
10 ounces dark chocolate candy coating
2 ounces baking chocolate or semisweet chocolate chips
Multicolored decorator sprinkles, chocolate decorator sprinkles, or colored decorator's sugar

Unwrap the caramels and set aside. Line a large countertop area or a large baking sheet with waxed paper.

In the top pan of a double boiler over hot but not boiling water, melt the candy coating and chocolate together, stirring until smooth. Using a fork or a specially designed dipping tool, dip the caramels in the melted chocolate until coated. Drop onto the waxed paper. Sprinkle the top of the caramels with decorative sprinkles while the chocolate is still warm. Let stand until the chocolate is firm. Store in an airtight container.

COOK'S NOTE: For helpful tips, see Dipping Candies in Chocolate (page 23). For alternate chocolate coating recipes, see Chocolate Coatings (page 151).

# Fondants

## Old-Fashioned Cooked Fondant

### Skill Level: Advanced

*Adventurous candy makers will love this old recipe from Kansas State University's 1942 cookbook because of the many ways this candy can be made. Keep in mind that this is a basic recipe and that the ingredients, flavorings, and methods may change based upon the type of candy desired. Read all instructions before beginning, choosing the combination of options that will produce the candy you desire. Suggested flavorings are vanilla extract, almond extract, strawberry extract, rum extract, maple extract, or butter flavoring.*

✳ **MAKES ABOUT 1 CUP**

**1 cup granulated sugar**
**½ cup water**
**1/16 teaspoon cream of tartar or 1 tablespoon light corn syrup**
**¼ to ½ teaspoon flavoring of choice**
**Few drops of food coloring as desired**
**2 to 4 tablespoons chopped nuts, chopped candied fruits, or sweetened flaked coconut (optional)**

In a small saucepan, combine the sugar, water, and cream of tartar, stirring until the sugar dissolves. Bring to a boil over medium heat, stirring until the sugar dissolves and the mixture begins to boil. Cover and cook 2 to 3 minutes to dissolve the sugar crystals on the sides of the pan. Remove the lid. Cook, without stirring, to the soft ball stage (234°F to 240°F, with 238°F recommended). Just before the candy reaches the desired temperature, rinse a platter with cold water; dry thoroughly.

Remove the boiling mixture from the heat. Pour onto the cool platter. Cool to 110°F, about 30 minutes. Work the mixture back and forth on the platter by hand until it is white and creamy, and then knead the candy by hand until it is perfectly smooth. Working the candy mixture can take 30 minutes or more. Professionals often use a special flat tool that looks somewhat like a scraper, scraping the candy on one side, lifting it up, and folding it over, and then scraping it on the other side, lifting it up, and folding it over.

Place the smooth, kneaded fondant into a bowl or an airtight container. Cover tightly. Let the fondant stand to ripen at room temperature at least 24 hours before using. The fondant may be stored several days if tightly covered. If the fondant becomes dry, place a damp cloth over it until it softens again. If the fondant sugars, add ⅞ cup water and cook it again.

When the fondant has ripened 24 hours, knead it by hand until it is soft and pliable, flavoring it as desired. Tint the fondant with a few drops of food coloring, if desired.

At this point, other ingredients, such as nuts, may be worked into the candy by hand, kneading the fondant only enough to mix the ingredients. The candy is now ready to shape or mold as desired.

**FINISHED FONDANT VARIATIONS**

*To Shape Bonbons:* Shape the ripened fondant into small balls. Place the balls on waxed paper and let stand until firm but not dry. If desired, dip the bonbons into melted chocolate. See Chocolate Coatings (page 151) for options. For useful tips, see Dipping Candies in Chocolate (page 23). Recipes found in Chocolate-Coated Candies (pages 148 to 161) can be used as examples. If desired, decorate the plain or chocolate-coated bonbons with chopped nuts or other candies. Store in an airtight container.

*To Mold a Cream Loaf:* Mold the ripened fondant into a small buttered loaf pan. Let the fondant stand, uncovered, until firm. Cover and slice as needed.

*To Mold a Marbled Cream Loaf:* Divide the ripened fondant into 2 or 3 portions and tint each a different color. (For example, tint 1 portion pink, 1 portion yellow, and leave 1 portion white.) Press the different colors together, twisting slightly to create a marbled effect, and place in a small buttered loaf pan. If preferred, layer the different colors of fondant when pressing into the buttered pan. Let the fondant stand, uncovered, until firm. Cover and slice as needed.

*To Make Cream Mints:* In the top pan of a double boiler over hot but not boiling water, heat about 1 cup of the ripened fondant at a time until the fondant is melted. Stir the fondant as little as possible. If the fondant does not melt rapidly, add a very small amount of water. Flavor the fondant with peppermint, wintergreen, clove, cinnamon, orange oil, or as desired. Tint the fondant using a few drops of food coloring if desired. Stir the fondant as little as possible when adding flavoring and coloring. Drop from the tip of a spoon onto waxed paper. Cool completely. If desired, dip the cream mints into melted chocolate. See Chocolate Coatings (page 151) for options. For useful tips, see Dipping Candies in Chocolate (page 23). Store in an airtight container.

**FONDANT COOKING VARIATIONS**

*To Make Easy Fondant:* Make the recipe and cool as directed. Spread 1 stiffly beaten egg white over the cooled fondant. Work the fondant back and forth in the saucepan used for cooking. Add the flavoring and form the fondant into the desired candy as soon as it is smooth and creamy, allowing the fondant to ripen in its finished form. (See Cook's Note about eating uncooked eggs on page 145.)

*To Make Bonbons:* Add ⅛ teaspoon glycerin as the fondant mixture comes to a boil. (Glycerin can be purchased in the pharmacy section of most large grocery stores.) Glycerin produces a very soft, fluffy fondant that is wonderful but sometimes difficult to handle. If adding glycerin to this recipe, do not allow the fondant to ripen 24 hours. Fondants that contain glycerin must be immediately worked back and forth after being poured onto the rinsed platter. If allowed to stand, they will soften and become difficult to handle.

**FONDANT FLAVOR VARIATIONS**

*Maple Fondant:* Decrease the water to ⅓ cup. Add ⅓ cup maple syrup.

*Caramel Fondant:* Decrease the water to ⅓ cup. Add ⅓ cup caramel syrup.

*Coffee Fondant:* Substitute clear, strong coffee for water.

*Brown Sugar Fondant:* Use ½ cup granulated sugar and ½ cup packed light brown sugar.

*Opera Cream Fondant:* Substitute heavy whipping cream for the water. Cook this option in a heavy aluminum saucepan to prevent scorching.

*Chocolate Fondant:* Add 1 to 2 ounces melted semisweet baking chocolate to finished fondant. Knead the candy by hand until well blended.

# Creamy Bonbon Fondant

## Skill Level: Advanced

*This soft, luscious fondant combines several options found under Old-Fashioned Cooked Fondant (page 162) to create the perfect centers for bonbons or chocolate creams.*

*For helpful tips, see Dipping Candies in Chocolate (page 23). For alternate chocolate coating recipes, see Chocolate Coatings (page 151). If desired, decorate the chocolate-coated bonbons with chopped nuts or other candies.*

✳ MAKES ABOUT 2 CUPS FONDANT

2 cups granulated sugar
1 cup water
1 tablespoon light corn syrup
¼ teaspoon glycerin

1 egg white, stiffly beaten
1 teaspoon vanilla extract (see Cook's Notes below)
Chocolate Coatings (page 151)

In a 2-quart saucepan over medium heat, bring the sugar, water, and corn syrup to a boil, stirring until the sugar dissolves and the mixture begins to boil. Add the glycerin just when the boiling begins. Cook, without stirring, to the soft ball stage (234°F to 240°F, with 238°F recommended). Just before the candy reaches the desired temperature, rinse a platter with cold water; dry thoroughly.

Remove the boiling mixture from the heat. Pour onto the cool platter. Cool to 110°F, about 30 minutes.

Spread the egg white over the cooled fondant. Work the mixture back and forth on the platter by hand until it is white and creamy. Working the candy mixture can take 30 minutes or more. Professionals often use a special flat tool that looks somewhat like a scraper, scraping the candy on one side, lifting it up, and folding it over, and then scraping it on the other side, lifting it up, and folding it over.

Flavor the candy with the vanilla, working the flavoring into the candy. Immediately shape the fondant into small balls. Place the balls on waxed paper. Dip the centers in melted chocolate as soon as the centers are firm. This candy will soften if allowed to stand too long. Store in an airtight container.

COOK'S NOTES: Glycerin used for bonbons can be purchased in the pharmacy section of most large grocery stores or craft stores.

Other extracts may be substituted for the vanilla. Suggested flavorings are maple extract, orange extract, cherry extract, coconut extract, strawberry extract, or peppermint extract.

. . . . . . . . . . . . . . . . . . . . . . . . .

# Manhattan Buttercream Fondant

## Skill Level: Novice, Super Simple

*This easy fondant recipe from Kansas State University in Manhattan, Kansas, creates a creamy filling for candies similar to those found in a box of assorted chocolates.*

✳ MAKES ABOUT 55

1 (1 pound) package powdered sugar

¼ cup butter, softened

Pinch salt

3 tablespoons boiling water or 4 tablespoons fruit juice

1 teaspoon flavoring of choice (see Cook's Note below)

Few drops food coloring (optional)

Chocolate Coatings (optional; page 151)

Make a mound of powdered sugar on a marble slab, a large cutting board, or a clean countertop. Put the softened butter and salt in the center of the mound. Knead the mixture by hand, adding the water to the mixture a few drops at a time. Add the flavoring and coloring, if using. Knead by hand until the fondant is very smooth and does not stick to the hands or fingers.

Pat the fondant into a ball or mound. Pinch off small amounts and shape as desired into small balls, squares, or wafers.

If desired, dip the fondant centers into melted chocolate using the techniques and recipes found in Dipping Candies in Chocolate (page 23) or Chocolate Coatings (page 151). Store in an airtight container.

COOK'S NOTE: Suggested flavorings are vanilla extract, maple extract, orange extract, cherry extract, coconut extract, strawberry extract, or peppermint extract. If preferred, fruit juices such as orange juice may be used in place of the boiling water, giving the candy additional flavor. If fruit juice is used, flavor the candy with vanilla extract or with an extract that complements the flavor of the fruit juice.

. . . . . . . . . . . . . . . . . . . . . . . . .

# Ultra-Creamy Fondant

## Skill Level: Novice, Super Simple

*Though similar to Manhattan Buttercream Fondant (at left), corn syrup makes this fondant creamy and slightly soft.*

✳ MAKES ABOUT 1⅓ POUNDS OR 50 TO 80 CANDIES

⅓ cup butter or margarine, softened

⅓ cup light corn syrup

1 teaspoon flavoring of choice (see Cook's Note, page 164)

½ teaspoon salt

Few drops of food coloring (optional)

1 (1-pound) package powdered sugar

Coating options: Sweetened flaked coconut, chopped nuts, multicolored decorator sprinkles, or Chocolate Coatings (page 151)

In a medium mixing bowl, blend the butter, corn syrup, flavoring, salt, and food coloring, if using, with a wooden spoon. Gradually add the powdered sugar, first mixing with the wooden spoon, and then kneading by hand until the mixture is smooth and well blended and no longer sticks to the hands. Shape the mixture into a ball or a mound.

TO MAKE BONBONS OR PATTIES: Line 2 large baking sheets with waxed paper. Pinch off small pieces of the fondant and shape into balls ¾ inch in diameter. Place the balls on the lined baking sheets. If making patties, flatten the balls with the palm of the hand or with a flat spatula. Roll in the coating of choice.

TO MAKE ROLLS: Cover the countertop with a large sheet of waxed paper. Shape the fondant into a roll about 1¼ inches in diameter. Secure the rolls in the waxed paper, sealing the ends tightly. Refrigerate 1 hour or until firm. Slice into ¼-inch rounds. Serve plain or cover with the coating of choice.

TO MAKE WAFERS: Place the ball or mound on a sheet of waxed paper. Cover with another sheet of waxed paper. Roll out like pie crust or cookie dough. Cut into shapes using cookie cutters. Decorate as desired.

COOK'S NOTES: If desired, this fondant may be prepared 1 to 2 days in advance and stored tightly wrapped in foil. It may also be stored in an airtight container in the freezer 1 to 2 months.

This fondant is the same filling recipe used for Chocolate-Covered Mint Patties (page 169).

# $M$ints

## Old-Fashioned Pastel Butter Mints

### Skill Level: Advanced

*At one time, these creamy pastel butter mints were just as essential to a proper Southern wedding as having a bride and groom. Traditionally served in a crystal bowl or silver compote, the mints were placed between the white wedding cake and the equally essential bowl of roasted cocktail nuts. We Southerners have loosened up a bit the past few decades, but not enough to stop loving this old-fashioned candy.*

✳ MAKES ABOUT 50

2 cups powdered sugar
1 cup cornstarch
2 cups granulated sugar
¾ cup water
¼ cup butter (do not use margarine)
¼ teaspoon cream of tartar or 2 tablespoons cider vinegar
Food coloring as desired
10 drops peppermint oil or ½ teaspoon peppermint extract

Butter a large platter or a 10 × 15-inch jelly roll pan. In a flat container that can be sealed, combine the powdered sugar and cornstarch, mixing well.

In a heavy 2-quart saucepan, bring the granulated sugar, water, butter, and cream of tartar to a boil, stirring until the sugar dissolves and the mixture begins to boil. Cover and cook 2 to 3 minutes to dissolve the sugar crystals on the sides of the pan. Remove the lid. Cook at a rapid boil, without stirring, to 265°F. When the temperature is nearly 265°F, drop in a few drops of food coloring, tinting the mixture to a light pastel color.

Remove from the heat. Quickly add the peppermint oil and turn onto the buttered platter to cool. As soon as the candy can be handled, knead by hand until it can be picked up and pulled. Pull or stretch the candy until it is firm. Stretch the candy into a rope about ½ inch in diameter. Using kitchen shears, snip the rope into ½- to 1-inch pieces, letting the pieces fall into the powdered sugar and cornstarch mixture. Store the mints with the sugar mixture in the airtight container until the mints soften and become creamy, 2 to 3 days. When the mints have softened, turn the mints and the sugar mixture into a sieve, shaking the sieve to remove the excess sugar. Store the softened mints in an airtight container at room temperature.

COOK'S NOTE: When pulling and stretching the candy, dip your fingers into a little cornstarch to prevent the candy from sticking.

# Marvelous Marbled Mints

### Skill Level: Novice, Super Simple

*Pretty as a picture and delicious to boot, this recipe is as much fun as opening your first can of Play-Doh. Whether you serve these mints for a special event or just as a special treat, everyone will want to know how you came up with such a marvelous creation.*

✳ MAKES ABOUT 100 SMALL MINTS

½ cup butter, softened
1 (1-pound) package powdered sugar
2 tablespoons half-and-half or evaporated milk
1 teaspoon peppermint or mint extract
Food coloring as desired

In a small mixing bowl, cream the butter with an electric mixer until fluffy. Gradually add half of the powdered sugar, mixing until smooth. Add the half-and-half and peppermint extract. Gradually add the remaining powdered sugar, blending thoroughly.

Divide the mixture into 3 parts. Tint 2 of the 3 parts as desired, leaving 1 part white. (For example, tint 1 portion pink, tint 1 portion yellow, and leave one portion white.)

Cover a countertop area with waxed paper. Lightly dust the waxed paper with a small amount of powdered sugar if desired. Place equal amounts of all 3 colors of the mixture on the waxed paper. Roll the 3 colors together into a long rope about ¾ to 1 inch in diameter, creating a marbled effect. Repeat until all the mixture is used. Secure the rolls in waxed paper, tightly sealing the ends. Transfer to a baking sheet and refrigerate until firm, about 1 hour.

Remove the rolls from the refrigerator. Slice into ¼-inch rounds. Cover an area of the countertop with waxed paper. Place the sliced mints on the waxed paper and cover lightly with another sheet of waxed paper. Let stand at room temperature until dry, 6 to 8 hours. Transfer the mints to an airtight container, separating each layer with waxed paper.

COOK'S NOTES: The mint fondant may be tinted a single color or any combination of colors desired. Though the three-color mints are beautiful, two-color mints can be equally as impressive.

If preferred, roll the mixture out like cookie dough and use small cookie cutters to give the mints unusual or festive shapes. For example, tint half of the mixture red, leaving the other half white. Roll the two colors together like cookie dough and cut into heart-shaped mints. Tiny amounts of contrasting colors may be shaped into small balls and pressed lightly into the mints as decorations.

# Luscious Cream Cheese Mints

### Skill Level: Novice, Super Simple

*Rich and creamy, these scrumptious little mints are always a popular choice.*

✳ MAKES ABOUT 100 MINTS

1 (8-ounce) package cream cheese, softened
¼ cup butter or margarine, softened
2 (1-pound) packages powdered sugar, plus extra for dipping
1 teaspoon peppermint or mint extract
Food coloring as desired

In a large mixing bowl, mix the cream cheese and butter with an electric mixer until smooth. Gradually add the powdered sugar, blending thoroughly. Add the peppermint extract, adjusting to taste if desired. Tint the mixture with food coloring as desired. Cover and refrigerate 1 hour or until firm enough to handle.

Line 2 to 3 large baking sheets with waxed paper.

Shape the mixture into balls 1 inch in diameter. Place the balls on the lined baking sheets. Dip the bottom of a glass into powdered sugar; press the bottom of the glass into each ball to flatten. Let stand, uncovered, 4 hours or until firm. Store in an airtight container, separating each layer with waxed paper. These mints may be refrigerated or frozen if desired.

# Chocolate-Covered Mint Patties

### Skill Level: Novice, Easy

*These are just as delicious as they sound, perfect for an after dinner treat.*

✳ MAKES ABOUT 80 MINTS

⅓ cup butter or margarine, softened
⅓ cup light corn syrup
1 teaspoon peppermint extract
½ teaspoon salt
1 (1-pound) package powdered sugar
10 ounces dark chocolate candy coatings
2 ounces baking chocolate or semisweet chocolate chips

In a medium mixing bowl, blend the butter, corn syrup, peppermint extract, and salt with a wooden spoon. Gradually add the powdered sugar, first mixing with the wooden spoon, and then kneading by hand until the mixture is smooth and well blended and no longer sticks to the hands. Shape the mixture into a ball or a mound.

Line 2 large baking sheets with waxed paper. Pinch off small pieces of the mint fondant and shape into balls ¾ inch in diameter. Place the balls on the lined baking sheets. Flatten the balls with the palm of the hand or with a flat spatula. Cover and refrigerate until firm, about 1 hour.

In the top pan of a double boiler over hot but not boiling water, melt the candy coating and chocolate together, stirring until smooth. Using a fork or a specially designed dipping tool, dip the mints into the melted chocolate until coated. Drop the mints onto the waxed paper. Let stand until the chocolate is firm. Store in an airtight container, separating each layer with waxed paper. These mints may be refrigerated or frozen if desired.

COOK'S NOTES: This basic fondant recipe can be used to create a variety of candies. Substitute the peppermint extract with an extract of choice, shape the mixture into balls or patties, and dip the candies into melted chocolate.

A Wilton hollow dipping spoon is a wonderful tool for dipping these mints, often leaving an attractive swirl pattern on the top.

For helpful tips, see Dipping Candies in Chocolate (page 23). For alternate chocolate coating recipes, see Chocolate Coatings (page 151).

# Sensational Orange Mint Patties

## Skill Level: Novice, Easy

*While I would love to claim these creamy, chocolate-covered orange mint patties as my own invention, this recipe comes from another candy maker named Jane, this one from Louisiana. Perfect for parties, gifts, or an after-dinner treat, these melt-in-your-mouth mints are truly sensational.*

❋ MAKES ABOUT 140 MINTS

½ **cup butter, softened**

1 **(14-ounce) can sweetened condensed milk**

1½ **teaspoons pure orange extract**

½ **teaspoon peppermint extract**

7 **cups powdered sugar (2 pounds minus ½ to ¾ cup)**

18 **to 20 ounces dark chocolate candy coating**

4 **to 6 ounces semisweet baking chocolate**

In a large mixing bowl, combine the butter, milk, orange extract, and peppermint extract with an electric mixer or by hand until smooth. Gradually add the powdered sugar, blending thoroughly after each addition. Cover and refrigerate 4 hours or until firm.

Cover 2 to 3 large baking sheets with waxed paper. Shape the mixture into balls 1 inch in diameter. Place the balls on the waxed paper and flatten with the palms of the hand or the back of a spatula. Cover and freeze 1 hour, or until firm.

Cover a large countertop area with waxed paper.

In the top pan of a double boiler over hot but not boiling water, melt the chocolate candy coating and semisweet chocolate together, stirring until smooth. Using a fork or a specially designed dipping tool, dip the mints into the melted chocolate until coated. Drop the mints onto the waxed paper. Let stand until the chocolate is firm. Store in an airtight container, separating each layer with waxed paper. These mints may be refrigerated or frozen if desired.

COOK'S NOTE: Not all mints must be shaped and dipped at once. If preferred, part or all of the mint filling may be sealed in an airtight container and stored in the freezer for at least 1 month.

Instead of shaping each individual mint by hand, shape the chilled fondant into several long, round rolls about 1¼ inches in diameter. Secure the rolls in waxed paper, tightly sealing the ends. Freeze for 1 hour or more. Remove the rolls from the freezer and slice into ¼-inch slices, using each slice as the center for an individual mint. If desired, these slices may be placed on a waxed paper-lined baking sheet, covered, and frozen again until ready to dip in melted chocolate. Shaping the fondant into rolls not only saves time, but it also gives the mints a uniform size.

A Wilton hollow dipping spoon is a wonderful tool for dipping these mints, often leaving an attractive swirl pattern on the top.

# Truffles

## Lynda's Gourmet Chocolate Truffles

### Skill Level: Novice, Easy

*After spending a day covered in chocolate, my cousin Lynda finally hit upon this delicious combination of milk chocolate, semisweet chocolate, cream, and liqueur as one of her favorites. It is one of my favorites, too.*
✳ MAKES ABOUT 48 TRUFFLES

1 (12-ounce) package Ghirardelli milk chocolate chips or other good-quality chocolate chips
6 ounces Ghirardelli semisweet block chocolate or other good-quality chocolate, finely chopped
¾ cup heavy cream
1 tablespoon liqueur of choice: Frangelico, Grand Marnier, amaretto, or coffee liqueur, or 1 tablespoon almond extract

*Coating Options*
1½ cups finely chopped hazelnuts or toasted almonds
¾ cup Williams Sonoma Pernigotti cocoa powder
¾ cup Ghirardelli Sweet Ground Chocolate and cocoa powder
8 ounces good-quality chocolate candy coating, such as Ghirardelli Double Chocolate Candy Making and Dipping Bar or a similar product

In a medium heatproof bowl, combine the milk chocolate chips and semisweet chocolate. Set aside.

In a small heavy saucepan over low heat, warm the cream until it comes to a low, simmering boil. Pour the hot cream over the chocolate in the bowl. Using a wire whisk, gently stir until the chocolate is completely melted and the mixture is smooth and well blended. Gently stir in the liqueur. Cover and refrigerate 1 hour or until firm enough to handle.

Line a large baking sheet with waxed paper. Drop the truffle mixture by rounded teaspoons onto the lined baking sheet, creating balls about ¾ inch in diameter. If preferred, place the truffle mixture into a pastry bag and squeeze onto the lined baking sheet through a plain decorator's tip, making rounded circles, one on top of the other, to create dome-shaped balls. (The pastry bag method is slightly more time-consuming, but often produces better looking truffles than the drop method.) Refrigerate 20 minutes or until firm.

If a nut or dry coating is desired, cover a large countertop area or a large baking sheet with waxed paper. Roll the balls in the coating of choice. Place the coated truffles onto the waxed paper while rolling the remaining truffles.

If a chocolate coating is desired, cover a large countertop area or a large baking sheet with waxed paper. In the top pan of a double boiler over hot but not boiling water, melt the chocolate candy coating, stirring until smooth.

(The chocolate candy coating may also be melted per package instructions.) Using a fork or specially designed dipping tool, dip the truffles into the melted chocolate until coated. Drop the truffles onto the waxed paper. Let stand until the chocolate is firm.

Store in an airtight container in the refrigerator. Let stand at room temperature 5 to 10 minutes before serving.

COOK'S NOTES: The chocolate-coated truffles may be rolled in chopped hazelnuts or toasted almonds while the chocolate coating is still warm.

For a slightly firmer center, use ⅔ cup heavy cream.

For helpful tips, see Dipping Candies in Chocolate (page 23). For alternate chocolate coating recipes, see Chocolate Coatings (page 151).

# Bittersweet Chocolate Truffles

## Skill Level: Novice, Easy

*When made with gourmet chocolate, these candies can be just as exquisite as the gourmet truffles found in exclusive specialty stores. Toasted hazelnuts may be added to the truffle centers, sprinkled on top of the chocolate coating, or omitted entirely.*

✳ MAKES ABOUT 30 TRUFFLES

**8 ounces good-quality bittersweet chocolate, such as Valrhona, coarsely chopped**
**1 cup heavy cream**
**Few grains sea salt, preferably fleur de sel**
**2 tablespoons unsalted butter, thinly sliced**
**½ to ¾ cup chopped toasted hazelnuts (optional)**
**8 ounces good-quality chocolate candy coating squares**

Place the coarsely chopped chocolate into a large heatproof bowl. Set aside.

In a small heavy saucepan over low heat, warm the cream until it reaches a low, simmering boil. Pour the hot cream over the chocolate in the bowl. Using a wire whisk, gently stir until the chocolate is completely melted. Add the salt and butter, a few small pieces at a time, and stir gently until the butter is completely melted and the mixture is smooth and well blended. Set aside at room temperature to cool 15 minutes.

Whip the truffle mixture briskly with a wire whisk until the chocolate lightens in color, 1 to 2 minutes. Stir in the hazelnuts, if desired. Set aside at room temperature until the truffle mixture becomes firm enough to handle, 30 to 35 minutes.

Line a large baking sheet with waxed paper. Drop the truffle mixture by rounded teaspoons onto the lined baking sheet. Refrigerate until the centers are firm enough to dip in melted chocolate, 30 minutes to 1 hour.

Cover a large countertop area or a large baking sheet with waxed paper.

In the top pan of a double boiler over hot but not boiling water, melt the chocolate candy coating, stirring until smooth. (The chocolate candy coating may also be melted per package instructions.) Using a fork or specially designed dipping tool, dip the truffles into the melted chocolate until coated. Drop the truffles onto the waxed paper. If the hazelnuts were not added to the filling mixture, sprinkle the coated truffles with the hazelnuts while the chocolate coating is still warm. Let stand until the chocolate is firm. Store in an airtight container in the refrigerator. Let stand at room temperature about 10 minutes before serving.

**COOK'S NOTES:** Valrhona bittersweet chocolate is a gourmet chocolate usually sold by the pound in large grocery stores and specialty stores in some large cities. If gourmet bittersweet chocolate is not available, more common brands of bittersweet chocolate may be substituted, though the candy may not be as rich.

Fleur de sel is a gourmet French sea salt. Other types of sea salt may be substituted. Though sea salt is best, a few grains of table salt may be substituted if sea salt is not available.

For helpful tips, see Dipping Candies in Chocolate (page 23). For alternate chocolate coating recipes, see Chocolate Coatings (page 151).

# Plain Jane Truffles

## Skill Level: Novice, Easy

*With all the gourmet recipes now available, it is nice to know that we can still make something quite delicious using ingredients we have on hand.*

✳ **MAKES ABOUT 18 TRUFFLES**

½ cup heavy whipping cream
2 tablespoons butter (preferably unsalted)
1 tablespoon granulated sugar
1 cup (6 ounces) semisweet chocolate chips
1 tablespoon almond extract, or to taste
¾ cup finely chopped toasted almonds

In a small heavy saucepan over low heat, warm the cream, butter, and sugar until it comes to a low, simmering boil. Remove from the heat. Add the chocolate chips, gently stirring until the chocolate is completely melted and the mixture is smooth and well blended. Gently stir in the almond extract. Cover and refrigerate 1 hour or until firm enough to handle.

Line a baking sheet with waxed paper. Shape the chilled mixture into balls ¾ inch in diameter. Place the balls on the lined baking sheet. Cover and chill or freeze 1 hour or until firm.

Cover a large countertop area with waxed paper. Place the chopped almonds into a small bowl or dish. Roll the chilled or frozen truffles in the chopped almonds until well coated. Place onto the waxed paper while rolling the remaining truffles. Store in an airtight container in the refrigerator. Let stand at room temperature 10 to 15 minutes before serving.

**COOK'S NOTES:** Other flavored extracts, such as mint, cherry, rum, or vanilla, may be substituted for the almond extract. Since the strength of extracts may vary, adjust flavorings to taste.

If preferred, the truffles may be coated in unsweetened cocoa powder, chocolate decorator sprinkles, powdered sugar, or other coatings as desired. Finely chopped walnuts or pecans may be substituted for the toasted almonds.

The truffles may also be dipped in melted chocolate if desired. For helpful tips, see Dipping Candies in Chocolate (page 23). For chocolate coating recipes, see Chocolate Coatings (page 151).

# Lynda's Luscious Lemon Truffles

## Skill Level: Average

*Add a touch of elegance to any event with these heavenly lemon truffles from my cousin Lynda.*

✳ **MAKES ABOUT 30 TRUFFLES**

**6 tablespoons heavy cream**
**Finely grated zest of 2 small lemons**
**9 ounces good-quality white chocolate, such as Ghirardelli block chocolate**
**4 tablespoons unsalted butter, thinly sliced**
**Few grains of sea salt, preferably fleur de sel (see Cook's Note, page 173)**
**4 teaspoons freshly squeezed lemon juice**

*Toasted Pecan Coating (optional)*
**1½ cups pecans**
**1 teaspoon unsalted butter**
**⅛ teaspoon sea salt, preferably fleur de sel**

**8 ounces good-quality white chocolate candy coating, such as Ghirardelli White Dipping Chocolate**

In a small heavy saucepan over low heat, warm the cream and lemon zest until it comes to a low, simmering boil. Remove from the heat, cover, and let stand at room temperature 15 to 20 minutes.

Coarsely chop the white chocolate by hand. Place the white chocolate into a food processor and chop again until it is very finely ground. (If a food processor is not available, chop the white chocolate by hand until very finely chopped.) Rinse a medium heatproof bowl in hot water; dry thoroughly. Place the white chocolate into the warmed bowl. Add the butter and sea salt. Set aside.

Place the saucepan containing the cream and lemon zest over low heat and bring to a low simmer a second time. Remove from the heat. Add the lemon juice, gently stirring to blend. Pour the hot cream mixture through a fine sieve placed over the white chocolate mixture. Discard the lemon zest trapped in the sieve. Using a small wire whisk, gently stir the cream and white chocolate mixture until the chocolate is completely melted and the mixture is smooth and well blended. Cover and refrigerate 4 hours or more.

Prepare the pecan coating, if desired: Preheat the oven to 350°F. Place the pecans in a shallow pan and toast in the oven, about 8 minutes or until light golden, stirring halfway through cooking. Remove from the oven and stir in the butter and sea salt. Cool. Finely chop the pecans by hand. Place in a small dish. Set aside.

Line a large baking sheet with waxed paper or parchment. Shape the chilled truffle mixture into balls ¾ inch in diameter. Place the balls on the lined baking sheet. Refrigerate or freeze until firm, about 20 minutes.

Cover a large countertop area or a baking sheet with waxed paper or parchment.

In the top pan of a double boiler over hot but not boiling water, melt the white chocolate candy coating, stirring until smooth. (The candy coating may also be melted per package directions.) Using two forks or a specially designed dipping tool, dip each chilled truffle into the melted chocolate until coated. If desired, immediately drop the chocolate coated truffle into the dish containing the pecan coating. Place the coated truffles onto the waxed paper. Let stand until the chocolate is firm. Store in an airtight container in the refrigerator. Let stand at room temperature about 10 minutes before serving.

COOK'S NOTES: For a special presentation, coat half the truffles in melted white chocolate and half in both melted white chocolate and the Toasted Pecan Coating. Place in fluted candy cups and serve on a beautiful china dish.

A MicroPlane grater is a kitchen tool designed to create very fine, fluffy zest. If a MicroPlane grater or a similar tool has been used to remove the lemon zest and the zest is very, very fine, the cream may be poured directly over the white chocolate without the use of a sieve.

For helpful tips, see Dipping Candies in Chocolate (page 23).

# Lemon Curd Truffles

## Skill Level: Novice, Easy

*This recipe requires slightly less effort than Lynda's Luscious Lemon Truffles (page 174), yet still has a rich lemon flavor.*

✳ MAKES ABOUT 30 TRUFFLES

**9 ounces good-quality white chocolate, such as Ghirardelli block chocolate**

**3 tablespoons unsalted butter, thinly sliced**

**6 tablespoons heavy cream**

**Few grains salt**

**2 to 3 teaspoons freshly squeezed lemon juice**

**⅓ cup prepared lemon curd**

**8 ounces good-quality white chocolate candy coating, such as Ghirardelli White Dipping Chocolate**

Coarsely chop the white chocolate by hand. Place the white chocolate into a food processor and chop again until it is very finely ground. (If a food processor is not available, chop the white chocolate by hand until very finely chopped.) Place the white chocolate and butter into a medium heatproof bowl.

In a small heavy saucepan over low heat, warm the cream until it comes to a low, simmering boil. Remove from the heat. Stir in the salt and lemon juice. Pour the hot cream mixture over the white chocolate mixture. Using a small wire whisk, gently stir until the chocolate is completely melted and the mixture is smooth and well blended. Add the lemon curd, gently stirring until blended and smooth. Cover and refrigerate until firm, about 1 hour.

Line a large baking sheet with waxed paper or parchment. Shape the chilled truffle mixture into balls ¾ inch in diameter. Place the balls on the lined baking sheet. Refrigerate or freeze until firm, about 20 minutes.

Cover a large countertop area or a baking sheet with waxed paper or parchment.

In the top pan of a double boiler over hot but not boiling water, melt the white chocolate candy coating, stirring until smooth. (The candy coating may also be melted per package directions.) Using a fork or specially designed dipping tool, dip each chilled truffle into the melted chocolate until coated. Drop the truffles onto the waxed paper. Let stand until the chocolate is firm. Store in an airtight container in the refrigerator. Let stand at room temperature about 10 minutes before serving.

COOK'S NOTE: Lemon curd is available in most grocery stores near the jellies and jams.

The amount of butter may be reduced by up to half if desired.

Roll the white chocolate–coated truffles in finely chopped pecans while the chocolate coating is still warm.

For helpful tips, see Dipping Candies in Chocolate (page 23).

# Marzipan Truffles

## Skill Level: Average

*This magnificent combination of scrumptious white chocolate and rich, almond flavoring is an unexpected surprise.*

✳ MAKES ABOUT 36 TRUFFLES

**9 ounces good-quality white chocolate, such as Ghirardelli block chocolate**

**6 tablespoons heavy cream**

**1 tablespoon amaretto liqueur or 1 teaspoon almond extract**

**1 (7-ounce) package marzipan**

**4 tablespoons unsalted butter, softened**

**8 to 10 ounces white or dark chocolate candy coating or 4 to 5 ounces each of white and dark chocolate coating**

**¼ cup ground or finely chopped almonds or ¼ cup white chocolate or dark chocolate shavings (optional)**

Coarsely chop the white chocolate by hand. Place the white chocolate into a food processor and chop again until it is very finely ground. (If a food processor is not available, chop the white chocolate by hand until very finely chopped.) Place the white chocolate in the top pan of a double boiler away from the heat. Set aside.

In a small heavy saucepan over low heat, warm the cream until it comes to a low, simmering boil. Gently stir in the liqueur. Pour the heated cream over the white chocolate, gently stirring until the white chocolate is fully melted. Add the marzipan and butter, stirring gently to blend.

Heat water in the bottom pan of the double boiler until hot but not boiling. Remove from the heat. Place the top double boiler pan con-

taining the white chocolate and marzipan mixture over the hot water, stirring until the mixture is completely melted and smooth.

Remove from the heat. Cover and refrigerate 3 to 4 hours or until firm enough to handle.

Line a large baking sheet with waxed or parchment paper. Shape the truffle mixture into balls ¾ inch in diameter. Place the balls on the lined baking sheet. Freeze until firm, about 15 minutes.

Cover a large countertop area or a large baking sheet with waxed paper.

In the top pan of a double boiler over hot but not boiling water, melt the chocolate candy coating, stirring until smooth. (The candy coating may also be melted per package directions.) Using a fork or specially designed dipping tool, dip the truffles into the melted chocolate until coated. Drop the truffles onto the waxed paper. Immediately sprinkle with the almonds or chocolate shavings, if desired. Let stand until the chocolate is firm. Store in an airtight container in the refrigerator. Let stand at room temperature 10 to 15 minutes before serving.

**COOK'S NOTES:** For a special presentation, dip half the truffles into melted white chocolate and half into melted dark chocolate. Decorate the tops of the truffles by sprinkling the white chocolate truffles with dark chocolate shavings and the dark chocolate truffles with white chocolate shavings.

For helpful tips, see Dipping Candies in Chocolate (page 23).

# Luscious Raspberry-Fudge Truffles

## Skill Level: Novice, Easy

*A longtime personal favorite, these "little bites of heaven" are worth the time it takes to make them.*

✳ MAKES ABOUT 75 TRUFFLES

1 (12-ounce) package semisweet chocolate
  chips
2 (8-ounce) packages cream cheese, softened
1 cup seedless raspberry preserves
2 tablespoons Chambord raspberry liqueur
1⅔ cups very finely crushed vanilla wafer
  crumbs (see Cook's Notes below)

*Chocolate Coating*
1 (12-ounce) package semisweet chocolate
  chips
2 (1.55-ounce) milk chocolate bars
4 teaspoons solid vegetable shortening

*Decorative White Chocolate Drizzle (optional)*
3 ounces white baking chocolate
1 tablespoon solid vegetable shortening

In a small heavy saucepan over low heat, melt the chocolate chips, stirring until smooth. Remove from the heat. Set aside to cool slightly.

In a large mixing bowl, beat the cream cheese with an electric mixer until smooth. Add the melted chocolate, raspberry preserves, and chambord, beating until well blended. Blend in the wafer crumbs, mixing well. Cover and freeze 1 hour or more.

Line a large baking sheet with waxed paper. Working with approximately one-third of the cold truffle mixture at a time, shape the mixture into balls ¾ inch in diameter. Place the balls on the lined baking sheet. Cover and freeze 1 hour or more.

Cover a large countertop area or 2 large baking sheets with waxed paper.

TO PREPARE THE COATING: In the top pan of a double boiler over hot but not boiling water, melt the chocolate chips, milk chocolate, and shortening together, stirring until smooth. Using a toothpick, fork, or specially designed dipping tool, dip the frozen balls into the melted chocolate until coated. Drop the coated truffles onto the waxed paper. Let stand until the chocolate is firm.

TO PREPARE THE WHITE CHOCOLATE DRIZZLE, IF DESIRED: Place the white chocolate and shortening in a small, heavy-duty self-sealing plastic bag. Seal the bag tightly. Submerge the bag in hot water until the chocolate melts. (The hot water left in the bottom of the double boiler pan that was used to melt the chocolate coating is usually perfect for melting the white chocolate.) Gently knead the bag until the chocolate and shortening are blended. Poke a tiny hole in one corner of the bag. Gently squeeze the white chocolate mixture through the hole in the bag, drizzling it over the tops of the dipped truffles in a decorative pattern. Let the truffles stand until the white chocolate is firm.

Store the truffles in an airtight container in the refrigerator for up to 3 weeks or in the freezer for up to 2 months. The truffles may be served at room temperature but taste best when chilled.

COOK'S NOTES: The key to making these truffles ultra smooth and delicious is to process the vanilla wafer crumbs in a food processor until they are almost the consistency of a powder.

This recipe appears to be more difficult

than it is. It is not necessary to shape or dip all truffles at one time. The filling may be placed in an airtight container and frozen for at least 2 months and then shaped and dipped as needed.

The mixture is much easier to form into balls when very cold. By working with approximately one-third of the mixture at a time, the remaining mixture remains cold until ready to be shaped.

If a toothpick is used to dip the truffles into the melted chocolate, the hole left by the toothpick must be covered with chocolate or the raspberry filling will ooze from the hole. Let the chocolate coating harden, and then use a spoon to dab a tiny amount of the melted chocolate over the hole.

For helpful tips, see Dipping Candies in Chocolate (page 23). For alternate chocolate coating recipes, see Chocolate Coatings (page 151).

Line an 8-inch square pan with waxed paper or foil, leaving a 1-inch overhang on the sides of the pan.

In the top pan of a double boiler over hot but not boiling water, melt the chocolate chips, stirring until smooth. Remove from the heat. Add the milk, salt, and vanilla, stirring only until blended. Gently stir in the nuts, if using.

Pour the mixture into the lined pan, spreading evenly. Cover and refrigerate until firm, about 2 hours. Remove the block of candy from the pan by gently lifting the edges of the waxed paper. Place the block on a cutting board. Remove the waxed paper or foil lining and cut into squares. Store in an airtight container in the refrigerator.

# Sooner Magic Truffles

## Skill Level: Novice, Easy

*Put a little Sooner magic into your life with these creamy fudge nuggets from my hometown newspaper, the* Ponca City News. *This recipe is so easy that you can make it during halftime.*

✳ MAKES ABOUT 64 TRUFFLES

1 cup (6 ounces) semisweet chocolate chips
½ cup plus 1 tablespoon sweetened condensed milk
Pinch salt
½ teaspoon vanilla extract
¼ cup finely chopped pecans or walnuts (optional)

# Farmhouse Favorites

Even the most devoted chocolate lovers need a change of pace now and then, and Farmhouse Favorites are the perfect choice. Packed with the treasures of a bountiful harvest, these candies are a gift from Mother Earth.

Savor a shiny red apple smothered in velvety smooth caramel or an oven-roasted pecan dressed in a bouquet of winter spices. Sample unusual jelly candies from the Pacific Northwest, where lush fruit orchards burst into bloom each spring to flaunt the beauty of nature's palette. Celebrate Indian summer with the crunchy goodness of popcorn candies flavored with nuts, orange, or natural sorghum syrup. Let the poetry of sugarplums hypnotize you with their charm as you prepare for that special Christmas Eve with loved ones.

Snacks made of fruits and honey date back thousands of years and were the first candies to be enjoyed by man. Whether tucked away in a backpack or served on a tray for guests, Farmhouse Favorites will always remind us of sunshine, springtime, and all things good.

# Candied and Spiced Nuts

## Roasted Cinnamon Pecans

### Skill Level: Novice, Easy

*Oh, my! The first time I made this recipe I ate the whole batch before anyone else could taste them. Roasting gives the pecans a deep, rich flavor, and a double dose of vanilla just makes them doubly delicious.*

✳ MAKES ABOUT 3 CUPS

> 2 cups pecan halves
> 1 cup granulated sugar
> 1 to 3 teaspoons ground cinnamon, to taste
> 1½ to 3 teaspoons vanilla extract, to taste
> 5 tablespoons water

Preheat the oven to 350°F. Scatter the pecans on a baking sheet. Roast the pecans 8 to 10 minutes, stirring once. Butter a large baking sheet.

In a heavy 2-quart saucepan, combine the sugar and cinnamon, mixing well. Stir in the vanilla and water. Bring to a boil over medium heat, stirring until the sugar dissolves. Cook at a medium boil, without stirring, about 5 minutes or until the mixture reaches the soft ball stage (234°F to 240°F; with 236°F recommended).

Remove from the heat. Stir vigorously about 1 minute. Add the pecans and stir until the syrup thickens and coats the pecans.

Pour the mixture onto the buttered baking sheet. Separate the pecans using two forks.

Cool. Store in an airtight container.

COOK'S NOTE: The amount of cinnamon and vanilla extract used is often a matter of personal preference and can easily be adjusted within the ranges listed. Although the timing method can be used in this recipe, a candy thermometer is preferred to make certain that the syrup has reached the soft ball stage.

. . . . . . . . . . . . . . . . . . . . . . . . . . . .

## Spiced Pecans

### Skill Level: Novice, Easy

*Nothing speaks of fall quite like fresh pecans smothered with the spices of your favorite apple pie.*

✳ MAKES ABOUT 3 CUPS

> 1 cup granulated sugar
> ½ teaspoon ground cinnamon
> ¼ teaspoon ground nutmeg
> ⅛ teaspoon ground allspice
> ½ teaspoon salt
> ½ cup water
> ½ teaspoon vanilla extract
> 2 cups pecan halves

Butter a large baking sheet.

In a heavy 2-quart saucepan, combine the sugar, spices, and salt, mixing well. Stir in the water. Bring to a boil over medium heat, stir-

## Gourmet Nuts

Candied and spiced nuts are so simple, so easy, and oh, so good; these wonderful delicacies are welcome any time of year. Serve them with ice cream or baked apples or just as a snack.

ring until the sugar dissolves. Cook, without stirring, to the soft ball stage (234°F to 240°F; with 236°F recommended).

Remove from the heat. Add the vanilla and stir vigorously about 1 minute. Add the pecans and stir until the syrup thickens and coats the pecans.

Pour onto the buttered baking sheet. Separate the pecans using two forks. Cool. Store in an airtight container.

## Pistol Pete Pecans

### Skill Level: Novice, Easy

*This creamy, spicy nut coating recipe is just one of many recipes my mother collected from colleagues while teaching in the school of Home Economics at Oklahoma State University.*
✳ MAKES ABOUT 3 CUPS

1 cup granulated sugar
¼ teaspoon salt
½ teaspoon ground cinnamon
6 tablespoons milk

½ teaspoon vanilla extract
2 cups pecan halves

Butter a large baking sheet.

In a heavy 2-quart saucepan, combine the sugar, salt, and cinnamon, mixing well. Stir in the milk. Bring to a boil over medium heat, stirring until the sugar dissolves. Cook, stirring occasionally to prevent scorching, to the soft ball stage (234°F to 240°F; with 236°F recommended).

Remove from the heat. Add the vanilla and stir vigorously about 1 minute. Add the pecans and stir until the syrup thickens and coats the pecans.

Pour onto the buttered baking sheet. Separate the pecans using two forks. Cool. Store in an airtight container.

## Crispy Sugared Walnuts

### Skill Level: Novice, Easy

*Sugared walnuts have a milder flavor than similar recipes made with pecans.*
✳ MAKES ABOUT 3 CUPS

2½ cups walnut halves
1 cup granulated sugar
1 teaspoon ground cinnamon
½ teaspoon salt
½ cup water
1 teaspoon vanilla extract

Preheat the oven to 350°F. Scatter the walnuts on a baking sheet. Roast the walnuts 5 minutes, stirring once. Butter a large baking sheet.

In a heavy 2-quart saucepan, combine the

sugar, cinnamon, and salt, mixing well. Stir in the water. Bring to a boil over medium heat, stirring until the sugar dissolves. Cook, without stirring, to the soft ball stage (234°F to 240°F; with 236°F recommended).

Remove from the heat. Add the vanilla and stir vigorously about 1 minute. Add the walnuts and stir until the syrup thickens and coats the walnuts.

Pour onto the buttered baking sheet. Separate the walnuts using two forks. Cool. Store in an airtight container.

# County Fair Nuts

### Skill Level: Novice, Super Simple

*My cousins Peggy and Lynda sent me this recipe after they had tasted the nuts at an arts and crafts fair in Shelby, North Carolina.*

✳ MAKES 3 TO 4 CUPS

**1 large egg white**
**1 tablespoon cold water**
**1 cup granulated sugar**
**1 teaspoon salt**
**1 tablespoon ground cinnamon**
**1 pound whole almonds, pecan halves, or**
 **walnut halves**

Preheat the oven to 275°F. Butter a large baking sheet or a 10 × 15-inch jelly roll pan.

In a small mixing bowl, beat the egg white and water with an electric mixer on high speed until frothy. In a separate small bowl, combine the sugar, salt, and cinnamon until well blended.

Drop the nuts, a few at a time, into the egg white mixture, turning with a fork until coated. Drop the coated nuts into the sugar mixture, turning with a fork until well coated with the sugar mixture. Place the nuts on the buttered baking sheet. Bake 45 minutes, stirring every 15 minutes, or until crispy. Remove from the oven. Cool. Store in an airtight container.

# Sugared Peanuts

### Skill Level: Novice, Easy

*With a crunchy sugar coating, these crispy peanuts are best eaten by the handful.*

✳ MAKES ABOUT 2½ CUPS

**1 cup sugar**
**½ cup water**
**2 cups raw, unsalted peanuts**

Preheat the oven to 325°F. Butter a 10 × 15-inch jelly roll pan or a large baking sheet.

In a heavy 2-quart saucepan, combine the sugar, water, and peanuts. Cook over medium-high heat, stirring occasionally, until the nuts are well coated in syrup and most of the moisture has evaporated.

Remove from the heat. Pour onto the buttered baking pan. Bake for 15 minutes, stirring twice. Remove from the oven. Cool. Store in an airtight container.

(*clockwise from top left*)
Aunt Lucy's Extra-Buttery Brittle;
Cherry-Almond Bark; Perfect Pralines;
Pistol Pete's Peanut Brittle

For Mary

(*clockwise from top left*)
Crazy Crunch; Glass Candy; Gourmet Layered
Peppermint Bark; Elegant Sparkling Strawberries;
Roasted Cinnamon Pecans; Pineapple Sherbet Fudge;
Charlotte's Extra-Good, Extra-Wicked Fudge;
Bittersweet Chocolate Truffles

# Candied Nuts

## Skill Level: Average

*A thick, light brown coating with a hint of sour cream gives these nuts a special flavor.*

✳ MAKES ABOUT 3 CUPS

**1 cup packed light brown sugar**
**½ cup granulated sugar**
**½ cup sour cream**
**1 teaspoon vanilla extract**
**2½ cups pecan halves**

Butter a large baking sheet.

In a heavy 2-quart saucepan, combine the sugars and sour cream. Bring to a boil over low heat, stirring until the sugar dissolves. Cover and cook 2 to 3 minutes to dissolve the sugar crystals on the sides of the pan. Remove the lid and cook slowly, stirring occasionally, until the mixture reaches the firm ball stage (244°F to 248°F, with 246°F recommended).

Remove from the heat. Add the vanilla and stir vigorously about 1 minute. Add the pecans and stir until the candy thickens and coats the pecans.

Pour onto the buttered baking sheet. Separate the pecans using two forks. Cool. Store in an airtight container.

# Glazed Nuts

## Skill Level: Average

*With a hard, clear, glossy coating, glazed nuts and fruits are usually used as a garnish.*

✳ MAKES ABOUT 3 CUPS

**1 cup granulated sugar**
**⅓ cup light corn syrup**
**½ cup water**
**2 cups pecan halves, walnut halves, or whole raw almonds**

Butter a large baking sheet or a large wire rack that has been placed over waxed paper.

In a very small saucepan, combine the sugar, corn syrup, and water. Bring to a boil over medium heat, stirring until the sugar dissolves. Cook, without stirring, to the hard crack stage (300°F).

Remove from the heat. Set the saucepan in a pan of boiling water to prevent the syrup from hardening. Drop the nuts, one at a time, into the syrup, coating the nuts well. Using a fork, remove the nuts and drop onto the buttered baking sheet. Do not stir the syrup while dipping the nuts. If the syrup becomes too thick to use, reheat the syrup over medium heat until it reaches a boil.

Cool. Store in an airtight container.

COOK'S NOTE: This recipe may also be used to glaze dried, candied, or fresh fruits such as cherries, pineapple, grapes, strawberries, or raisins, though fresh fruits will not store well and should be used immediately.

# Popcorn Candies

## Cowboy Crunch

### Skill Level: Average

*This is a personal favorite, and one batch of this buttery gourmet candied popcorn is never enough to satisfy friends and family.*

❋ MAKES ABOUT 11 CUPS

    8 cups freshly popped popcorn, unsalted
    1 cup coarsely chopped pecans, toasted
    1 cup sliced almonds, toasted
    1⅓ cups granulated sugar
    1 cup butter or margarine
    ½ cup light corn syrup
    1 teaspoon vanilla extract

In a very large mixing bowl, combine the popcorn and nuts, tossing them together until the nuts are evenly distributed. Spray a 9 × 13-inch pan or a large roasting pan with nonstick spray. Pour the popcorn mixture into the pan.

In a heavy 2-quart saucepan over medium heat, bring the sugar, butter, and corn syrup to a boil, stirring until the sugar dissolves and the mixture begins to boil. Cook, stirring constantly to prevent scorching, to a point between the hard ball and soft crack stages (265°F to 268°F), about 15 minutes. The syrup will not darken significantly and will be a very light golden color when cooked.

Remove from the heat. Stir in the vanilla. Pour the hot syrup over the popcorn mixture and stir until the popcorn and nuts are well coated. Cool slightly, 5 to 10 minutes. Break the candy apart into small pieces. Cool completely. Store in an airtight container.

COOK'S NOTE: The cooking temperature for the syrup can vary a few degrees without harming the candy. Do not cook the syrup beyond 270°F, or the popcorn will be hard and difficult to chew.

## Orange-Nut Popcorn

### Skill Level: Average

*Not your usual popcorn candy, this zesty version has a wonderful orange flavor.*

❋ MAKES ABOUT 14 CUPS

    12 cups freshly popped popcorn, unsalted
    1 cup coarsely chopped pecans, walnuts, or
        toasted almonds
    2 cups granulated sugar
    ½ cup half-and-half
    Freshly grated zest of 1 orange
    ½ cup orange juice
    Dash salt
    1 tablespoon butter or margarine

In a very large mixing bowl, combine the popcorn and nuts, tossing them together until the nuts are evenly distributed. Spray a 9 × 13-inch pan or a large roasting pan with nonstick spray. Pour the popcorn mixture into the pan.

In a heavy 2-quart saucepan over medium-low heat, bring the sugar, half-and-half, orange zest, orange juice, and salt to a boil, stirring until the sugar dissolves and the mixture begins to boil. Cook, stirring only as needed to prevent scorching, to the soft ball stage (234°F to 240°F, with 236°F recommended).

Remove from the heat. Stir in the butter until melted. Slowly pour the hot syrup over the popcorn mixture and stir until the popcorn and nuts are coated. Cool slightly, 5 to 10 minutes. Break the candy apart into small pieces. Cool completely. Store in an airtight container.

COOK'S NOTE: If preferred, the mixture may be shaped into popcorn balls. Wrap each cooled popcorn ball in plastic wrap.

# Honey-Nut Popcorn

## Skill Level: Novice, Easy

*Sweet, golden honey slowly baked onto popcorn, almonds, pecans and cashews creates a magnificent combination.*

✳ MAKES ABOUT 12 CUPS

> 8 cups freshly popped popcorn, unsalted
> 1 cup blanched slivered almonds
> 1 cup coarsely chopped pecans
> 1 cup roasted salted cashews
> 1 cup packed light brown sugar
> ½ cup butter or margarine
> ¼ cup honey
> 1 teaspoon vanilla extract

Preheat the oven to 250°F. Butter a very large roasting pan. Pour the popcorn and nuts into the pan, tossing them together until the nuts are evenly distributed.

In a heavy 2-quart saucepan over medium heat, bring the sugar, butter, and honey to a boil, stirring until the sugar dissolves and the mixture begins to boil. Boil 5 minutes without stirring.

Remove from the heat. Stir in the vanilla. Pour the hot syrup over the popcorn mixture and stir the popcorn and nuts until well coated. Bake 1 hour, stirring every 15 minutes. Remove from the oven and cool completely. Break into pieces. Store in an airtight container.

# Old-Fashioned Caramel Popcorn

## Skill Level: Average

*With a crunchy texture and rich molasses flavor, it is no wonder that this recipe has been enjoyed by many generations.*

✳ MAKES ABOUT 12 CUPS

> 12 cups freshly popped popcorn, unsalted
> 1 cup granulated sugar
> ½ cup molasses
> ½ cup water
> 1½ teaspoons cider vinegar
> 2 tablespoons butter
> ½ teaspoon baking soda
> 1 teaspoon vanilla extract

Pour the popcorn into a large mixing bowl.

In a heavy 3-quart saucepan over medium

heat, bring the sugar, molasses, water, vinegar, and butter to a boil, stirring until the sugar dissolves and the mixture begins to boil. Cook, stirring gently a few times, to the soft crack stage (270°F).

Remove from the heat. Stir in the baking soda. Add the vanilla. Pour the hot syrup over the popcorn and stir until the popcorn is well coated. Cool and separate into pieces. Store in an airtight container.

. . . . . . . . . . . . . . . . . . . . . . . . . . .

# Southern-Style Caramel Popcorn

## Skill Level: Average

*Made with Southern-style sorghum syrup, this gooey, flavorful caramel-coated popcorn may taste familiar, especially to seniors who remember the days when sorghum was used as a sugar substitute.*
✳ **MAKES ABOUT 16 CUPS**

**16 cups freshly popped popcorn, unsalted**
**1 cup pure sorghum syrup or sorghum with molasses**
**1 cup packed light brown sugar**
**¼ cup butter**
**¼ cup water**

Pour the popcorn into 2 large or one very large mixing bowl.

In a heavy 3-quart saucepan over medium heat, bring the sorghum, sugar, butter, and water to a boil, stirring until the sugar dissolves and the mixture begins to boil. Cook, stirring gently a few times, to the soft ball stage (240°F)

Remove from the heat. Cool slightly, 1 to 2 minutes. Pour the hot syrup over the popcorn, stirring the popcorn until well coated. Cool and separate into pieces. Store in an airtight container. If preferred, the coated mixture may be shaped into popcorn balls. Wrap each cooled popcorn ball in plastic wrap.

**COOK'S NOTE:** Sorghum syrup is made from sorghum cane and was once quite common in the South. It is becoming popular as a sweetener again because of its high antioxidant content. One brand of sorghum is Mackin's Louisiana sorghum with molasses.

. . . . . . . . . . . . . . . . . . . . . . . . . . .

# Popcorn-and-a-Prize

## Skill Level: Average

*Popcorn, peanuts, and a prize, this candy might have a familiar taste.*
✳ **MAKES ABOUT 22 CUPS**

**20 cups freshly popped popcorn, unsalted**
**1 cup salted peanuts**
**2 cups packed light brown sugar**
**½ cup butter**
**½ cup light corn syrup**
**⅛ teaspoon cream of tartar**
**1 teaspoon baking soda**
**1 small toy prize (optional)**

Preheat the oven to 200°F. In 2 large mixing bowls, combine the popcorn and peanuts, tossing them together until the peanuts are evenly distributed. Butter 2 large baking sheets with sides.

In a heavy 3-quart saucepan over medium

heat, bring the sugar, butter, corn syrup, and cream of tartar to a boil, stirring until the sugar dissolves and the mixture begins to boil. Boil 5 minutes without stirring.

Remove from the heat. Stir in the baking soda. Pour the hot syrup over the popcorn mixture, stirring the popcorn and peanuts until well coated. Bake 40 minutes, stirring every 10 minutes. Remove from the oven and cool completely. Break into pieces. Hide the toy prize inside the popcorn, if using. Store in an airtight container.

# Microwave Caramel Popcorn

### Skill Level: Novice, Easy

*One bite of this microwave popcorn will leave you "shaking" for more.*

✳ MAKES ABOUT 16 CUPS

16 cups freshly popped popcorn, unsalted
1 cup packed light brown sugar
6 tablespoons butter or margarine
¼ cup light corn syrup
¼ teaspoon salt
1 teaspoon vanilla extract
½ teaspoon baking soda

Pour the popcorn into a large brown paper bag. Spray a very large roasting pan with nonstick spray.

In a large mixing bowl, combine the sugar, butter, corn syrup, and salt, stirring to blend. Microwave uncovered on High for 2 minutes. Stir. Microwave on High 3 minutes, stirring af-

## Sorghum Syrup

During the Depression of the 1930s, sugar was a luxury item that few could afford. Like many Southerners, my grandfather built a mule-operated sorghum mill on his land so that his family could still enjoy sweets. Once a year, the family harvested their sorghum cane by hand, hauled it to my grandfather's mill in a horse-drawn wagon, and then cooked the sorghum juice in a flat pan over a large open fire until it thickened into a sweet, brown syrup. With a few days of hard work, the family had enough sorghum syrup to last an entire year, plus a little extra to share with neighbors.

ter each minute. Stir in the vanilla and baking soda until well blended.

Pour the hot syrup over the popcorn in the paper bag. Seal the top of the bag. Microwave on High 1 minute. Shake the bag. Microwave 1 minute and shake the bag. Microwave 30 seconds and shake the bag. Microwave 30 seconds and shake the bag.

Pour the popcorn into the roasting pan. Cool and break into pieces. Store in an airtight container.

# Old-Fashioned Popcorn Balls

## Skill Level: Average

*These classic white popcorn balls are just as tasty as you remember them being.*

✳ MAKES ABOUT 12 BALLS

**12 cups freshly popped popcorn, unsalted**
**1 teaspoon salt**
**1 cup granulated sugar**
**1 cup light corn syrup**
**1 tablespoon cider vinegar**
**1 tablespoon butter or margarine**

Pour the popcorn into a large mixing bowl. Sprinkle with the salt.

In a 1-quart saucepan over medium to medium-high heat, bring the sugar, corn syrup, and vinegar to a boil, stirring until the sugar dissolves and the mixture begins to boil. Cook, without stirring, to the hard ball stage (265°F).

Remove from the heat. Stir in the butter. Slowly pour the hot syrup over the popcorn and stir until the popcorn is well coated. Let the popcorn cool slightly. Using lightly buttered hands, quickly form the popcorn mixture into balls 3 inches in diameter. (Use caution when forming the balls; the syrup can be dangerously hot. See Cook's Note below.) Cool completely. Wrap each cooled popcorn ball in plastic wrap.

COOK'S NOTE: If the syrup is too hot to handle, use two large spoons to loosely form the popcorn into balls or large clusters, and then drop the clusters onto a buttered baking sheet. Cool slightly, and then finish forming the balls by hand.

# Painter's Popcorn Balls

## Skill Level: Average

*Always a favorite, these tinted popcorn balls make a wonderful party favor for a child's birthday.*

✳ MAKES ABOUT 20 BALLS

**20 cups freshly popped popcorn, unsalted**
**2 cups granulated sugar**
**1 cup light corn syrup**
**2 teaspoons cream of tartar**
**1 tablespoon butter**
**Few drops food coloring of choice**
**1/2 teaspoon baking soda**

Pour the popcorn into a large mixing bowl.

In a 2-quart saucepan over medium heat, bring the sugar, corn syrup, cream of tartar, and butter to a boil, stirring until the sugar dissolves and the mixture begins to boil. Cook, without stirring, to the hard ball stage (265°F).

Remove from the heat. Stir in a few drops of food coloring as desired. Stir in the baking soda. Slowly pour the hot syrup over the popcorn, stirring the popcorn until well coated. Let the popcorn cool slightly. Using lightly buttered hands, quickly form the popcorn mixture into balls 3 inches in diameter. (Use caution when forming the balls because the syrup can be dangerously hot; see Cook's Note, at left.) Cool completely. Wrap each cooled popcorn ball in plastic wrap.

COOK'S NOTE: Up to 1½ cups chopped pecans may be mixed with the popcorn in the bowl. Omit the food coloring if desired.

# Kid Pleasin' Popcorn Cake

## Skill Level: Novice, Easy

*Aunt Lucy always knew how to bring out the kid in all of us, especially through food. This was one of her best kid pleasers.*

✳ MAKES ABOUT 12 SERVINGS

**16 cups freshly popped popcorn, unsalted**
**8 ounces small gumdrops**
**8 ounces salted peanuts**
**1 pound large or miniature marshmallows**
**½ cup butter**
**½ cup vegetable oil**

Butter a 10-inch tube cake pan and a large roasting pan. Combine the popcorn, gumdrops, and peanuts in the roasting pan.

In a heavy 3-quart saucepan over low heat, melt the marshmallows, butter, and oil together, stirring until smooth.

Remove from the heat. Pour the marshmallow mixture over the popcorn mixture, stirring until the popcorn is well coated. Press the popcorn mixture into the coated tube pan. Cool completely. Remove the cake from the pan. Wrap the cake in foil until ready to serve. To serve, slice into pieces.

## VARIATION

*Candy Popcorn Cake:* Substitute plain M&M's chocolate candies for the gumdrops. Let the marshmallow mixture cool slightly before pouring it over the popcorn mixture so the candies do not melt. Mixed nuts may be substituted for the peanuts if desired.

# Popcorn Party Cake

## Skill Level: Average

*Packed with peanuts and sweet, flaky coconut, this version of popcorn cake is held together with an old-fashioned cooked syrup, much like syrups used in popcorn balls.*

✳ MAKES ABOUT 8 SERVINGS

**6 cups popped popcorn, unsalted**
**½ cup salted peanuts**
**1 cup sweetened flaked coconut**
**1 cup granulated sugar**
**½ cup half-and-half**
**1 cup light corn syrup**
**Dash of salt**
**1 tablespoon butter**
**1 teaspoon vanilla extract**

Combine the popcorn, peanuts, and coconut in a large mixing bowl. Spray a 10-inch tube pan with nonstick spray.

In a heavy 2-quart saucepan over medium heat, bring the sugar, half-and-half, corn syrup, and salt to a boil, stirring until the sugar dissolves and the mixture begins to boil. Cook, stirring occasionally to prevent scorching, to the soft ball stage (234°F to 240°F with 238°F recommended).

Remove from the heat. Stir in the butter and vanilla until the butter melts. Pour the hot syrup over the popcorn mixture and stir until the popcorn mixture is well coated. Press the popcorn mixture into the coated tube pan. Cool. Remove the cake from the pan. Wrap the cake in foil until ready to serve. To serve, slice into pieces.

# Nutty Popcorn Candy

## Skill Level: Novice, Easy

*Chewy and packed with peanut butter, this unusual popcorn candy may be like none you have ever tasted.*

✳ **MAKES ABOUT 1¼ POUNDS**

> **3 cups ground popped popcorn (see Cook's Note below)**
> **1 cup finely chopped salted peanuts**
> **½ cup granulated sugar**
> **½ cup light corn syrup**
> **½ cup peanut butter**
> **½ teaspoon vanilla extract**

Butter an 8-inch square pan. In a large mixing bowl, combine the popcorn and peanuts, stirring until well mixed.

In a very small saucepan over medium-high heat, bring the sugar and corn syrup to a boil, stirring until the sugar dissolves and the mixture begins to boil. Boil 1 to 2 minutes without stirring.

Remove from the heat. Add the peanut butter and vanilla, stirring until smooth. Pour the syrup over the popcorn and peanuts, mixing well. Pack into the buttered pan. Cool and cut into squares. Store in an airtight container.

**COOK'S NOTE:** To make this candy like our grandmothers did, grind popcorn in a food grinder, measuring 3 cups when finished. If a food grinder is not available, a food processor may be used, although many food processors only chop the popcorn into slightly smaller pieces.

# Popcorn Snap

## Skill Level: Average

*Almost like peanut brittle but made with ground popcorn, this interesting old recipe may be one of a kind.*

✳ **MAKES ABOUT 1½ POUNDS**

> **1½ cups granulated sugar**
> **½ cup packed light brown sugar**
> **½ cup light corn syrup**
> **Butter the size of a walnut (2 tablespoons butter)**
> **½ cup water**
> **Pinch salt**
> **¼ teaspoon baking soda**
> **3 cups ground popped popcorn (see Cook's Note, at left)**
> **½ cup ground peanuts**

Butter 2 large baking sheets.

In a heavy 5-quart kettle over medium heat, bring the sugars, corn syrup, butter, water, and salt to a boil, stirring until the sugars dissolve and the mixture begins to boil. Cook, stirring gently a few times, to the hard crack stage (300° F).

Remove from the heat. Stir in the baking soda until well blended. Add the popcorn and peanuts. Quickly pour the mixture onto the buttered baking sheets, spreading evenly across both pans. Cool slightly and cut into pieces or cool completely and break into pieces. Store in an airtight container.

# Fruit Candies

## Washington State Apple Squares

### Skill Level: Average

*Similar to Washington state's famous Aplets candy, these fruity squares are a popular treat throughout the Pacific Northwest.*

✳ MAKES ABOUT 3 POUNDS

3 cups applesauce, at room temperature, divided
4 envelopes (1-ounce box) unflavored gelatin
4 cups granulated sugar
1 cup coarsely chopped walnuts
1 teaspoon vanilla extract
Pinch salt
2 to 3 cups powdered sugar, for rolling

In a small bowl, combine 1 cup of the applesauce and the gelatin, stirring until blended. Butter an 8 × 11-inch pan. Line the bottom of a large airtight plastic container with waxed paper.

In a heavy 4- to 5-quart kettle over medium heat, bring the remaining 2 cups applesauce and the sugar to a boil over medium heat, stirring until the sugar dissolves and the mixture begins to boil. Gradually add the gelatin mixture, by spoonfuls, working out the lumps with the back of a spoon as the mixture cooks. Boil rapidly, stirring occasionally, over medium heat 20 minutes.

Remove from the heat. Cool slightly, 5 to 10 minutes. Stir in the walnuts, vanilla, and salt. Pour into the buttered pan. Cool at room temperature about 30 minutes. Cover and refrigerate until firm.

Cut into 1-inch squares. Roll each square in the powdered sugar once a day for 2 to 3 days or until they have a white coating. After the first coating, place the squares in the lined plastic container, separating each layer with waxed paper to prevent sticking. Place the squares back in the same container after the second rolling. If needed, roll a third time. Store at room temperature several days. Once they begin to lose their eye appeal, they are spoiled and should be discarded.

# Apricot or Apple Squares

## Skill Level: Average

*This version of Washington state's famous candy offers a slightly different cooking method to Washington State Apple Squares (page 191).*

✳ MAKES ABOUT 2 POUNDS

2 (15.25-ounce) cans apricots or 2 cups
　applesauce
2 tablespoons unflavored gelatin
½ cup cold water
2 cups light corn syrup
1 tablespoon lemon juice
1 cup chopped walnuts
About 2 cups powdered sugar, for rolling

If using canned apricots, drain the apricots in a colander, removing as much excess juice as possible. Chop the apricots in a food processor until reduced to a puree; measure 2 cups. In a small bowl, dissolve the gelatin in the cold water, stirring to mix. Butter an 8-inch square pan.

In a heavy 3-quart saucepan over medium heat, bring the apricot puree or applesauce and the corn syrup to a boil, stirring constantly. Cook at a medium boil, stirring constantly, about 20 minutes or until the excess moisture has evaporated and the mixture is very thick.

Remove from the heat. Add the gelatin mixture and stir until the lumps dissolve. Cool slightly, about 3 minutes. Stir in the lemon juice and walnuts. Pour into the buttered pan. Cool completely. When firm, cut into squares and roll in the powdered sugar. Store in an airtight container, separating each layer with waxed paper to prevent sticking. After 24 hours, roll the squares in powdered sugar again. The squares should maintain a white, powdery coating. If not, wait a few hours and

roll in powdered sugar a third time. Store in an airtight container at room temperature for several days. Once they begin to lose their eye appeal, they are spoiled and should be discarded.

COOK'S NOTES: The easiest way to make this candy is to use canned applesauce or canned apricots. If preferred, 2 cups cooked sauce from Jonathan or Winesap apples may be substituted for the applesauce, and 2 cups cooked fresh apricot puree may be substituted for the canned apricots. If using fresh apples or apricots, peel, core, and slice the fruit into thin slices. Cook over low heat in a small saucepan until tender, using as little water as possible. Sieve and place in the heavy 3-quart saucepan.

. . . . . . . . . . . . . . . . . . . . . . . . . . .

# Apple-Cinnamon Walnut Squares

## Skill Level: Average

*The combination of apples, cinnamon, and strawberry just makes these gelatin candies more flavorful.*

✳ MAKES ABOUT 1 POUND

1 cup canned applesauce
1 tablespoon small hot cinnamon candies
1 (3-ounce) package strawberry gelatin
1 cup granulated sugar
¾ cup chopped walnuts
About 1 cup granulated or powdered sugar, for
　rolling

Butter a 9 × 5-inch loaf pan.

In a heavy 2-quart saucepan over low heat,

## A Candy Memory

Many of the people I met while writing this book shared their memories of homemade candy with me, often reminiscing about their childhoods with stories such as this one.

"I remember making apricot candy when I was a child," one man told me. "We were very poor and could not afford gifts, so every year my family made little balls of apricot candy and gave them to family and friends for Christmas. I am not sure what recipe we used, but it sure was good!"

All of those who heard this story agreed that a gift of homemade candy is always special.

# Apricot Bars

## Skill Level: Average

*The addition of orange gives a slightly different spin to Washington's famous Cotlets candy.*

✳ **MAKES ABOUT 2 POUNDS**

> 4 envelopes (1-ounce box) granulated gelatin
> 1½ cups apricot juice
> 2 cups granulated sugar
> ¼ cup orange juice
> 2 teaspoons freshly grated orange zest
> 1 cup pureed or cooked dried apricots
> About 1 cup powdered or granulated sugar for rolling

bring the applesauce and candies to a boil. Stir in the gelatin and sugar. Bring to a second boil, stirring constantly. Boil 2 minutes, stirring constantly.

Remove from the heat. Add the walnuts and mix well. Pour into the buttered pan. Cover and refrigerate until firm, about 3 hours. Cut into squares and roll the squares in the sugar. Place in an airtight container, separating each layer with waxed paper to prevent sticking. After 24 hours, roll the squares in sugar again. Store in an airtight container at room temperature for several days. Once they begin to lose their eye appeal, they are spoiled and should be discarded.

Line an 8-inch square pan with waxed paper, leaving a 1-inch overhang on the sides of the pan.

Soften the gelatin in 1 cup of the apricot juice.

In a heavy 3-quart saucepan over medium heat, bring the sugar, remaining apricot juice, orange juice, orange zest, and gelatin mixture to a boil, stirring until the sugar dissolves and the mixture begins to boil. Cook at a medium boil 20 minutes, stirring constantly. Add the apricot puree and cook 2 minutes longer.

Remove from the heat. Cool 10 to 20 minutes. Pour into the lined pan. Cool completely, refrigerating if desired. When the candy is firm, remove it from the pan and cut into bars or squares. Roll each piece in sugar and place on waxed paper or a wire rack to dry. If needed, roll in sugar again until the candy can be handled and no longer has a sticky coating. Store in an airtight container.

COOK'S NOTE: These candies will spoil within about 1 week of being cooked, perhaps sooner.

Once they begin to lose their eye appeal, it is time to dispose of them.

. . . . . . . . . . . . . . . . . . . . .

# Aunt Shirley's Apricot Sugarplums

## Skill Level: Average

*Each holiday season, Aunt Shirley enchants her family and friends with these elegant apricot sugarplums. To spice up your holidays, try adding a dash of ginger.*

✳ **MAKES 30 TO 36**

**1 (11-ounce) package dried apricots**
**3 cups water, divided**
**2 cups granulated sugar, plus about 1 cup for rolling**
**2 tablespoons light corn syrup**
**1 tablespoon orange or almond liqueur or a dash of ginger (optional)**
**About 3 cups walnut halves**

In a 3-quart saucepan over medium heat, combine the apricots and 2 cups of the water. Cover and bring to a boil. Remove from the heat. Cool 10 minutes. Drain the apricots, discarding the water.

In a 10-inch skillet over medium heat, bring the 2 cups sugar, remaining 1 cup water, and corn syrup to a boil, stirring until the sugar dissolves. Cook, without stirring, 15 minutes. Add the apricots, stirring gently to separate them. Gently stir in the liqueur, if using. Simmer, uncovered, until the apricots are translucent, about 20 minutes.

Remove from the heat. Cool to room temperature, about 1½ hours.

Remove each apricot half from the skillet and place on a wire rack. Let stand, uncovered, at room temperature until dry. Fill the cavity of each apricot with a walnut half. Roll the stuffed apricots in the sugar. Store in an airtight container at room temperature for up to 3 days or freeze for up to 1 month.

. . . . . . . . . . . . . . . . . . . . .

# Apple Crystals

## Skill Level: Average

*When cut into fancy shapes, these dried apple crystals make an elegant garnish for a favorite cake or dessert.*

✳ **MAKES ABOUT 72 PIECES**

**6 firm apples**
**2 cups granulated sugar, plus 2 cups for rolling**
**2 tablespoons small hot cinnamon candies**
**2 drops red food coloring**
**1 cup water**

Peel the apples and cut into halves or quarters. Remove the cores using a half-teaspoon measuring spoon or a French ball cutter (melon baller). Cut the apples into fancy shapes or rings or slice the apple halves crosswise using a fluted edge cutter. Cut each apple half into about 6 slices.

Cover a large countertop area or 2 large baking sheets with waxed paper.

In a 1- to 2-quart saucepan over medium heat, bring the sugar, candies, food coloring, and water to a boil, stirring until the sugar dissolves and the mixture begins to boil. Drop up to 12 pieces of apple (no more than one apple at a time) into the syrup and cook until the apple pieces are tender when pierced with a toothpick. Remove the apple pieces from the syrup, drain, and place on the waxed paper to cool. Repeat until all of the apple pieces are cooked, adding ¼ cup more water to cook each apple (or 12 pieces) until all the apples are cooked or the syrup gets too low to use (the syrup will be absorbed by the apples).

Let the apple pieces stand, uncovered, for 24 hours. Roll the pieces in the sugar. Roll twice again at 24-hour intervals, turning the apples and keeping them in as dry a location as possible, especially if weather is damp. Dry the apples at room temperature until they have no moisture. Pack in an airtight container and store in a cool, dry location. Use as a candy or as a garnish.

## Fresh Coconut Chips

### Skill Level: Novice, Easy

*For a simple, elegant dessert, fill stemmed glasses with scoops of vanilla ice cream, add a spoonful of Kahlua, and top with oven-toasted coconut chips.*
✳ MAKES ABOUT 2 CUPS

**1 fresh coconut**
**Salt, to taste**

Preheat the oven to 350°F. Using an ice pick or a large nail, punch holes into the coconut eyes. Drain the coconut milk, discarding the milk or saving it for another recipe. Place the coconut

on a baking sheet and bake for 30 to 40 minutes. Remove the coconut from the oven and cool until it is comfortable to the touch.

Using a hammer, crack the center of the coconut shell. Run a knife blade between the coconut meat and the shell, loosening the coconut meat from the shell. Remove any shell fragments from the coconut meat by rinsing under cold water.

Using a vegetable peeler, cut the coconut into thin ribbons by drawing the peeler toward you. Use a paring knife to cut the ribbons into smaller pieces.

Spread the thinly sliced coconut on 2 baking sheets. Place in the oven and reduce the temperature to 200°F. Dry the coconut in the oven for 2 to 3 hours, stirring occasionally. If desired, increase the oven temperature to 250°F the last few minutes to toast the chips. Sprinkle the toasted chips with salt. If the chips lose their crispness, heat in the oven a few minutes. Cool the chips completely. Store in an airtight container.

# Candied Citrus Peel

## Skill Level: Average

*Candied citrus peel makes a wonderful garnish for the top of a special cake or a holiday tray filled with other sweets.*

✳ MAKES ABOUT 2 CUPS

> 4 medium oranges, 6 lemons, or 2 grapefruits
> 1 cup granulated sugar, plus about 1 cup for coating
> 1/3 cup water

Select thick-skinned fruit. Remove the peel and cut into slender strips using a sharp knife or kitchen shears. Place the strips in a small saucepan and cover with cold water. Bring to boil over medium heat. Boil for 10 to 15 minutes; drain. Add fresh cold water, repeating the process up to three times or until the peel is tender. (Changing water helps remove excess bitterness.) Do not mix different types of fruit peels because cooking times vary with different fruits.

In a small saucepan over low heat, bring the sugar and the water to a boil, stirring until the sugar dissolves and the mixture begins to boil. Add the peel, boiling until the syrup is almost completely absorbed by the peel, stirring occasionally.

Lift the peel from the syrup and place into a strainer to drain. Spread in a single layer on waxed paper to cool. Sprinkle sugar over the peel, mixing with a fork so that each piece is coated with sugar. Let dry 12 to 24 hours. Add more sugar as needed so that the candied peel does not stick together. Store in an airtight container.

# Banana Tidbits

## Skill Level: Novice, Super Simple

*This recipe was a favorite with an elderly woman I knew as a child. Ruby would be thrilled to have you try her peanut-and-coconut-covered treats.*

✳ MAKES ABOUT 16 PIECES

> 2 ripe medium bananas
> 1/2 cup sweetened condensed milk
> 1/2 cup finely chopped peanuts
> 1/2 cup sweetened flaked coconut

Peel the bananas and cut into 1-inch slices. Dip each banana piece into the milk. Roll half of the banana pieces in the peanuts and half in the coconut. Cover and refrigerate until ready to serve. This treat is best served within 1 day.

# Cuppa Fruit Candy

## Skill Level: Novice, Super Simple

*A cup of this, a cup of that, add a little honey, and you have a natural, healthy candy.*

*Using a food processor, grind or finely chop the fruit before measuring. Grind or chop the nuts after measuring.*

✳ MAKES 40 TO 45 PIECES

> 1 cup ground or finely chopped dried peaches or apricots
> 1 cup ground or finely chopped raisins
> 1 cup ground or finely chopped figs
> 1 cup ground or finely chopped dried apples
> 1 cup ground or finely chopped dates

**1 cup toasted almonds, ground or finely chopped**
**About 1 cup honey**
**½ cup sesame seeds**
**½ cup sunflower seeds**

In a large mixing bowl, combine the fruits and almonds. Blend together, adding just enough honey to hold the fruit together. Shape small bits of the fruit mixture into patties. Roll the patties in the sesame seeds and sunflower seeds. Store in an airtight container.

COOK'S NOTE: If the fruit is particularly dry, cover it in water and soak for 30 minutes. Drain off the liquid before chopping the fruits.

# Nature's Candy

## Skill Level: Novice, Super Simple

*Choosy mothers may want to choose this candy as an after-school treat.*
✳ MAKES ABOUT 12

**½ cup peanut butter**
**⅝ cup ground or very finely chopped sunflower seeds**
**½ cup chopped raisins**
**¼ cup instant nonfat dry milk**
**½ teaspoon salt**
**4 tablespoons honey**
**About ¼ cup wheat germ**
**About ½ cup sweetened flaked coconut, for rolling**

In a medium mixing bowl, combine the peanut butter, sunflower seeds, raisins, dry milk, salt,

and honey. Shape the mixture into balls 1 inch in diameter. Roll the balls in the wheat germ and the coconut. Cover and refrigerate until chilled. Store in an airtight container.

COOK'S NOTE: If desired, 1 tablespoon brewers yeast can be added to the mixture if you like its unusual flavor.

# Persian Sweets

## Skill Level: Novice, Super Simple

*This is the perfect snack for skiers and hikers to stash away in their pockets.*
✳ MAKES ABOUT 18 PIECES

**4 ounces pitted dates**
**4 ounces figs**
**1 cup raisins**
**1 cup pecans or walnuts**
**Honey or fruit juice, if needed**
**About ¼ cup powdered or granulated sugar, for rolling**

Finely chop the dates, figs, raisins, and nuts; place into a bowl. Blend or knead the mixture by hand until thoroughly mixed. If the mixture is too dry to hold together, stir in honey, by teaspoons, to moisten.

The mixture may be pressed into a small pan and cut into squares, shaped into logs and sliced, or shaped into small balls. Roll each piece of candy in powdered or granulated sugar. Store in an airtight container.

# Figgie Nuggets

## Skill Level: Novice, Super Simple

*Loaded with figs and apricots, this tasty treat is packed with sunshine.*

✳ MAKES 45 TO 50 PIECES

1 pound dried figs
8 ounces pitted dates
½ cup raisins
1 pound dried apricots
2 cups walnuts or pecans
1 teaspoon grated orange zest
Honey or orange juice, if needed
1½ to 2 cups sweetened flaked coconut, for rolling

Grind the figs, dates, raisins, apricots, and nuts in a food grinder until finely ground. Transfer to a medium bowl; stir in the orange zest. Mix the ingredients by hand until well blended. If the mixture is too dry to hold its shape, stir in a few teaspoons of honey to moisten.

Press into an 8-inch square pan. Cut into squares and roll each square in the coconut. Store in an airtight container.

COOK'S NOTE: If a food grinder is not available, very finely chop the fruits and nuts in a food processor or by hand.

# Carnival Candied Apples

## Skill Level: Average

*Remember those delicious, sticky, bright cinnamon red apples you loved as a kid? Once a common carnival treat, they can easily be made at home.*

✳ MAKES 8

8 medium red apples
3 cups granulated sugar
½ cup water
½ cup light corn syrup
1 drop cinnamon oil, or to taste
1 teaspoon red food coloring

Wash, dry, and polish the apples. Remove the stems. Insert a wooden skewer into the stem end of each apple, using a twisting motion so that the apple will not split. Line a large baking sheet with aluminum foil. Spray the foil with nonstick spray.

In a large, heavy, deep saucepan over medium heat, bring the sugar, water, and corn syrup to a boil, stirring until the sugar dissolves and the mixture begins to boil. Cook, without stirring, to the soft crack stage (285°F).

Remove from the heat. Stir in the cinnamon oil and food coloring just until mixed.

Working very quickly, hold an apple by the wooden skewer and quickly twirl it into the syrup, tilting the pan to cover the apple. Remove the apple from the syrup, allow the excess syrup to drip into the pan, and then twirl the apple again to spread the syrup smoothly over the apple. Place on the lined baking sheet. Repeat with remaining apples and syrup. Let stand until firm. Store in a cool, dry place.

COOK'S NOTE: These apples are lightly flavored with cinnamon. The amount of cinnamon oil may be increased if desired.

. . . . . . . . . . . . . . . . . . . . . . . . .

# Mrs. McDonald's Red Candied Apples

## Skill Level: Average

*Once upon a time, every child in a small Oklahoma town knocked on Mrs. McDonald's door on Halloween night to get one of her very special red candied apples. These softly wrapped apples are just as rich and creamy today as my sister-in-law remembers them.*

✳ MAKES 20

20 small apples
2 cups granulated sugar
1¾ cups milk
1½ cups light corn syrup
¼ cup margarine
¹⁄₁₆ teaspoon baking soda
½ ounce red food coloring

Wash, dry, and polish the apples. Remove the stems and insert round, pointed sticks into the cores. Butter 2 large baking sheets.

In a heavy 5-quart kettle over medium-low to medium heat, bring the sugar, milk, corn syrup, margarine, and baking soda to a boil, stirring until the sugar dissolves and the mixture begins to boil. Cook, stirring occasionally to prevent scorching, to between 240°F and 242°F, about 40 minutes. Add the food coloring, stirring until well blended.

Remove from the heat. Working very quickly,

hold an apple by the wooden skewer and quickly twirl it into the syrup, tilting the pan to cover the apple. Remove the apple from the syrup, allow the excess syrup to drip into the pan, and then twirl the apple again to spread the syrup smoothly over the apple. Place on the lined baking sheet. Repeat with remaining apples and syrup. Let stand until firm. Wrap each apple in plastic wrap.

COOK'S NOTE: If preferred, this recipe may be doubled and cooked in a heavy 8-quart kettle.

. . . . . . . . . . . . . . . . . . . . . . . . .

# Old-Fashioned Caramel Apples

## Skill Level: Average

*What could be better than a crisp fall apple smothered in rich, creamy homemade caramel? Here is the real McCoy.*

✳ MAKES 12

12 medium apples
2 cups granulated sugar
1 cup packed light brown sugar
⅔ cup light corn syrup
½ cup butter or margarine
1 cup half-and-half or evaporated milk
1 teaspoon salt
2 teaspoons vanilla extract
2 cups chopped pecans, 1½ cups sweetened flaked coconut, or 2 cups crisp rice cereal (optional)

Wash and dry the apples. Remove the stems. Insert a wooden skewer into the stem end of each apple, using a twistlike motion so that the apple will not split. Cover a large countertop area or a large baking sheet with waxed paper.

In a large, heavy kettle over medium-low heat, bring the sugars, corn syrup, butter, half-and-half, and salt to a boil, stirring until the sugars dissolve and the mixture begins to boil. Cook, gently stirring to prevent scorching, to the firm ball stage (246°F). Stir in the vanilla.

Remove from the heat. Cool until the mixture thickens slightly. Hold each apple by the wooden skewer and quickly twirl into the caramel, tilting the pan to cover the apple with caramel. Remove the apple from the caramel, allow the excess caramel to drip into the pan, and then twirl the apple again to spread the caramel smoothly over the apple. Use a spoon to coat any part of the apple not covered with caramel. If desired, roll the coated apples in the pecans before the caramel sets. Place on the waxed paper until the coating is firm. Store in a cool, dry place.

### VARIATION

*Red Caramel Apples:* Use ⅔ cup butter or margarine. Stir in about ½ ounce red food coloring with the vanilla.

# Short and Sweet

**S**ometimes just the simplest combination of ingredients is enough to satisfy a screaming sweet tooth or feed a starving crowd. When those busy days arrive, nothing pleases us more than to have a ready supply of easy recipes that we can make in a matter of minutes.

Perfect for everyday entertaining or filling a holiday gift tin, the cool, refreshing taste of peppermint bark is always a favorite, no matter which recipe is used. Chocolate, butterscotch, and peanut butter lovers will delight in the many simple clusters and confections they can make using ingredients already on hand. And what grandparent can resist introducing the grandkids to fun and creative recipes such as Caramel Nut Marshmallows, Chocolate Birds' Nests, or Chipper Nutty Fudge?

With a little something for everybody, the only difficult part about these recipes is choosing just one favorite.

# Simple Barks

## Cherry-Almond Bark

### Skill Level: Novice, Easy

*Aunt Lucy's simple, colorful candy will brighten up any holiday gift tin.*

※ MAKES ABOUT 1 POUND

**12 ounces white chocolate baking squares**
**½ cup chopped almonds, toasted**
**½ cup chopped candied red cherries**

Line a large baking sheet with waxed paper.

In the top pan of a double boiler over hot but not boiling water, melt the white chocolate, stirring until smooth. Stir in the almonds and cherries. Spread the mixture onto the lined baking sheet in an even layer. Refrigerate 1 hour or until firm. Break into pieces. Store in an airtight container.

### VARIATIONS

This candy may also be made using 8 ounces white chocolate baking squares and 4 ounces white chocolate candy coating or 12 ounces white chocolate candy coating in place of the white chocolate.

Pistachio nuts may be substituted for the toasted almonds, and dried cranberries may be substituted for the candied red cherries.

## White Chocolate Peppermint Bark

### Skill Level: Novice, Easy

*A bag of this cool, mint-flavored bark is the perfect gift for those you want to remember during the holiday season. For stronger flavor, add more crushed peppermint.*

※ MAKES ABOUT ¾ POUND

**12 ounces white chocolate candy coating**
**¼ cup crushed peppermint candies or candy canes, or to taste, divided**
**½ teaspoon peppermint extract**

Line a baking sheet with waxed paper.

In the top pan of a double boiler over hot but not boiling water, melt the white chocolate, stirring until smooth. Stir in half of the peppermint candy and the peppermint extract, blending well. Spoon the mixture onto the lined baking sheet. Using a flat metal spatula or knife, spread the mixture evenly to about a ¼-inch thickness. Sprinkle the remaining crushed peppermint on top. Refrigerate 1 hour or until firm. Break into small pieces. Store in an airtight container.

COOK'S NOTE: This candy can be made using 12 ounces white chocolate in place of the white chocolate candy coating.

# Mary Fallin's Peppermint Almond Bark

## Skill Level: Novice, Easy

*Oklahoma Lieutenant Governor Mary Fallin shares a favorite family recipe for this festive, two-toned microwave peppermint bark.*

✳ MAKES ABOUT 2 POUNDS

**20 ounces chocolate almond bark**
**1 large or 6 medium peppermint candy canes**
**20 ounces white chocolate almond bark**

Line a 10 × 15-inch jelly roll pan or a large baking sheet with waxed paper.

Melt the chocolate almond bark in the microwave according to package directions. Spread the chocolate in a thin layer across the lined pan or baking sheet. Cool about 30 minutes.

Seal the candy canes in a plastic bag. Crush the candy canes into small pieces by gently pounding the outside of the bag with a mallet or hammer.

Melt the white chocolate almond bark in the microwave according to package directions. Stir the crushed peppermint into the melted white chocolate almond bark. Spread the white mixture evenly over the cooled chocolate layer. Cool and break into pieces. Store in an airtight container.

# Gourmet Layered Peppermint Bark

## Skill Level: Novice, Easy

*This double-layered peppermint bark is as beautiful as it is delicious. A stunning gift, this is a personal favorite.*

✳ MAKES ABOUT 1½ POUNDS

**8 ounces dark chocolate candy coating**
**4 ounces (⅔ cup) semisweet chocolate chips or baking squares**
**2 teaspoons peppermint extract, divided**
**12 ounces white chocolate candy coating or**
    **8 ounces white chocolate candy coating and**
    **4 ounces white chocolate, finely chopped**
**¾ cup crushed peppermint candies or candy canes**

Line a baking sheet with waxed paper.

In the top pan of a double boiler over hot but not boiling water, melt the dark chocolate candy coating and chocolate chips, stirring until smooth. Remove from the heat. Stir in 1 teaspoon of the peppermint extract until well blended. Pour the chocolate mixture onto the lined baking sheet, spreading into a thin, even layer. Cool about 30 minutes or until the chocolate is firm.

In the top pan of a double boiler over hot but not boiling water, melt the white chocolate candy coating, stirring until smooth. Remove from the heat. Stir in the remaining peppermint extract until well blended. Pour the white chocolate on top of the dark chocolate layer, spreading evenly. Sprinkle with the crushed peppermint. Cool and break into pieces. Store in an airtight container.

# Chocolate-Nut Bark

## Skill Level: Novice, Easy

*This old favorite can be made in a matter of minutes.*

❋ MAKES ABOUT 2 POUNDS

1 cup pecans in large pieces, toasted
10½ ounces (2⅔ bars) German's sweet
    chocolate bar
1 tablespoon butter or margarine
1½ pounds large marshmallows, halved
1 teaspoon vanilla extract

Butter a large baking sheet and sprinkle with the pecans.

In a large glass bowl in the microwave or in the top of a double boiler pan over hot but not boiling water, melt the chocolate and butter together. Blend well.

Remove from the microwave or heat. Stir in the marshmallows. The marshmallows will only partially melt. Stir in the vanilla. Quickly pour the chocolate mixture over the nuts on the baking sheet. Cool until the chocolate is firm, about 1 hour. Break into pieces. Store in an airtight container.

# Speedy Candy Rolls

## Marshmallow Date Roll

**Skill Level: Novice, Super Simple**

*For a simple dessert, top a few slices of this old favorite with dollops of freshly whipped cream or your favorite ice cream.*

✳ **MAKES ABOUT 1½ POUNDS**

1 cup chopped pitted dates
1 cup miniature marshmallows
1 cup golden raisins
½ cup finely chopped pecans or walnuts
1 cup finely crushed graham cracker crumbs
About ⅓ cup evaporated milk or half-and-half

In a medium mixing bowl, combine the dates, marshmallows, raisins, nuts, and graham cracker crumbs, mixing well. Stir in just enough milk to moisten the ingredients so they can be shaped into a roll.

Tear 2 large sheets of waxed paper. Divide the mixture evenly, spooning half the mixture onto each piece of waxed paper. Shape each portion into a roll about 2 inches in diameter. Wrap tightly in the waxed paper; seal in foil. Refrigerate until firm, about 2 hours. Slice as needed. Store covered in the refrigerator.

## Pineapple Date Roll

**Skill Level: Novice, Super Simple**

*Pineapple Date Roll is another old-time treat that tastes particularly good when smothered in whipped cream.*

✳ **MAKES ABOUT 3 POUNDS**

1½ cups chopped pitted dates
2 cups miniature marshmallows
1 cup chopped pecans
½ cup crushed pineapple, drained
3 cups graham cracker crumbs
About ½ cup evaporated milk or half-and-half

In a medium mixing bowl, combine the dates, marshmallows, pecans, pineapple, and graham cracker crumbs, mixing well. Stir in just enough milk to moisten the ingredients so they can be shaped into a roll.

Cover the countertop with 2 to 3 large sheets of waxed paper. Divide the mixture evenly, spooning equal portions onto each piece of waxed paper. Shape each portion into a roll about 2 inches in diameter. Wrap tightly in the waxed paper, and then wrap again in aluminum foil. Refrigerate until firm, about 2 hours. Slice as needed. Store covered in the refrigerator.

**COOK'S NOTE:** If preferred, ½ to 1 cup graham cracker crumbs may be reserved and patted onto the outside of the roll before sealing it in waxed paper.

. . . . . . . . . . . . . . . . . . . . . . . .

# Rushin' Raisin Roll

## Skill Level: Novice, Easy

*I'm not sure where this candy got its name. The Russians never heard of it, but rushin' people love its easy preparation.*

✳ **MAKES ABOUT 4 POUNDS**

**1 pound large or miniature marshmallows**
**1 cup evaporated milk**
**1 pound graham crackers, finely crushed**
**1 pound raisins**
**4 cups chopped pecans**

In a heavy 3-quart saucepan over low heat or in the top pan of a double boiler over hot but not boiling water, melt the marshmallows and milk together, stirring until smooth. Remove from the heat. Reserve 1 cup of the graham cracker crumbs. Stir the remaining crumbs, raisins, and pecans into the melted marshmallow mixture, blending well. Let the mixture stand until slightly thickened so that it can be shaped into a roll.

Cover a countertop area with 2 to 3 large sheets of waxed paper. Sprinkle the reserved crumbs evenly onto the sheets of waxed paper. Divide the marshmallow mixture evenly, spooning equal portions onto the crumbs. Shape into rolls and roll in the crumbs to coat. Wrap tightly in the waxed paper, and then wrap in aluminum foil. Refrigerate until firm, about 1 hour. Slice as needed. Store wrapped in the refrigerator.

# Chocolate Raisin Roll

## Skill Level: Novice, Easy

*Chocolate velvet, chewy raisins, and crunchy coconut—with all these textural contrasts, this candy must have been invented by an artist.*

✳ **MAKES ABOUT 1½ POUNDS**

**1 cup (6 ounces) semisweet chocolate chips**
**20 large marshmallows, halved or quartered**
**1 tablespoon milk**
**1 cup finely chopped pecans**
**1 cup raisins**
**1 to 1½ cups sweetened flaked coconut,**
    **toasted (see page 195)**

In the top pan of a double boiler over hot but not boiling water, melt the chocolate chips, marshmallows, and milk together, stirring until smooth.

Remove from the heat. Stir in the pecans and raisins. Let the mixture cool slightly, about 5 minutes, or until it begins to thicken and can be shaped into a roll.

Cover the countertop with a large sheet of waxed paper. Sprinkle the coconut on the waxed paper. Spoon the cooled mixture on top the coconut. Shape the chocolate mixture into a long roll about 2 inches in diameter, sprinkling with the coconut while rolling. Wrap tightly in the waxed paper, and then wrap again in foil. Refrigerate until firm, about 2 hours. Slice as needed. Store in an airtight container in the refrigerator.

**COOK'S NOTE:** Snip the marshmallows in halves or quarters using a pair of kitchen shears.

. . . . . . . . . . . . . . . . . . . . . . .

# Cherry-Topped Fruit Roll

## Skill Level: Novice, Easy

*Bright red and green cherries adorn this fluffy white marshmallow, raisin, and pecan roll, but the best part may be the spiced outer coating.*

✳ MAKES ABOUT 1½ POUNDS

¼ cup whole red candied cherries, divided
¼ cup whole green candied cherries, divided
½ cup coarsely chopped candied pineapple
1 cup golden raisins
1 cup coarsely chopped pecans
2 cups miniature marshmallows
½ cup dry bread crumbs, divided
½ teaspoon ground cinnamon
½ teaspoon ground nutmeg

Reserve half of the red candied cherries and half of the green candied cherries. Coarsely chop the remaining cherries.

In a medium microwave-proof bowl, combine the remaining red and green cherries with the pineapple, raisins, pecans, and marshmallows, mixing well. Microwave the mixture, uncovered, 1½ to 2 minutes on High or until the marshmallows have melted. Stir the ingredients together until well blended.

Cover the countertop with a large sheet of waxed paper. Lightly sprinkle the waxed paper with about half of the bread crumbs, and then sprinkle the bread crumbs with the cinnamon and nutmeg. Using alternating colors of the reserved red and green cherries, place the cherries down the center of the bread crumbs in a straight line, spacing them about ½ inch apart. Spoon the marshmallow mixture into a row next to the row of cherries. Shape the marshmallow mixture into a roll and sprinkle with the remaining bread crumbs. Roll in the waxed paper, pressing the red and green cherries into the marshmallow mixture while rolling, creating a decorative cherry-topped design. Wrap tightly in the waxed paper, and then wrap in aluminum foil and freeze.

To serve, remove the foil and cut into thin slices, leaving the waxed paper in place while slicing. Let stand at room temperature 10 to 15 minutes, removing the waxed paper before serving. Store tightly wrapped in the refrigerator or freezer.

# Simple Peanut Butter Roll

## Skill Level: Novice, Super Simple

*So simple that a child can make it, this candy is ready to enjoy in a matter of minutes.*

✳ MAKES ABOUT ½ POUND

1 cup light corn syrup
1 cup smooth peanut butter
1 cup powdered sugar
1½ cups instant nonfat dry milk
1 cup crushed vanilla wafer cookies or
    cornflakes cereal

In a medium mixing bowl, combine the corn syrup and peanut butter, blending until smooth. Gradually stir in the powdered sugar and dry milk until well blended. Shape the candy into small logs and roll in the crushed cookies. Slice into pieces to serve. Store wrapped in plastic wrap.

COOK'S NOTE: If preferred, omit the crushed cookies or cereal and roll the candies into balls. The ball can be rolled in crushed cookies or cereal.

# Candies in Short Order

## Chocolate Fudge Turtles

**Skill Level: Novice, Super Simple**

*This 1964 prizewinning recipe from the* Ponca City News *annual recipe contest was so popular that, nearly twenty years later, someone put another new spin on it and won another award. See the 1983 version, Chocolate Marshmallow Turtles at right.*

✳ MAKES 40 TO 50

3 cups (18 ounces) semisweet chocolate chips
1 (14-ounce) can sweetened condensed milk
1 (7-ounce) jar marshmallow creme
2 teaspoons vanilla extract
4 cups pecans in large pieces

Cover a large countertop area or 2 large baking sheets with waxed paper.

In the top pan of a double boiler over hot but not boiling water, melt the chocolate chips, stirring until smooth. Remove from the heat. Stir in the milk, marshmallow creme, vanilla, and pecans. Drop by spoonfuls onto the waxed paper. Cool. Store in an airtight container.

## Chocolate Marshmallow Turtles

**Skill Level: Novice, Easy**

*This 1983 prizewinning recipe from the* Ponca City News *annual recipe contest will feed an army of kids. If the kids do not like nuts, just add a few more marshmallows.*

✳ MAKES 50 TO 60

3 cups (18 ounces) semisweet chocolate chips
1 (14-ounce) can sweetened condensed milk
1 (7-ounce) jar marshmallow creme
Pinch salt
1 teaspoon vanilla extract
1 cup walnuts in large pieces
1 cup pecans in large pieces
1 (10.5-ounce) package miniature
   marshmallows

In the top pan of a double boiler over hot but not boiling water, melt the chocolate chips, stirring until smooth. Remove from the heat. Cool slightly, about 10 minutes.

Cover a large countertop area or 2 large baking sheets with waxed paper.

In a large mixing bowl, mix together the sweetened condensed milk and marshmallow creme, blending well. Stir in the salt, vanilla, and melted chocolate until smooth. Stir in the nuts and marshmallows until coated. Drop by spoonfuls onto the waxed paper. Let stand until firm. Store in an airtight container.

# Ultra-Smooth Chocolate Clusters

### Skill Level: Novice, Easy

*When I can no longer fight that urge for chocolate, I whip up a batch of these smooth clusters.*
✳ MAKES 12 TO 18

- 1 cup (6 ounces) semisweet chocolate chips
- 3 tablespoons light corn syrup
- 1 tablespoon water
- 1 cup sweetened flaked coconut or pecans in large pieces

Cover a countertop area or medium baking sheet with waxed paper.

In a heavy 1-quart saucepan over low heat, heat the chocolate chips, corn syrup, and water together, stirring until smooth. Remove from the heat. Add the pecans. Drop by spoonfuls onto the waxed paper. Let stand until the chocolate is firm. Store in an airtight container.

# Chocolate Coconut Drops

### Skill Level: Novice, Easy

*Moist and chewy, these addictive little chocolate drops are halfway between a candy and a cookie.*
✳ MAKES ABOUT 36

- 2 ounces unsweetened baking chocolate, coarsely chopped
- 1 (14-ounce) can sweetened condensed milk
- 1 (7-ounce) package sweetened flaked coconut
- ½ cup pecans or walnuts in large pieces

Line a baking sheet with aluminum foil. Spray the foil with nonstick spray. Preheat the oven to 350°F.

In a small heavy saucepan over low heat, melt the chocolate, stirring until smooth. Remove from the heat. Stir in the milk, coconut, and nuts. Drop by spoonfuls onto the lined baking sheet.

Place the baking sheet into the oven. Turn off the heat. Leave in the oven until the candy has a glazed appearance, about 20 minutes. Remove from the oven and cool completely before removing the candy from the baking sheet. Store in an airtight container.

# Chocolate Peanut Clusters

## Skill Level: Novice, Easy

*These simple little candies will always be one of America's favorites.*

✳ MAKES ABOUT 2½ DOZEN

**1½ cups (9 ounces) semisweet chocolate chips**
**1 cup roasted peanuts**

Cover a large countertop area or 2 large baking sheets with waxed paper.

In the top pan of a double boiler over hot but not boiling water, melt the chocolate chips, stirring until smooth. Stir in the peanuts. Drop by spoonfuls onto the waxed paper. Let stand until firm. Store in an airtight container.

# Sweet Chocolate Clusters

## Skill Level: Novice, Easy

*This chocolate is as smooth as velvet.*

✳ MAKES ABOUT 25

**2 (4-ounce) German's sweet chocolate bars**
**⅔ cup sweetened condensed milk**
**1 cup peanuts or raisins**

Cover large baking sheet with waxed paper. Spray with nonstick spray.

In the top pan of a double boiler over hot but not boiling water, melt the chocolate, stirring until smooth. Remove from the heat. Stir in the milk and peanuts, mixing well. Drop by spoonfuls onto the waxed paper. Refrigerate until the chocolate is firm. Store in an airtight container in the refrigerator.

# Twice-as-Nice Peanut Clusters

## Skill Level: Novice, Easy

*These clusters have a double dose of flavor.*

✳ MAKES ABOUT 24

**1 cup (6 ounces) semisweet chocolate chips**
**1 cup (6 ounces) butterscotch chips**
**1 tablespoon solid vegetable shortening**
**1 to 2 cups roasted peanuts**

Cover a large countertop area or 2 large baking sheets with waxed paper.

In the top pan of a double boiler over hot but not boiling water, melt the chocolate chips, butterscotch chips, and shortening together, stirring until smooth. Stir in the peanuts. Drop by spoonfuls onto the waxed paper. Let stand until firm. Store in an airtight container.

# Triple Delight Pecan Patties

## Skill Level: Novice, Easy

*Good things come in threes, such as these three-flavor pecan patties.*
✳ MAKES ABOUT 36

1 (4-ounce) German's sweet chocolate bar
1 cup (6 ounces) peanut butter chips
1 cup (6 ounces) butterscotch chips
1 tablespoon solid vegetable shortening
2 to 3 cups pecans in large pieces

Cover a large countertop area or 2 large baking sheets with waxed paper.

In the top pan of a double boiler over hot but not boiling water, melt the chocolate, peanut butter chips, butterscotch chips, and shortening together, stirring until smooth. Stir in the pecans. Drop by spoonfuls onto the waxed paper. Let stand until firm. Store in an airtight container.

. . . . . . . . . . . . . . . . . . . . . .

# Triple Delight Marshmallow Squares

## Skill Level: Novice, Easy

*Three great flavors blended with marshmallows make this candy every kid's dream.*
✳ MAKES ABOUT 30 SQUARES

1 (11-ounce) package butterscotch chips
1 (12-ounce) package semisweet chocolate chips

1 cup smooth peanut butter
1 (10.5-ounce) bag miniature marshmallows

Spray a 9 × 13-inch pan with nonstick spray.

In a heavy 2-quart saucepan over low heat, melt the butterscotch chips, chocolate chips, and peanut butter together, stirring until smooth. Remove from the heat. Stir in the marshmallows until coated. Pour the mixture into the prepared pan. Chill in the refrigerator until firm. Cut into squares. Store in an airtight container.

. . . . . . . . . . . . . . . . . . . . . .

# Rocky Road

## Skill Level: Novice, Easy

*The rocky road of life is always easier to travel when first paved with chocolate.*
✳ MAKES ABOUT 2 POUNDS

3 cups (18 ounces) semisweet or milk chocolate chips
3 cups miniature marshmallows
¾ cup pecans or walnuts in large pieces

Butter an 8-inch square pan.

In the top pan of a double boiler over hot but not boiling water, melt the chocolate, stirring until smooth. Remove from the heat. Cool slightly, 3 to 5 minutes. Stir in the marshmallows and nuts. Spread into the buttered pan. Cover and chill until firm. Cut into squares. Store refrigerated in an airtight container.

. . . . . . . . . . . . . . . . . . . . . .

# Heavenly Hash

### Skill Level: Novice, Easy

*An old favorite deserving of its name, this recipe of-fers two versions.*

✳ MAKES ABOUT 2½ POUNDS

> 1 (12-ounce) package semisweet chocolate chips
> 1 (14-ounce) can sweetened condensed milk
> 1 (10.5-ounce) package miniature marshmallows
> 2 cups pecans in large pieces

Butter a 9 × 13-inch pan.

In a heavy 2-quart saucepan over low heat, melt the chocolate chips with the milk, stirring until smooth. Remove from the heat. Stir in the marshmallows and pecans.

Spread in the buttered pan. Cover and chill until firm. To serve, cut into squares. Store in an airtight container in the refrigerator.

### VARIATION

*Coconut Heavenly Hash:* Reduce the amount of miniature marshmallows to 1 cup. Reduce the pecans to 1½ cups and add 1 to 2 cups sweetened flaked coconut and 1 teaspoon vanilla.

COOK'S NOTE: If preferred, the candy may be dropped by spoonfuls onto waxed paper.

# Fudgy Goody Squares

### Skill Level: Novice, Easy

*Peanut butter lovers will appreciate the ease of mak-ing this delicious nutty candy.*

✳ MAKES ABOUT 2 POUNDS

> 1 (12-ounce) package semisweet chocolate chips
> 1 cup (6 ounces) peanut butter chips or butterscotch chips
> 1 (14-ounce) can sweetened condensed milk
> ½ teaspoon vanilla extract
> 1½ cups pecans or walnuts in large pieces

Line an 8-inch square pan with aluminum foil, leaving a 1-inch overhang on the sides of the pan. Lightly coat the foil with nonstick spray.

In a heavy 2-quart saucepan over low heat, melt the chocolate chips and peanut butter chips with the milk, stirring until the chips are melted and the mixture is smooth.

Remove from the heat. Stir in the vanilla and nuts. Pour into the lined pan. Chill until firm, about 2 hours. Lift the candy from the pan and remove the foil lining. Cut into squares. Store in an airtight container in the refrigerator.

# Marshmallow Trivia

10 miniature marshmallows=
  1 large marshmallow
110 miniature marshmallows=1 cup
11 large marshmallows=1 cup

# Chocolate Rum Squares

## Skill Level: Novice, Easy

*Rum extract adds a rich flavor to these tasty candies.*
✳ MAKES ABOUT 2 POUNDS

2½ cups (15 ounces) semisweet chocolate
   chips
1 cup sweetened condensed milk
Dash salt
2 teaspoons rum extract or almond extract
1½ cups chopped pecans or walnuts

Line an 8-inch square pan with aluminum foil, leaving a 1-inch overhang on the sides of the pan. Spray the foil lightly with nonstick spray.

In the top pan of a double boiler over hot but not boiling water, melt the chocolate chips with the milk, stirring until smooth. Remove from the heat. Stir in the salt, rum extract, and nuts. Pour into the prepared pan. Cover and refrigerate 24 hours. Lift the candy from the pan and remove the foil lining. Cut into squares. Store in an airtight container in the refrigerator.

# Chocolate Honey Squares

## Skill Level: Novice, Easy

*This old 1950s recipe was designed with children in mind.*
✳ MAKES ABOUT ½ POUND

1 cup (6 ounces) semisweet chocolate chips
¼ cup honey
2 tablespoons water
⅔ cup instant nonfat dry milk

Line a 9 × 5-inch loaf pan with waxed paper.

In the top of a double boiler over hot but not boiling water, melt the chocolate, stirring until smooth. Remove from the heat. Stir in the honey and water, blending thoroughly. Add the dry milk, a few spoonfuls at a time, blending well after each addition. Pour the mixture into the lined pan, spreading into an even layer. Chill until firm. Cut into squares. Store in an airtight container.

# Caramel Nut Marshmallows

## Skill Level: Novice, Easy

*Kids enjoy making these caramel-coated marshmallows almost as much as they enjoy eating them.*
✳ MAKES ABOUT 30

1 pound caramels, unwrapped
3 tablespoons evaporated milk
30 large marshmallows
1½ cups pecans in large pieces

Cover a countertop area or a small baking sheet with waxed paper.

In a heavy 1-quart saucepan over low heat, melt the caramels and milk together, stirring until smooth. Using a fork, toothpick, or specially designed dipping tool, dip the marshmallows into the hot caramel until coated. Immediately roll the dipped marshmallows in the pecans. Place on the waxed paper. Let stand until firm. Store in an airtight container.

# Chipper Nutty Fudge

## Skill Level: Novice, Super Simple

*This yummy peanut butter candy comes with an endorsement from my cousin Travis, who hails from a long line of expert candy tasters. It will be an instant favorite with your family, too.*

✳ **MAKES ABOUT 2½ POUNDS**

- 1½ cups packed light brown sugar
- 1 (14-ounce) can sweetened condensed milk
- 1½ teaspoons vanilla extract
- 1 cup crunchy peanut butter
- 1 cup (6 ounces) semisweet chocolate chips or miniature semisweet chocolate chips
- ½ to 1 cup salted roasted peanuts, finely chopped

Butter a 9 × 13-inch pan.

In a medium bowl, combine the brown sugar, milk, and vanilla, stirring until the sugar dissolves. Stir in the peanut butter until well blended and smooth. Add the chocolate chips and peanuts, mixing well. Spread into the buttered pan. Refrigerate until firm. Cut into squares. Store in an airtight container in the refrigerator.

# Peanut Butter Graham Squares

## Skill Level: Novice, Super Simple

*This candy may remind you of one of America's favorite candy bars.*

✳ **MAKES ABOUT 24**

- 1½ cups smooth peanut butter
- 1½ cups graham cracker crumbs
- 1 cup butter or margarine, softened
- 1 (1-pound) package powdered sugar
- 1 (12-ounce) package semisweet chocolate chips, melted

Coat a 9 × 13-inch pan with nonstick spray.

In a medium mixing bowl, combine the peanut butter, crumbs, butter, and powdered sugar, mixing well. Press into the prepared pan. Spread the chocolate on top of the peanut butter layer. Chill until firm. Cut into squares. Store in an airtight container.

# Mom's Peanut Butter Candy

## Skill Level: Novice, Super Simple

*I might not have made it through grade school without this candy. Whether I had a scraped knee or just needed an after-school treat, this yummy-for-the-tummy candy was my solution to all of life's problems.*

*My youngest cousin Anne was so enamored with Mom's special candy that she requested the recipe when she was only six years old. Here are Anne's in-*

structions: *"Peanut butter. White Shugger. and Creame. Miks them all tell the shugger goes Away and the creame goes Away then roll them in balls and eat."*

✳ MAKES 8 TO 10 PIECES

3 to 4 tablespoons smooth or crunchy peanut butter
2 cups powdered sugar
About 2 tablespoons half-and-half or milk
¼ teaspoon vanilla extract (optional)

In a small bowl, mix the peanut butter and powdered sugar together. Stir in just enough half-and-half to bind the ingredients and make the candy smooth. Add the vanilla, if desired. Shape the candy into balls ¾ to 1 inch in diameter. Store in an airtight container.

. . . . . . . . . . . . . . . . . . . . . . . . . .

# Pine Cones

## Skill Level: Novice, Super Simple

*Who can resist smooth peanut butter candy rolled in crispy peanuts?*

✳ MAKES 12 TO 16 PIECES

1 cup smooth peanut butter
½ cup sweetened condensed milk
⅓ cup powdered sugar
½ cup chopped roasted peanuts

In a small bowl, mix the peanut butter, milk, and powdered sugar together, blending until well mixed. Knead the candy by hand until smooth. Shape the candy into small logs ¾ to 1 inch long; roll in the chopped peanuts to re-

semble pine cones. Store in an airtight container.

# Peanut Butter Log

## Skill Level: Novice, Super Simple

*This creamy peanut butter roll coated with coconut is a fun candy to make, and eat, with your kids.*

✳ MAKES ABOUT 12 PIECES

¼ cup smooth peanut butter
¼ cup light corn syrup
2 teaspoons water
3 tablespoons instant nonfat dry milk
1⅔ cups powdered sugar
¼ teaspoon salt
½ cup sweetened flaked coconut

In a small mixing bowl, combine the peanut butter and corn syrup until well mixed. Stir in the water, dry milk, powdered sugar, and salt, blending well. Shape the candy into a log. Roll the log in the coconut. To serve, slice into pieces. Store in an airtight container.

. . . . . . . . . . . . . . . . . . . . . . . . . .

# Honey Do Candy

## Skill Level: Novice, Super Simple

*This classic combination of peanut butter and honey may help you get those household chores done more quickly.*

✳ MAKES ABOUT ½ POUND

1 cup instant nonfat dry milk
1 cup creamy peanut butter
1 cup honey
½ teaspoon vanilla extract
½ cup chopped peanuts

In a medium mixing bowl, combine the dry milk, peanut butter, honey, and vanilla, blending until smooth. Shape into balls ¾ inch in diameter. Roll in the peanuts. Store in an airtight container in the refrigerator.

# Kwik-Fix Cereal Candies

## Rhonda Walters' Chocolate-Topped Cereal Bars

### Skill Level: Novice, Easy

*Oklahoma's former First Lady Rhonda Walters shares her recipe for a favorite Walters family treat, Special K bars.*

✴ MAKES ABOUT 24 BARS

6 cups Special K cereal
1 cup light corn syrup
1 cup granulated sugar
1½ cups creamy peanut butter
1¼ cups (about 7½ ounces) semisweet
 chocolate chips
1¼ cups (about 7½ ounces) butterscotch chips

Spray a 9 × 13-inch pan with nonstick spray. Pour the cereal into a large mixing bowl.

In a 1-quart saucepan over medium heat, bring the corn syrup and sugar to a boil, stirring until the sugar dissolves and the mixture begins to boil. Boil 1 minute.

Remove from the heat. Stir in the peanut butter, blending well. Pour the hot syrup over the cereal, stirring the cereal until well coated. Spread evenly in the buttered pan. Cool.

In a heavy 1-quart saucepan over low heat, melt the chocolate chips and butterscotch chips together, stirring until smooth. Spread the melted chocolate-butterscotch mixture over the cereal mixture. Cool and cut into squares. Store in an airtight container.

COOK'S NOTE: The chocolate chips and butterscotch chips may be melted together in the microwave if preferred.

## Special Request Candy-Topped Brownies

### Skill Level: Novice, Easy

*At the request of her friends, budding gourmet Elizabeth Walters, youngest daughter of Oklahoma's former governor David Walters and his wife, Rhonda, makes these gooey, chewy, multilayered candy-topped brownies for all birthday celebrations.*

✴ MAKES ABOUT 24

1 (1-pound 3.5-ounce) box brownie mix, baked
 and cooled as directed
1 (7-ounce) jar marshmallow creme
1 cup smooth peanut butter
1 (12-ounce) package semisweet chocolate chips
3 cups crispy rice cereal

Spread the marshmallow creme in an even layer across the cooled brownies. Refrigerate until firm.

In a medium microwave-proof bowl, combine the peanut butter and chocolate chips. Microwave on High 1 minute or until the chocolate is almost completely melted. Stir until the mixture is well blended and smooth. Stir in the cereal until well coated. Spread the mixture in an even layer across the marshmallow layer. Refrigerate until firm. To serve, cut into squares. Store in an airtight container.

# Chocolate Birds' Nests

## Skill Level: Novice, Easy

*Perfect for an Easter celebration, these egg-filled birds' nests will put a twinkle into any child's eye.*
✳ MAKES ABOUT 40

> 1 (12-ounce) package semisweet chocolate
>   chips
> 1 (12-ounce) jar smooth or crunchy peanut
>   butter
> ¼ teaspoon vanilla extract
> 10 cereal shredded wheat cereal biscuits,
>   crushed
> Colored jellybeans

Cover a large countertop area or 2 large baking sheets with waxed paper.

In the top pan of a double boiler over hot but not boiling water, melt the chocolate chips, stirring until smooth. Add the peanut butter, vanilla, and cereal, stirring until the peanut butter has melted and the mixture is well blended.

Remove from the heat. Quickly drop by spoonfuls onto the waxed paper. Using a thumb or the back of a spoon, make an indention in the center of each candy. Lightly press

2 to 5 brightly colored jellybeans into each indentation before the chocolate cools completely. Cool. Store in an airtight container.

COOK'S NOTE: If desired, slightly less peanut butter may be used.

# Chocolate-Covered Turtles

## Skill Level: Novice, Easy

*Crunchy noodles and roasted cashews make these extra good.*
✳ MAKES ABOUT 50

> 1 (12-ounce) package semisweet chocolate
>   chips
> 1 (11-ounce) package butterscotch chips
> 1 cup roasted salted cashews
> 1 (3- to 5-ounce) can chow mein noodles

Cover a large countertop area or 2 large baking sheets with waxed paper.

In the top pan of a double boiler over hot but not boiling water, melt the chocolate chips and butterscotch chips together, stirring until smooth.

Remove from the heat. Stir in the cashews and noodles. Quickly drop by spoonfuls onto the waxed paper. Cool. Store in an airtight container.

# Butterscotch Bonbons

## Skill Level: Novice, Easy

*Butterscotch and peanut butter are always a favorite combination, regardless of what else is added.*
✳ MAKES ABOUT 30

1 cup (6 ounces) butterscotch chips
½ cup smooth peanut butter
1½ cups cornflakes cereal
1 cup miniature marshmallows
½ cup chopped candied cherries, raisins, or
   unsalted peanuts

Cover a large countertop area or a large baking sheet with waxed paper.

In the top pan of a double boiler over hot but not boiling water, melt the butterscotch chips and peanut butter together, stirring until smooth.

Remove from the heat. Stir in the cereal, marshmallows, and cherries. Refrigerate until lightly set, 10 to 15 minutes. Drop by spoonfuls onto the waxed paper. Cool. Store in an airtight container.

### VARIATIONS

*Double Butter Clusters:* Omit the marshmallows and the fruit or nuts. Substitute crunchy peanut butter for the smooth peanut butter. Use 2 cups slightly crushed cornflakes cereal. Stir in ½ teaspoon vanilla extract with the cereal.

*Crazy Candy:* Omit the cornflakes, marshmallows, and the fruit or nuts. Reduce the peanut butter to 4 teaspoons. Stir in 1 (1.5-ounce) can shoestring potatoes.

# Hopscotch Candy

## Skill Level: Novice, Easy

*An oldie but a goody, this recipe combines soft, fluffy marshmallows with crisp chow mein noodles to create the ultimate quick-style treat.*
✳ MAKES ABOUT 30

1 cup (6 ounces) butterscotch chips
½ cup peanut butter
1 (3-ounce) can (2 cups) chow mein noodles
2 cups miniature marshmallows

Cover a large baking sheet with waxed paper.

In the top pan of a double boiler over hot but not boiling water, melt the butterscotch chips and peanut butter together, stirring until smooth.

Remove from the heat. Stir in the noodles and marshmallows. Quickly drop by spoonfuls onto the waxed paper. Chill until firm. Store in an airtight container.

### VARIATION

*Chinese Candy:* Omit the marshmallows.

# Butterscotch Crispies

## Skill Level: Novice, Easy

*Peanuts give this quick candy an extra punch.*
✳ MAKES ABOUT 30

1 (11-ounce) package butterscotch chips
1 (5-ounce) can chow mein noodles
1 (7.5-ounce) package Spanish peanuts

Cover a large countertop area or a large baking sheet with waxed paper.

In the top pan of a double boiler over hot but not boiling water, melt the butterscotch chips, stirring until smooth.

Remove from the heat. Stir in the noodles and peanuts. Quickly drop by spoonfuls onto the waxed paper. Cool. Store in an airtight container.

### VARIATION
*Butterscotch Crunch:* Use 1 (3-ounce) can chow mein noodles and 1 cup salted peanuts.

# Chocolate Caramel Quickies

### Skill Level: Novice, Easy

*This recipe from the 1962* Ponca City News *recipe contest came with a note saying, "It costs 64 cents to make these." Imagine what our thrifty chef would think now.*

✳ MAKES ABOUT 1¼ POUNDS

8 ounces caramels, unwrapped
8 ounces chocolate caramels, unwrapped
1 (3- to 5-ounce) can chow mein noodles

Cover a large countertop area or a large baking sheet with waxed paper.

In a heavy 1-quart saucepan over low heat, melt the caramels together, stirring until smooth. Remove from the heat. Stir in the noodles. Pour onto the waxed paper. Let stand until firm. Cut into squares. Store in an airtight container.

# Easy Peanut Butter Candy

### Skill Level: Novice, Easy

*This peanut butter and cereal candy is sure to find some new fans among peanut butter lovers.*
✳ MAKES ABOUT 30

4 cups crushed cornflakes cereal
¾ cup granulated sugar
¾ cup light corn syrup
1 cup plus 1 teaspoon peanut butter

Cover a large countertop area or a large baking sheet with waxed paper. Pour the cornflakes into a medium mixing bowl.

In a 1-quart saucepan, bring the sugar and corn syrup to a boil. Remove from the heat. Add the peanut butter, stirring until smooth. Pour the hot syrup over the cornflakes, stirring until the cornflakes are well coated. Quickly drop by spoonfuls onto the waxed paper. Cool. Store in an airtight container.

# Peanut Butter Crumb Bars

### Skill Level: Novice, Easy

*Peanut butter and marshmallows with a slightly different twist.*
✳ MAKES ABOUT 16

1 (7-ounce) jar marshmallow creme
3 tablespoons butter or margarine
⅓ cup crunchy peanut butter
4 cups crisp rice cereal squares, crushed to make 2 cups crumbs

Spray an 8-inch square pan with nonstick spray.

In the top pan of a double boiler over hot but not boiling water, melt the marshmallow creme, butter, and peanut butter together, stirring until smooth.

Remove from the heat. Stir in the cereal. Press the mixture into the buttered pan. Cool and cut into squares. Store in an airtight container.

# Crispy Peanut Butter Treats

## Skill Level: Novice, Easy

*Surprise your kids with ice cream served in these crispy candy cups.*

✳ MAKES ABOUT 16 SQUARES OR 6 ICE CREAM CANDY CUPS

2½ cups crispy rice cereal
16 large marshmallows
3 tablespoons butter or margarine
¼ cup peanut butter
½ teaspoon vanilla extract

Spray a large mixing bowl and an 8-inch square pan with nonstick spray. Pour the cereal into the mixing bowl.

In the top pan of a double boiler over hot but not boiling water, melt the marshmallows, butter, and peanut butter together, stirring until smooth.

Remove from the heat. Stir in the vanilla. Pour the marshmallow mixture over the cereal, stirring until the cereal is well coated. Press the mixture into the buttered pan. Cool and cut into squares. Store in an airtight container.

**COOK'S NOTE:** If preferred, the mixture can be pressed into the bottom and sides of 6 buttered custard cups to make candy cups used for serving ice cream.

# S'Mores

## Skill Level: Novice, Easy

*What a marvelous invention!*

✳ MAKES ABOUT 16

⅓ cup light corn syrup
1 cup (6 ounces) semisweet chocolate chips
½ teaspoon vanilla extract
4 cups graham cracker cereal
1½ cups miniature marshmallows

Butter a 9-inch square pan.

In a 2-quart saucepan, bring the corn syrup to a boil. Remove from the heat. Stir in the chocolate chips until melted. Stir in the vanilla, cereal, and marshmallows until well coated. Turn into the buttered pan. Cool and cut into squares. Store in an airtight container.

# No-Bake Cookies: Homeroom Mother Classics

**N**othing evokes that warm, fuzzy feeling quite like the memory of homeroom mothers floating into our childhood classrooms to place delicious homemade treats upon our desks. Whether dressed in Halloween costumes or cotton shirtwaist dresses, women across America thrilled a generation of Baby Boomers by interrupting math and history lessons with goodies that made our schooldays special. No-bake cookies were always at the top of the list: Mothers adored them for their ease, and kids adored them for their taste.

For some of us, just reading these recipes can transform us into gleeful children again. Classics such as Cathedral Cookies or Cow Chips immediately conjure up images of Campfire Girl meetings, Girl Scout badges and which of our childhood friends was ultimately named playground tetherball champion. We smile at names like Kookie Klusters and Peanut Dandies, remembering when those names were as much fun as dodge ball, Little League, jumping into puddles, and riding our bikes.

Today we are soccer moms, business leaders, single parents and corporate CEOs—attorneys, grandparents, sportswriters and clerks. We have grown, we have changed, but one thing is still certain: All across America, Baby Boomers are sitting wistfully behind their desks wishing that someone would arrive with no-bake cookies to make our workdays special.

# No-Bake Cookies with Peanut Butter

## Cow Chips

### Skill Level: Novice, Easy

*My brother-in-law once said that no cookbook is complete without Cow Chips. I agree. My sister's chocolate-oatmeal-peanut butter cookies disappear from my kitchen almost as quickly as they appear.*

❋ MAKES ABOUT 30 COOKIES

- **2 cups granulated sugar**
- **¼ cup butter or margarine**
- **½ cup milk**
- **¼ cup unsweetened cocoa powder**
- **½ cup smooth peanut butter**
- **2 cups quick rolled oats**
- **1 teaspoon vanilla extract**

Cover a large countertop area or a large baking sheet with waxed paper.

In a 2-quart saucepan over medium heat, bring the sugar, butter, milk, and cocoa to a boil, stirring until the sugar dissolves and the mixture begins to boil. Boil 1 minute.

Remove from the heat. Stir in the peanut butter, oats, and vanilla until combined. Quickly drop by spoonfuls onto the waxed paper. Cool. Store in an airtight container.

## Chocolate Nut Cookies

### Skill Level: Novice, Easy

*With an extra dose of butter, these cookies are a little richer than Cow Chips (at left). The nuts are a nice addition.*

❋ MAKES ABOUT 30 COOKIES

- **2 cups granulated sugar**
- **½ cup butter or margarine**
- **½ cup milk**
- **3 tablespoons unsweetened cocoa powder**
- **½ cup smooth peanut butter**
- **2½ cups quick rolled oats**
- **2 teaspoons vanilla extract**
- **¼ cup chopped pecans or walnuts**

Cover a large area of the countertop or a large baking sheet with waxed paper.

In a 2-quart saucepan over medium heat, bring the sugar, butter, milk, and cocoa to a boil, stirring until the sugar dissolves and the mixture begins to boil. Boil 3 minutes.

Remove from the heat. Stir in the peanut butter, oats, vanilla, and nuts until combined. Quickly drop by spoonfuls onto the waxed paper. Cool. Store in an airtight container.

### VARIATION

*Butterscotch Nut Cookies:* Omit the cocoa powder. Stir in ¼ cup butterscotch chips with the peanut butter, stirring until the chips melt. Stir in the oats, vanilla, and nuts.

# Puddin's Chocolate Oatmeal Cookies

## Skill Level: Novice, Easy

*This creamy version of chocolate-oatmeal-peanut butter cookies was the specialty of the house with my aunt Erma, better known to her family as Puddin'.*

✳ MAKES ABOUT 30 COOKIES

  1 cup granulated sugar
  ½ cup butter
  ½ cup milk
  ½ cup unsweetened cocoa powder
  ½ cup light corn syrup
  ½ cup smooth peanut butter
  2 cups quick rolled oats
  1 teaspoon vanilla extract

Cover a large area of the countertop or a large baking sheet with waxed paper.

In a 2-quart saucepan over medium heat, bring the sugar, butter, milk, cocoa, and corn syrup to a boil, stirring until the sugar dissolves and the mixture begins to boil. Boil less than 1 minute.

Remove from the heat. Stir in the peanut butter, oats, and vanilla until combined. Quickly drop by spoonfuls onto the waxed paper. Cool. Store in an airtight container.

COOK'S NOTE: Aunt Erma preferred to pour her cookies onto a buttered plate and store covered in the refrigerator, cutting as needed.

# Chocolate Cereal Cookies

## Skill Level: Novice, Easy

*Put a new spin on an old favorite by using chocolate chips in place of cocoa.*

✳ MAKES ABOUT 50 COOKIES

  1 cup granulated sugar
  1 cup light corn syrup
  1 (12-ounce) jar crunchy peanut butter
  1 cup (6 ounces) semisweet chocolate chips
  5 cups quick rolled oats or cornflakes
  1 teaspoon vanilla extract

Cover a large countertop area or 2 large baking sheets with waxed paper.

In a 2-quart saucepan over medium heat, bring the sugar and corn syrup to a rapid boil, stirring until the sugar dissolves and the mixture begins to boil. Boil less than 1 minute.

Remove from the heat. Stir in the peanut butter and chocolate chips until melted. Stir in the cereal and vanilla until combined. Quickly drop by spoonfuls onto the waxed paper. Cool. Store in an airtight container.

# Kookie Klusters

## Skill Level: Novice, Easy

*Any recipe that can be made with just three ingredients is not the least bit kookie to busy moms and dads.*

✳ MAKES ABOUT 30 COOKIES

  1 cup (6 ounces) semisweet or milk chocolate
    chips
  ½ cup smooth or crunchy peanut butter

**3 cups quick rolled oats, cornflakes, or bran flakes**

Cover a large countertop area or a large baking sheet with waxed paper.

In a heavy 2-quart saucepan over low heat, melt the chocolate chips and peanut butter, stirring constantly to prevent scorching.

Remove from the heat. Stir in the cereal, mixing well. Quickly drop by spoonfuls onto the waxed paper. Cool. Store in an airtight container.

COOK'S NOTE: If preferred, the cookies can be poured into a buttered 8-inch square pan and cut into squares.

# Chocolate Frosty Treats

## Skill Level: Novice, Easy

*By now, the beloved chocolate-oatmeal-peanut butter cookie has taken so many spins that it must be dizzy. This version is made with chocolate frosting mix.*

✳ MAKES ABOUT 40 COOKIES

**1 (15.25-ounce) box chocolate frosting mix**
**⅓ cup butter or margarine**
**⅓ cup water**
**1 cup smooth or crunchy peanut butter**
**1 teaspoon vanilla extract**
**3 cups quick rolled oats**

Cover a large countertop area or 2 large baking sheets with waxed paper.

In a 2-quart saucepan over low heat, bring the frosting mix, butter, and water to a boil,

stirring constantly. Stir in the peanut butter until melted. Stir in the vanilla and oats.

Remove from the heat. Stir until well blended. Quickly drop by spoonfuls onto the waxed paper. Cool. Store in an airtight container.

# Peanut Dandies

## Skill Level: Novice, Easy

*An oldie but a goody, this no-chocolate version has both peanuts and peanut butter.*

✳ MAKES 20 TO 25 COOKIES

**1 cup granulated sugar**
**¼ cup butter or margarine**
**⅓ cup evaporated milk**
**½ cup smooth peanut butter**
**½ teaspoon vanilla extract**
**1 cup quick rolled oats**
**½ cup peanuts**

Cover a large countertop area or a large baking sheet with waxed paper.

In a heavy 2-quart saucepan over medium heat, bring the sugar, butter, and milk to a boil, stirring until the sugar dissolves and the mixture begins to boil. Boil 3 minutes, stirring to prevent scorching.

Remove from the heat. Stir in the peanut butter and vanilla until well blended. Stir in the oats and peanuts. Drop by spoonfuls onto the waxed paper. Cool. Store in an airtight container.

# Peanut Butter–Coconut Cookies

## Skill Level: Novice, Easy

*If you are caught sneaking too many of these, just explain that you found a new way to take vitamins.*

\* MAKES ABOUT 35 TO 40 COOKIES

1 cup granulated sugar
1 cup light corn syrup
1½ cups smooth peanut butter
4 cups Special K cereal
1 cup sweetened flaked coconut
1 teaspoon vanilla extract

Cover a large countertop area or 2 large baking sheets with waxed paper.

In a 2-quart saucepan, bring the sugar and corn syrup to a rolling boil, stirring until the sugar dissolves and the mixture begins to boil.

Remove from the heat. Stir in the peanut butter until melted. Stir in the cereal, coconut, and vanilla until combined. Quickly drop by spoonfuls onto the waxed paper. Cool. Store in an airtight container.

### VARIATIONS

*Chewy Peanut Butter Cookies:* Omit the coconut. Increase the sugar to 1½ cups granulated sugar.

*Cornflakes Candy:* Omit the coconut. Decrease peanut butter to 1 cup and use 6 cups cornflakes cereal instead of the Special K cereal.

# Peanut Butter Quickies

## Skill Level: Novice, Easy

*Peanut butter, oats, nuts, and coconut make these quick cookies crunchy and delicious.*
\* MAKES 35 TO 40 COOKIES

1½ cups granulated sugar
½ cup butter or margarine
¾ cup all-purpose flour
½ cup milk or ⅔ cup evaporated milk
⅔ cup smooth peanut butter
1½ cups quick rolled oats
½ cup chopped walnuts or pecans
½ cup sweetened flaked coconut
¼ teaspoon salt
1 teaspoon vanilla extract

Cover a large countertop area or 2 large baking sheets with waxed paper.

In a 2-quart saucepan over medium heat, bring the sugar, butter, flour, and milk to a boil, stirring until the sugar dissolves and the mixture begins to boil. Boil rapidly, stirring constantly, for 3 minutes.

Remove from the heat. Stir in the peanut butter, oats, nuts, coconut, salt, and vanilla, blending well. Quickly drop by spoonfuls onto the waxed paper. Cool. Store in an airtight container.

### VARIATION

*Peanut Butter–Coconut Quickies:* Drop the cookies into 1 cup sweetened flaked coconut, rolling the cookies until well coated. Place on the waxed paper to cool.

# No-Bake Cookies without Peanut Butter

## Rich Chocolate Cookies

### Skill Level: Novice, Easy

*Did you know that the beloved chocolate-oatmeal-peanut butter no-bake cookies can be made without the peanut butter? They are great for those kids who love no-bake cookies but are allergic to peanuts.*

✳ MAKES ABOUT 30

2½ cups granulated sugar
¼ cup unsweetened cocoa powder
½ cup milk
½ cup butter or margarine
1 teaspoon vanilla extract
2½ cups quick oats
½ cup pecans or walnuts in large pieces

Cover a large countertop area or a large baking sheet with waxed paper.

In a heavy 2-quart saucepan over medium heat, bring the sugar, cocoa, milk, and butter to a full boil, stirring constantly. Boil 2 minutes, stirring constantly.

Remove from the heat. Stir in the vanilla. Stir in the oats and nuts. Quickly drop by spoonfuls onto the waxed paper. Cool. Store in an airtight container.

. . . . . . . . . . . . . . . . . . . . .

## Coco-Nut Cookies

### Skill Level: Novice, Easy

*Coconut and nuts wrapped in delicious chocolate, doesn't that sound divine?*

✳ MAKES ABOUT 30

2 cups granulated sugar
3 tablespoons unsweetened cocoa powder
½ cup milk
½ cup butter
1 teaspoon vanilla extract
3 cups quick oats
1 cup sweetened flaked coconut
½ to 1 cup pecans in large pieces

Cover a large countertop area or a large baking sheet with waxed paper.

In a heavy 2-quart saucepan over medium heat, bring the sugar, cocoa, milk, and butter to a full boil, stirring constantly. Boil 3 minutes, stirring constantly.

Remove from the heat. Stir in the vanilla. Stir in the oats, coconut, and pecans. Quickly drop by spoonfuls onto the waxed paper. Cool. Store in an airtight container.

. . . . . . . . . . . . . . . . . . . . .

# Fudge Nut Cookies

### Skill Level: Novice, Average

*These no-bake cookies are filled with graham cracker crumbs and have a rich chocolate flavor.*

✳ MAKES ABOUT 30

2 cups granulated sugar
½ cup unsweetened cocoa powder
1 cup evaporated milk
5 tablespoons butter or margarine
1 teaspoon vanilla extract
1 cup graham cracker crumbs
1 cup pecans or walnuts in large pieces

Cover a large countertop area or a large baking sheet with waxed paper.

In a heavy 2-quart saucepan over medium heat, bring the sugar, cocoa, and milk to a boil, stirring until the sugar dissolves. Cook, stirring occasionally to prevent scorching, to the soft ball stage (234°F to 240°F, with 236°F recommended).

Remove from the heat. Stir in the butter and vanilla until the butter is melted. Stir in the crumbs and nuts. Quickly drop by spoonfuls onto the waxed paper. Cool. Store in an airtight container.

# Fudge Nougats

### Skill Level: Novice, Easy

*Anyone who loved chocolate-coated graham cracker cookies as a kid will think these Fudge Nougats are heaven-sent.*

✳ MAKES ABOUT 40 PIECES

2 cups granulated sugar
½ cup butter or margarine
1 cup evaporated milk
1 cup (6 ounces) semisweet chocolate chips
¾ cup all-purpose flour
1 cup graham cracker crumbs
¾ cup walnuts in large pieces
1 teaspoon vanilla extract

Butter a 9-inch square pan.

In a heavy 2-quart saucepan over medium heat, bring the sugar, butter, and milk to a rolling boil, stirring constantly. Boil 10 minutes, stirring frequently to prevent scorching.

Remove from the heat. Stir in the chocolate chips, flour, crumbs, walnuts, and vanilla. Spread into the buttered pan. Cool and cut into squares. Store in an airtight container.

# Sugar Shock Special

### Skill Level: Novice, Super Simple

*Years ago, a houseguest walked into the kitchen late at night to find me indulging in a childhood favorite of rich chocolate buttercream frosting spread between crisp graham crackers. She appropriately dubbed me "Sugar Shock Sharrock," but only because I did not share.*

*This "quaint" old family recipe makes a delicious lunchbox treat.*

✳ MAKES ABOUT 12 PIECES

2 cups powdered sugar
2 to 3 tablespoons unsweetened cocoa powder
¼ cup butter or margarine, melted
½ to 1 tablespoon milk or half-and-half
About 12 whole graham crackers

In a small bowl, combine the powdered sugar, cocoa, and butter, blending well. Stir in a few drops of milk at a time until the frosting reaches a spreading consistency. Spread the frosting on whole graham crackers and top with another whole graham cracker. Break into halves or quarters. If stored in an airtight container, these cookies soften.

COOK'S NOTE: For a really quick version, use canned chocolate frosting.

# Marshmallow Fudge Cookies

## Skill Level: Average

*What kid can resist marshmallow chocolate treats?*
✳ MAKES ABOUT 40

- 2 cups granulated sugar
- 3 tablespoons unsweetened cocoa powder
- 1 cup milk
- 2 tablespoons butter or margarine
- 24 large marshmallows, quartered
- 3 cups graham cracker crumbs
- 1 cup chopped pecans or walnuts
- 2 teaspoons vanilla extract

Cover a large countertop area or 2 large baking sheets with waxed paper.

In a heavy 2-quart saucepan over medium heat, bring the sugar, cocoa, and milk to a boil, stirring until the sugar dissolves. Cook, stirring occasionally to prevent scorching, to the soft ball stage (234°F to 240°F, with 236°F recommended).

Remove from the heat. Cool slightly, about 3 minutes. Stir in the butter and marshmallows just until blended. Stir in the crumbs, nuts, and vanilla. Quickly drop by spoonfuls onto the waxed paper. Cool. Store in an airtight container.

# Peppermint Chocolate Squares

## Skill Level: Novice, Easy

*Chocolate peppermint frosting? Some things are too good to be true.*
✳ MAKES ABOUT 20

- 1 cup granulated sugar
- ¾ cup butter or margarine
- 2 eggs
- ½ cup sweetened flaked coconut
- 1 teaspoon vanilla extract
- 24 large marshmallows, quartered
- 17 graham crackers, crushed
- 1 cup chopped walnuts or pecans, divided
- ½ teaspoon peppermint extract
- ¾ (1-pound) can chocolate buttercream frosting

In the top pan of a double boiler over hot but not boiling water, combine the sugar, butter, and eggs. Cook until the mixture is thick and creamy, stirring constantly.

Remove from the heat. Cool. Add the coconut and vanilla. Cover and chill 30 minutes to 1 hour.

Spray an 8 × 11-inch pan with nonstick spray. In a large mixing bowl, combine the marshmallows, crumbs, and ½ cup of the nuts. Stir in the chilled coconut mixture until well mixed. Press the mixture into the pan.

Stir the peppermint extract into the chocolate frosting. Spread the frosting over the top of the coconut mixture. Sprinkle with the remaining nuts. Cover and chill until firm. To serve, cut into squares. Store covered in the refrigerator.

COOK'S NOTE: Homemade chocolate buttercream frosting may be substituted if desired.

. . . . . . . . . . . . . . . . . . . . . . . . . .

# Eskimo Cookies

### Skill Level: Novice, Super Simple

*These tasty little chocolate balls are sure to warm your tummy on a cold, snowy day.*
✳ MAKES ABOUT 40

¾ **cup butter or margarine, softened**
¾ **cup granulated sugar**
1 **tablespoon cold water**
½ **teaspoon vanilla extract**
3 **tablespoons unsweetened cocoa powder**
2 **cups rolled oats**
⅓ **cup powdered sugar**

In a large mixing bowl, blend the butter, sugar, water, and vanilla together until well mixed. Stir in the cocoa, mixing well. Stir in the oats. Cover and chill 30 minutes. Shape the chilled mixture into balls 1 inch in diameter. Roll in powdered sugar. Store in an airtight container in the refrigerator.

. . . . . . . . . . . . . . . . . . . . . . . . . .

# Chewy Coconut Cookies

### Skill Level: Novice, Easy

*Loaded with chewy coconut, these nutty little cookies may remind you of the coconut-pecan frosting used on German chocolate cakes.*
✳ MAKES ABOUT 30

½ **cup granulated sugar**
1½ **cups packed light brown sugar**
½ **cup milk**
½ **cup butter**
½ **teaspoon vanilla extract**
2½ **cups quick rolled oats**
1½ **cups sweetened flaked coconut**
½ **cup chopped pecans**

Line a large baking sheet with waxed paper.

In a heavy 2-quart saucepan over medium heat, bring the sugars, milk, and butter to a full boil, stirring constantly. Boil 1 minute.

Remove from the heat. Stir in the vanilla. Add the oats, coconut, and pecans. Quickly drop by spoonfuls onto the waxed paper. Chill until firm. Store in an airtight container in the refrigerator.

### VARIATION
*Coconut-Walnut Cookies:* Substitute 2 cups granulated sugar for the ½ cup granulated sugar and 1½ cups brown sugar. Use 3 cups quick rolled oats and ½ to 1 cup sweetened flaked coconut. Substitute walnuts for the pecans.

. . . . . . . . . . . . . . . . . . . . . . . . . .

# Butter Nut Cookies

## Skill Level: Novice, Easy

*Crispy shredded rice gives these cookies an extra crunch.*

✳ MAKES ABOUT 30

1 cup packed light brown sugar
½ cup evaporated milk
2 tablespoons butter or margarine
½ cup pecans in large pieces
½ teaspoon vanilla extract
3½ cups bite-size shredded rice biscuits

Cover a large countertop area or a large baking sheet with waxed paper.

In a heavy 2-quart saucepan over medium heat, bring the sugar, milk, butter, and pecans to a full boil, stirring constantly. Boil, stirring constantly, 5 minutes.

Remove from the heat. Stir in the vanilla. Add the shredded rice biscuits and mix well. Quickly drop by spoonfuls onto the waxed paper. Cool. Store in an airtight container.

# Maple Praline Cookies

## Skill Level: Average

*The maple lovers in your life will kiss you for making this one.*

✳ MAKES ABOUT 40

1¼ cups maple syrup
¼ cup light corn syrup
¼ cup butter

1 cup chopped pecans
2 cups quick rolled oats
1½ cups pecan halves (optional)

Cover a large countertop area or a large baking sheet with waxed paper.

In a 1-quart saucepan over medium heat, bring the maple syrup and corn syrup to a boil, stirring until the mixture begins to boil. Cook to the soft ball stage (236°F) without stirring.

Remove from the heat. Stir in the butter until melted. Stir in the pecans and oats. Quickly drop by spoonfuls onto the waxed paper. If desired, press a pecan half on the top of each cookie. Cool. Store in an airtight container.

### VARIATION
*Maple Cream Cookies:* Substitute ½ cup half-and-half for the corn syrup. Cook in a heavy saucepan, stirring as needed to prevent scorching. Finish as above.

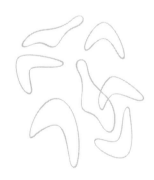

# Cathedral Cookies

## Skill Level: Novice, Easy

*If you have never heard of this 1960s "homeroom mother classic," you are in for a real treat. The pastel marshmallows inside these chocolate rolls create "stained glass windows" when sliced, hence the name Cathedral Cookies.*

✳ MAKES ABOUT 36 COOKIES

- 1 (12-ounce) package semisweet chocolate chips
- ½ cup butter or margarine
- 1 (10.5-ounce) package multicolored miniature marshmallows
- ¾ cup chopped pecans (optional)
- 1 (7-ounce) package sweetened flaked coconut or 1½ cups sifted powdered sugar, for rolling

In the top pan of a double boiler over hot but not boiling water, melt the chocolate chips and butter, stirring until smooth.

Remove the pan containing the chocolate from the double boiler. Let stand away from the heat until the mixture cools to lukewarm and is slightly thickened, 10 to 15 minutes. Gently stir in the marshmallows until coated, being careful not to let the marshmallows melt. Add the pecans if desired. Let the mixture cool until it begins to hold its shape, 20 to 30 minutes.

Cover a large countertop with three large pieces of waxed paper. Sprinkle generously with the coconut. Divide the mixture into three parts, gently spooning the mixture onto the waxed paper. Shape each portion into a 2-inch log by hand or with a spoon or knife. Sprinkle the excess coconut on top of the logs. Roll the logs in the waxed paper, and then roll in a dry cloth or towel. Gently transfer the logs to a baking sheet and refrigerate until firm, 1 to 2 hours. To serve, slice the chilled rolls into 1-inch slices using a wet knife.

- - - - - - - - - - - - - - - -

# Frying Pan Cookies

## Skill Level: Novice, Easy

*These old-time favorites are far more delicious than you might think.*

✳ MAKES ABOUT 50

- 1 cup granulated sugar
- 2 teaspoons butter
- 2 eggs
- 1½ cups chopped pitted dates
- ¼ teaspoon salt
- 2 cups crisp rice cereal
- ¾ cups chopped pecans
- ½ teaspoon vanilla extract
- 1 cup sweetened flaked coconut, for rolling

Place the sugar, butter, eggs, dates, and salt into a cold heavy frying pan. Turn the heat to medium. Cook 10 minutes, stirring constantly.

Remove from the heat. Stir in the cereal, pecans, and vanilla. Cool slightly, 5 to 10 minutes or until the mixture can be handled. Shape into balls 1 inch in diameter. Roll the balls in the coconut. Place on waxed paper to cool. Store in an airtight container.

COOK'S NOTE: For similar recipes, see Skillet Cookies (page 233), Humdinger Date Balls (page 144), and Snowballs (page 144).

- - - - - - - - - - - - - - - -

# Skillet Cookies

## Skill Level: Novice, Easy

*Skillet Cookies put a slightly different twist on Frying Pan Cookies (page 232) by using less sugar and more butter.*

✳ MAKES ABOUT 50

½ cup butter or margarine
¾ cup granulated sugar
2 egg yolks
6 ounces pitted dates, chopped
2 cups crisp rice cereal
1 cup chopped pecans
1 cup sweetened flaked coconut, for rolling

In a large, heavy skillet over medium heat, heat the butter and sugar until the butter is melted. Stir in the egg yolks and dates. Cook 5 to 6 minutes, stirring constantly.

Remove from the heat. Stir in the cereal and pecans. Cool slightly, 5 to 10 minutes or until the mixture can be handled. Shape into balls 1 inch in diameter. Roll the balls in shredded coconut. Place on waxed paper to cool. Store in an airtight container.

COOK'S NOTE: For similar recipes, see Frying Pan Cookies (page 232), Humdinger Date Balls (page 144), and Snowballs (page 144).

# Tutti-Frutti Bars

## Skill Level: Novice, Easy

*Baby boomers know that this dressed-up version of crispy rice bars would have been a smash hit with Ozzie of 1950s "reality TV."*

✳ MAKES ABOUT 24 BARS

1 (15½-ounce) package crisp rice cereal
¼ cup butter or margarine
½ pound marshmallows
½ teaspoon vanilla extract
½ cup chopped candied cherries
½ cup chopped pecans
¼ cup halved candied cherries or pecan halves (optional)

Butter a 9-inch square pan. Pour the rice cereal into a large mixing bowl.

In the top pan of a double boiler over hot but not boiling water, heat the butter and marshmallows until melted and thick, stirring to blend. Stir in the vanilla. Add the chopped cherries and pecans. Pour the marshmallow mixture over the cereal and quickly stir to combine. Press into the buttered pan. If desired, press candied cherry halves into the top of the mixture to decorate. Let stand until firm enough to cut, about 1 hour.

# Metric Charts

## COMPARISON TO METRIC MEASURE

| When You Know | Symbol | Multiply By | To Find | Symbol |
|---|---|---|---|---|
| teaspoons | tsp | 5.0 | milliliters | ml |
| tablespoons | tbsp | 15.0 | milliliters | ml |
| fluid ounces | fl. oz. | 30.0 | milliliters | ml |
| cups | c | 0.24 | liters | l |
| pints | pt. | 0.47 | liters | l |
| quarts | qt. | 0.95 | liters | l |
| ounces | oz. | 28.0 | grams | g |
| pounds | lb. | 0.45 | kilograms | kg |
| Fahrenheit | F | 5/9 (after subtracting 32) | Celsius | C |

## FAHRENHEIT TO CELSIUS

| F | C |
|---|---|
| 200–205 | 95 |
| 220–225 | 105 |
| 245–250 | 120 |
| 275 | 135 |
| 300–305 | 150 |
| 325–330 | 165 |
| 345–350 | 175 |
| 370–375 | 190 |
| 400–405 | 205 |
| 425–430 | 220 |
| 445–450 | 230 |
| 470–475 | 245 |
| 500 | 260 |

## LIQUID MEASURE TO MILLILITERS

| | | | |
|---|---|---|---|
| ¼ teaspoon | = | 1.25 | milliliters |
| ½ teaspoon | = | 2.5 | milliliters |
| ¾ teaspoon | = | 3.75 | milliliters |
| 1 teaspoon | = | 5.0 | milliliters |
| 1¼ teaspoons | = | 6.25 | milliliters |
| 1½ teaspoons | = | 7.5 | milliliters |
| 1¾ teaspoons | = | 8.75 | milliliters |
| 2 teaspoons | = | 10.0 | milliliters |
| 1 tablespoon | = | 15.0 | milliliters |
| 2 tablespoons | = | 30.0 | milliliters |

## LIQUID MEASURE TO LITERS

| | | | |
|---|---|---|---|
| ¼ cup | = | 0.06 | liters |
| ½ cup | = | 0.12 | liters |
| ¾ cup | = | 0.18 | liters |
| 1 cup | = | 0.24 | liters |
| 1¼ cups | = | 0.3 | liters |
| 1½ cups | = | 0.36 | liters |
| 2 cups | = | 0.48 | liters |
| 2½ cups | = | 0.6 | liters |
| 3 cups | = | 0.72 | liters |
| 3½ cups | = | 0.84 | liters |
| 4 cups | = | 0.96 | liters |
| 4½ cups | = | 1.08 | liters |
| 5 cups | = | 1.2 | liters |
| 5½ cups | = | 1.32 | liters |

# Index